THE HOME GARDEN COOKBOOK

KEN & PAT KRAFT

THE
HOME GARDEN
COOKBOOK
From Seed to Plate

GARDEN CITY, NEW YORK

Doubleday & Company, Inc.

Acknowledgment is made to the following for permission to reprint their material:

"Batter-Fried Squash Blossoms" from THE ART OF AMERICAN INDIAN COOKING by Yeffe Kimball and Jean Anderson. Copyright © 1965 by Yeffe Kimball and Jean Anderson. Reprinted by permission of Doubleday & Company, Inc. and McIntosh & Otis, Inc.

Copyright © 1970 by Ken and Pat Kraft
All Rights Reserved
Printed in the United States of America

This book is for Maud Van Cortland Oakes,
a joyous gardener, cook, and friend;
and for Anyá Oakes (alias Bonbon), who was always
willing to help with the experiments that failed.

ACKNOWLEDGMENTS

Many persons have helped us with information and advice on this book, and have given us their time freely. We have called on friends again and again to taste the results of recipes, and to give us their opinion on whether we were making ourselves clear in wording the recipes. Among those to whom our special thanks are due are Ivan N. Anderson, Mrs. D. A. Brown, Mr. and Mrs. David Burpee, John Coniglio, Mrs. Frank L. Culin, Floris Hartog, Jerome Kantor, the Countess of Kinnoull, Mr. and Mrs. Gordon Baker Lloyd, Mr. and Mrs. William J. Park, Ed Pazzaglia, K. E. Relyea, Michael Roach, and Mr. and Mrs. R. A. Tracy.

And, as always, we owe much to the diligence and patience of the staff of the Harrison Memorial Library of Carmel, California, and in particular to the kindness of Mrs. Ruth G. Thornburg and Mrs. Edith J. Chester.

KEN AND PAT KRAFT

Carmel, California

CONTENTS

Recipes for items marked with an asterisk (*) may be located by consulting the Index.

THE HOME GARDEN COOKBOOK

Chapter 1

IN THE KRAFT GARDEN . . . from seed . . .

This is a cookbook for home gardeners—and for future home gardeners. We invite you to take a Cook's Gardening Tour with us in these pages, in the interest of fine dining on superb food well grown. We will be talking almost entirely about our own kitchen gardens and our own kitchens—and we use the plurals because we've had quite a number of each. At the end of this chapter you will find plans of two of our kitchen gardens.

If we have become adept at certain gardening and cooking abilities it is from practical experience and from a steady regard for the convenience, natural bounty, the deliciousness, and the economy of a home garden. We are still learning, every season, but it is the experience we want to pass along. It is, we think, the most helpful help.

The most important reason we have a kitchen garden is to get the kind of food we cannot find on sale. Offhand that sounds as if we must be growing exotics. We aren't. With a few exceptions everything in our garden is known to nearly everyone who sees it: Lettuces, chard, broccoli, beets, squash, carrots, cress, mustard, and so on.

But . . . you *can* find these things on sale at the stores, can't you?

Sorry, but you cannot. What you can buy is store lettuce, store chard, store broccoli, and the like. What you *cannot* buy is garden-fresh lettuce, garden-fresh chard, garden-fresh anything.

And this is no small difference.

Garden-fresh food is succulent, brimming with flavor and health. Such home-garden food should be cooked differently from truck-farm food, which has been bred to take the hardships of industrialized farming and long-distance shipping, not to mention storage. Quite plainly, the cooking and seasoning of such foods is not the cooking and seasoning that best suits tender home-garden freshness, nor is the commercial frozen vegetable the same vegetable that was growing in your garden ten minutes ago and is now in your kitchen for cooking.

In her well-known *Let's Cook It Right,* Adelle Davis says: "Vegetables to be cooked should be handled in the same manner as salad vegetables. Ideally they should be gathered immediately before being cooked."

Yet, most vegetable recipes must necessarily train their sights on vegetables that aren't really fresh. This is the real underneath reason why vegetables are the stepchildren of the menu makers. It is, we are sure, the reason some people are indifferent or even hostile to vegetables. We had a good friend, a veteran combat army man, who thought the only vegetables worth eating were beans, dried ones. We did get him to eat some corn on the cob once, but the thing that probably appealed was that we were roasting it over a primitive outdoor grill, as if on bivouac.

Still, we can't really blame anyone for this attitude if the only vegetables available to him are store vegetables. Here is a note we made after a weekly grocery shopping trip last September:

Seen in produce section—2 bunches chard, 25 cents. Small bunches, perhaps 10 stalks, the cut ends black, the leaves limp. Our chard in the garden at this moment is so huge and beautiful a visiting artist friend took some home for a leafy decoration. And zucchini squash—at the market, 25 cents a pound, sad little things, partly dehydrated, lacking a good green, not the firm and upright fruits on the squash plants currently in our garden. Yesterday we estimated from cut stem ends that each plant has had from 2 dozen to over 3 dozen fruits so far. The huge green-mottled leaves and wide golden blossoms are lovely.

Listen—do you know what lettuce really tastes like? You never will unless you taste it young and virginal, its milk-white juice dewing the cut stalk. Its botanical name, Lactuca, is from the Latin word for milk. Go to a garden in early morning and from a new row thin out a young lettuce no taller than your finger. Eat it unadorned. You will surprise a light springtime delicacy of flavor no

other vegetable duplicates. Or shell a pea from a pod as you pick it
from the vine, and eat it at once. It will taste a shade more robust
than the lettuce, with a texture that snaps crisply between the
teeth like the glassy crackle of some apples, and with a freshly sweet
flavor—which is perhaps why some good cook long ago thought of
adding a harmonizing pinch of sugar to new peas. And to fresh
young carrots, as you'll understand perfectly when you nibble one
just out of the garden.

And in the merest dab of space—a strip no wider than your
hand along a walk, even—you can grow lettuce, you can grow carrots. And peas will flatten themselves agreeably against a fence. The
more space the better, within reason. Of course. But you can grow
delicious food for your table on even the most ridiculously small and
overlooked bit of ground.

If you enjoy the brief oriental style of cooking, raising some of
the vegetables for it is the difference between superb and so-so. In
this connection we urge your particular attention to Jerusalem artichokes, edible-podded peas, and Belgian endive. All are covered
in the chapters that follow.

Throughout this book we are talking from experience, as we said,
which means failures along with successes—and you learn faster from
the failures. We've always been curious about trying new things, so
we've grown and cooked nearly every plant a home gardener finds
available to him, and in a variety of climates.

We've moved around the country a good deal, so we've had
many sizes and kinds of gardens. Our Missouri farm garden was half
the size of a football field, and our smallest garden was about the
size of a throw rug, though in even it we raised enough lettuce to
give some to the neighbors. In every case our idea was to provide
unbuyable food for our table, but we also got bonuses of pleasure
and of economy. Don't let anyone tell you a home garden isn't a big
help to the food dollar. You can fritter money on a garden, certainly, just as you can on a car or a house, but that's a matter of
choice, not have-to.

SEED PACKETS

And vegetables for your table are easier to grow than most people
think. If anyone doubts this we call his attention to any seed packet.

In addition to being such attractive little things that a rack of them in a store courts browsers in the way flowers court honey bees, these packets are little mines of how-to information. On each you'll find directions for growing the seed it contains—and if the growing were complicated, there wouldn't be room for it on a packet. As we write this we have a packet of lettuce seed before us. The variety is Deer Tongue, a favorite of ours, and here's what the packet says:

A compact, semi-heading type of leaf lettuce. Leaves are slightly blistered or savoyed, attractive green, excellent quality with thick, succulent mid-rib. Fully grown plants are 12 inches across, 6 to 7 inches high, leaves oblong to triangular with rounded tip.

Lettuce does best where the seasons remain reasonably cool, and for that reason it is grown extensively during the spring and in the fall. A good rich soil, retaining a fair amount of moisture, is essential, as lettuce develops its best qualities if it is grown quickly, without any checks in growth. Sow the seed very thinly outdoors as early in the spring as possible and again in late summer in rows 18 inches apart. Thin so that individual plants have ample room to develop.

That's a thumbnail education in growing lettuce. What's more, the packet is an instant reference, right there along with you in the garden as you plant. And may we suggest that instead of using it as a row label, you keep it and jot on it the date of seeding and those of any succession seedings? It will be a useful record, for it will tell you later what *you* did that season in *your garden*. The packet is your personal score card.

SEED CATALOGUES

This brings up another point—the value of a seed catalogue to you. Just the other day we asked a seed house to send a catalogue to the daughter of a friend of ours, and we heard that the daughter and her husband spent a whole happy weekend poring over it. It was the first seed catalogue they'd ever owned. Another friend always saved her own garden seed and had never realized there were such things as seed catalogues. And a third friend once said wistfully in our hearing, "I do wish I knew how to get a catalogue." Yet each of these persons is a normal intelligent citizen. On the assumption they aren't the only ones in the world not informed about sources of supply, we have included a chapter, "Where to Get It," with a list of some seed houses and nurseries that sell what we talk about in this book. We think there are few things more annoying than to read so enthusiastic an account of something that you're dying to have it, and then be left hanging without any clue on where to find it.

Furthermore we have another reason for recommending seed catalogues to you. They are one more valuable source of down-to-earth and accurate gardening know-how. Some are issued by regional houses and stress the vegetable varieties adapted to their regions—a good point in the case of a temperamental vegetable. Some have detailed planting and cultural tables, and most tell how to grow each plant, what it looks like, how long it takes to mature, the special merits of each variety, and often how to use and store the harvest.

Here and there in this book organic gardeners may frown at our acceptance of commercial fertilizers and other such helps. Years ago we were organic gardeners ourselves, and we feel righteously organic all over again when a spray rig drenches an oak tree across the street with DDT that then drifts all over the community. But, like it or not, this is the way things are, so we are only as organic about gardening as life lets us be. We like an interesting garden, for example, and usually plant several things in the same small bed, including flowers, something organic gardeners favor. We too hope that such companion planting will help things grow, and meanwhile we enjoy looking at them.

What follows now are a few pointers on ways to run a home vegetable garden, and have a good time doing it.

COMPOST

We will speak frequently of compost in this book. Composting is an ancient way of giving back to the soil what plants take away from it. Compost is vegetable matter that has been worked on by chemical action and bacteria until it is like good garden soil full of humus. After years of trying various ways of making compost we now use a very simple one. We build an oblong bottomless and topless box 6 feet long and 3 feet wide (or 3 feet square if we're running a small garden). The best materials are planks 2 inches thick and 12 inches wide.

We put this box on the ground in a shady place near the garden, and spade out the earth it encloses, going down about a foot. As garden waste, weeds, grass clippings, potato peelings, and so forth, accumulate, we throw them into this compost pit until we have about a 6-inch depth. We then chop it coarsely with a spade, sprinkle half a coffee can of any commercial fertilizer over it, cover it with an inch of the earth we had dug out, and wet it down.

This process is repeated until the pile reaches near the top of the box. We then build a second box, put it on top of the first one, and go on building up the pile until we need a third box. When the pile reaches to the top of this third one, we finish it off with a final layer of earth, flattening and dishing the top so water won't run off. If we get to it, we spade up the top few layers of the pile after about a month, to hurry it. The compost is ready to use in two or three months in this climate, though we've known it to take six months elsewhere.

We keep three compost piles going—one we're building, one that is built and on the way to becoming compost, and one that *is* compost and which we are using. The sectionalized boxes make it easier to get at the compost, as well as easier to build the pile.

Fats, meat scraps, and cloth have no place in a compost pile. They attract animals and create odors. The compost pile described above will not create a nuisance and will give you compost that is the equivalent of the well-rotted manure you are always being advised to get for the garden but can't find.

MULCHING

Mulching is a way to protect plants from dying of thirst or heat. Lacking enough water, we depended on mulches for our farm garden. A mulch is something laid on the ground to keep water from evaporating quickly from the soil. Such litter as grass clippings, chopped weeds, sawdust, straw, or leaves make good mulches. Newspaper sheets have been used, and black sheet plastic is sold for the purpose. Compost is a good mulch and also feeds the plant it mulches. It and a fine-grained mulch such as sawdust need be only about 2 inches thick, but 4 to 6 inches is about right for others. Peek underneath the mulch now and then to see if you need to kill unwelcome residents such as slugs.

When you apply any mulch except compost or an unorganic one such as plastic, sprinkle a handful of commercial fertilizer for each 4 or 5 feet of row, to keep the mulch from impoverishing the soil as it decomposes.

LAYING OUT A GARDEN

Here's how we decide on the dimensions of a new vegetable garden if there is enough water available: We pick the sunniest spot available on the house grounds, set a lawn sprinkler in the middle of it, and turn on the sprinkler. We usually use a sprinkler that makes an oblong pattern, and when it has wet the ground enough to show the coverage, we mark these boundaries. That becomes the garden, and from then on we water it by simply placing the sprinkler in the same spot and turning it on. This is the most reasonable way we've ever thought of to mark off a garden, and unless you are living in the country where you can't spare the water (as we could not, on our farm), we recommend it to you.

No matter what size our garden is, we extend it with small annexes in the form of pots or planters of herbs conveniently close to the kitchen, as mentioned in Chapter 34, "Herbs." Our object is practical but the effect is aesthetic; a tiny forest of herbs on window sill or terrace cheers the eye and embraces the spirit.

GARDEN PLANTING PLAN

If you work best in a pleasant chaos you won't have any use for a garden plan showing where plants are to go, but if you like things organized you'll make a plan. There is something to be said for either view. If you do make a plan based on our sprinkler system (or Instant Rain, as we think of it), you'll know the garden's dimensions at once and can take it from there. Here are a few guidelines:

DON'T CROWD PLANTS. For best air circulation, rows should be 18 inches apart for fairly compact growers such as scallions, leaf lettuce, radishes, spinach, carrots, and beets. If you plant closer, do so with the knowledge that this may invite disease and insects. Closer plantings also demand extra water and feeding. (But when we are short of space, we throw the rules to the winds, and crowd everything. We don't recommend it; we merely confess it.)

Except for most tomatoes, corn, and vine crops, which need more room, 2 feet between rows is right for the rest of the garden. Miniature vegetables can be planted closer than others; there is a tomato now, Tiny Tim, that needs less than a foot between plants.

Put What Where? Tall plants such as corn and climbing beans should go where they won't shade others; the north side of the garden is best.

If your garden must be tiny, forget about corn and watermelons unless you want nothing else, and think radishes, lettuce, bush beans, and perhaps chard and a few tomatoes. This depends on what your climate permits, too. Yet there are many pleasures in a small garden. One is that you may gather in it a leaf of this, a sprig of that, a root of some other—just in the quantity you may need, and only a step away. And gloriously succulent and flavorful. Even in a tiny garden we try to work in a few flowers and herbs even if we have to keep them in pots and shift them about to make room now and then.

A not tiny but not immense garden can accommodate everything in the tiny one and in greater quantity, plus more leafy greens and salad plants, broccoli, peas, lima beans, bush squash, garlic, leeks, a few celery plants, more herbs, and perhaps a bed of Belgian endive.

If you have room for a big garden—from 1,000 square feet upward—you can grow anything described in this book if your climate suits it. Too big a garden to take care of isn't good, of course, but it's a mistake you have to make for yourself. We did, and we're glad we did; now we know.

We always make paths in a garden, about 2 feet wide if we have enough space, and surface them with sand or something that looks good and is easy to walk on. We've also used grass paths. The paths automatically divide the garden into beds and we like this effect. Beds can then be edged with low-growing herbs, flowers, or vegetables.

When you plant your garden the *second* year and thereafter, shift the arrangement around so that root crops go where non-root ones were. Also, neither the same vegetable nor its close relatives should be planted in the same place two years running, and three years between plantings is better. A general guide to a vegetable's relatives is its botanical name, especially its genus, the first part of its name. Thus, you'll notice in the vegetable chapters that kohlrabi is *Brassica caulorapa*, and rutabaga is *Brassica napobrassica*, so don't follow one with the other even though one is a root vegetable and the other isn't. Most importantly, don't follow brassicas with brassicas, cucurbits (vine crops) with cucurbits, or legumes (peas and beans) with legumes. This shifting about in the garden with the seasons is called rotation planting. The idea is to deprive disease organisms in the earth from continuing to live, season after season, on the plants they need.

STARTING SEEDS EARLY

Some things take so long to grow that starting seeds early is the only way to give them time enough to mature. Celery is an example. Tomatoes are usually started ahead of time to prolong the harvest. Other plants that repay an early start are the cabbage group, lettuces, and peppers. If your average last spring frost comes in mid-April, plan on seeding early-starters about Valentine's Day.

If you have a cold frame, you can plant directly in it. We have often made a simple cold frame in a few minutes if we had a spare window sash on hand. Merely nail four boards together to make a box without a bottom and for which the window can serve as the top. Boards 12 inches wide are best, but even 8-inch ones are better than nothing. Put this frame where it will get all the sun it can, such as against a south wall. Spade up the patch of earth it encloses, dig in compost or peat moss, and make a seed bed by raking it all smooth and fine. Or fill flats with a planting mixture as given below, and put them inside the cold frame. Prop the window sash open to ventilate the frame on warm days.

Indoors you can grow seeds in a pot at a sunny window. Put an inch of gravel in the pot first, for drainage, fill it with the same mixture we give next for flats, and set it on an old plate.

A flat is a shallow wooden box about 3 inches high, a foot wide, and 1½ feet long. Sizes vary, but not greatly, because when filled with soil the flat must be light enough to be easily lifted. A nursery-man will sell you flats, or if you buy a flatful of plants you get the flat too.

A good planting mixture for a flat is 2 parts of garden soil and one part sand. Use builders' sand or any other sharp sand except from a salt-water beach. Screen the soil through a piece of fine hardware cloth to eliminate lumps. Fill the flat to within ½ inch of the top, and finish with a ¼-inch layer of sphagnum peat moss. The moss is a little trouble to wet but it helps keep down fungus that can kill seedlings.

To plant, water the flat well and let it drain. Make rows 2 inches apart by pressing the edge of a small board into the surface ¼ inch deep. Disinfect seed with a fungicide such as Arasan by dropping a pinch of it into the packet, closing the packet, and shaking vigorously. Drop the seeds into the rows, spacing them about ¼ inch apart if you can. Cover them with ¼-inch layer or less of the peat moss and press it down with your fingers. The tiniest seeds don't have to be covered.

Water flats and pots you have seeded only when the upper part of the soil becomes a little dry. You can tell by poking your finger in it. It should feel just barely moist. Lukewarm water is better than cold water on germinating seeds and on tiny new seedlings.

In a week or two, usually, seedlings will appear. Until you become adept, it is best to wait until they form a pair of true leaves (the first ones don't count) before transplanting. And since it is hard to plant seeds as thinly as you'd prefer, you will probably have to thin surplus plants even before you start transplanting. Do this thinning with a scissors, cutting at ground level, if you don't trust yourself to pull these tiny plants out by the roots without disturbing their neighbors.

We usually transplant little seedlings to another flat, spacing them 2 inches apart each way, with a final transplanting to the garden later. When transplanting these small plants, handle them by the leaves, not by the stems. You can transplant to peat pots or other small pots, if you prefer, or to plant bands; all these make for easy transfer to the garden when the weather permits.

A more expensive but good way to seed a flat is to ask your nurseryman to do it for you, with seeds you supply. Get the seeds to him about 2 months before you'll want the plants. By furnishing the seeds you'll control the varieties, and the nurseryman will deliver the flat of little plants when they are ready to set out.

We keep flats working all the time, using them as temporary little gardens to populate the regular garden with new plants as needed. The point here is to save space. Thus the garden can use most of its area for plants instead of having to be a seed bed for everything too. The things we seed in flats during the growing season are those adaptable for succession plantings and which can be transplanted. They include lettuces, broccoli, kale, kohlrabi, mustard, and chard.

OUTDOOR PLANTING

Early in the spring you might want to have your garden soil tested for acidity if you haven't grown a good garden there the year before. This is the safe, conservative approach. Your county agricultural agent at your county seat can make the soil test, or you can buy a simple testing kit. Most seed houses sell them. A thorough test will inform you on fertilizer needs as well as lime requirements for acidity correction, if any. In the absence of a test, a very general rule for 100 square feet of garden is: Add 5 pounds each of hydrated lime and commercial fertilizer, say a 5–10–5 formula (meaning 5 percent of nitrogen, 10 percent of phosphorus, and 5 percent of potash; the figures always read in that order, from left to right).

If lime is added, work it in when you spade the garden, and also spade in compost or peat moss. Work in commercial fertilizer with a rake just before you seed or transplant.

When you plant seeds, don't plant them too deeply. This is the commonest fault in gardening and is the reason a lot of plants never come up. Check the seed packet for depth. A frequent depth is ¼ inch, and if it helps, you might remember that a penny is about three times as wide as that.

In mild coastal and southern regions you can plant some things in the fall—hardy leafy greens, salad plants, peas, some root crops, and most of the cabbage family. Elsewhere, mid-March is about the earliest safe time to work the soil. Peas and potatoes can go in then. In April, seed the vegetables that can take some chill—those mentioned above for fall planting in milder climates. We'll have to admit we're always planting things earlier than they should be planted in the spring, and later than they should be in the fall. But we consider this part of the sport, a little like betting on a race.

When the spring chill is over and the night air is mild, seed or transplant the tender things such as squash and other vine crops, beans, peppers, tomatoes, eggplant, and corn. For small transplants, plastic berry boxes make good protectors from sun and birds for the first week or so.

Also at this time arm yourself with an all-purpose dust to keep damage from insects and disease at bay if necessary. We find a little chlordane another very useful protection to have on hand; when sprinkled around broccoli and other cabbage plants, turnips, mustard, and radishes, it stops any attack from maggots, which hatch from eggs laid by a fly common in many regions.

In the chapters that follow, we use the word "hill" for a form of plant spacing. It is an accepted gardening word, and it means not a hill in the sense of a mound, but a group of seeds rather than a row. In such a hill the seeds are planted in a circle about the size of a dinner plate. Six or eight seeds may be planted, and the seedlings are later thinned to the best two or three. Vine crops are so planted, pole beans often are, and corn may be.

Care of a garden during the growing season consists largely of keeping weeds hoed or pulled, keeping plants growing well with enough feeding and watering, protecting them from troubles if necessary, and keeping up with the harvest. Mulching will help with keeping weeds down and keeping moisture in the soil. If you must water, use enough to wet the soil 6 or 8 inches deep. A simple gauge is a length of wire coat hanger; push it into the soil; it will penetrate easily only the well-soaked soil.

A general rule for feeding (side-dressing) plants when they are half grown or just starting a long bearing season, is: 1 pound of commercial fertilizer to 20 feet of row.

One more tip. Vegetables that mature quickly can be planted more than once in a season (succession planting), and so to keep the seed in good condition between plantings, do this: Put the packet in a plastic bag and put the bag in the refrigerator. This will keep them cool and dry, the two storage conditions seeds need. If well kept, most seeds will live for more than one year even though some in each packet will expire. Here is a guide on how many years

IN THE KRAFT GARDEN . . . FROM SEED . . .   13

the seeds of most vegetables covered in this book will live in good
storage; the figures are conservative:

Beans	3	Lettuces	5
Beets	5	Melons	4–5
Belgian Endive	8	Mustard	4
Broccoli	4	Okra	4
Cabbage	4	Onions	2
Carrots	3	Parsley	1
Celery	3	Parsnips	1
Celeriac	3	Peas	3
Chard	5	Peppers	2
Corn	3	Radishes	4
Cucumber	5	Rhubarb	3
Eggplant	4	Salsify	1
Endive	10	Squash	4
Florence Fennel	4	Tomatoes	6–7
Kohlrabi	5	Turnips	4
Leek	3	Herbs	3 for most

KRAFT CALIFORNIA HOME GARDEN

Figures 1, 2, and 3 show a plan of the small home garden we
have been running for the past few years in Carmel, California. The
arrangement of plantings changes each year and each season of the
year, but we have kept the same general bed layout. The garden
measures 31 feet long, north and south, and 17 feet wide—a shape
governed by the coverage of the sprinkler we are using. The garden
is divided by sanded paths into five beds, and the planting space
amounts to about 400 square feet. In addition, we plant some potatoes outside the garden, and the Jerusalem artichoke planting is
slightly outside. By starting new plants in flats and then transplanting them to the garden when room is available, we can raise a good
deal of food in this fairly small space. We recommend this system
even for a large garden, as tiny plants can be more easily protected
and tended in flats. We usually transplant them to another flat when
they are still quite small, even before true leaves form, spacing them
about 2 inches apart. This lets us take cubes of soil with them when
they move to the garden and entirely prevents transplanting shock.
The flat-to-garden method lets us keep the garden working the year

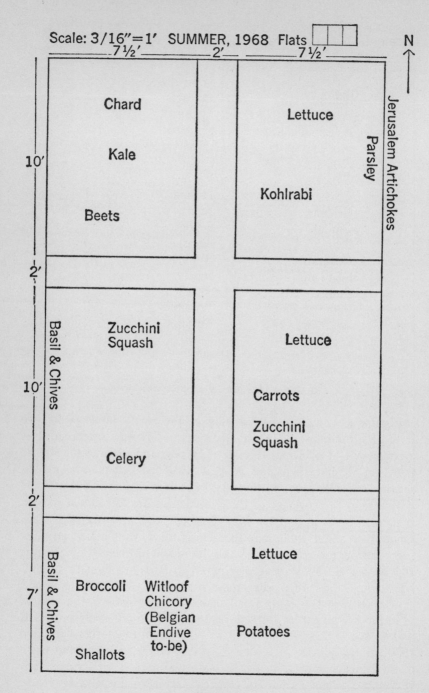

Scale: 3/16"=1' SUMMER, 1968 Flats

N

7 ½' 2' 7 ½'

10'

2'

10'

2'

7'

Chard

Kale

Beets

Lettuce

Kohlrabi

Zucchini
Squash

Celery

Lettuce

Carrots

Zucchini
Squash

Broccoli   Witloof
             Chicory
             (Belgian
              Endive
Shallots   to-be)

Lettuce

Potatoes

Basil & Chives

Basil & Chives

Parsley

Jerusalem Artichokes

figure 1

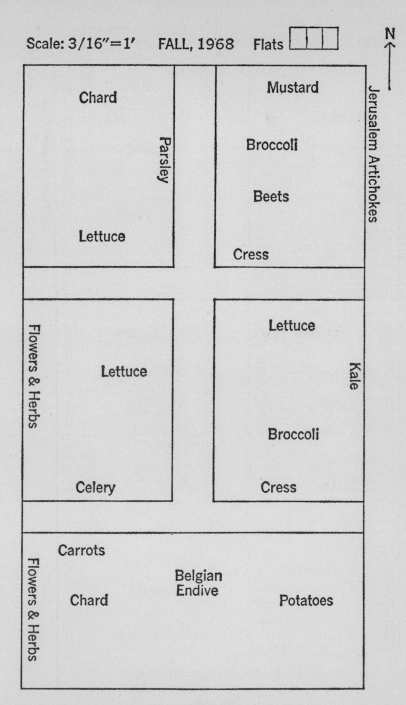

Scale: 3/16″=1′   FALL, 1968   Flats

N

Jerusalem Artichokes

Chard

Parsley

Lettuce

Mustard

Broccoli

Beets

Cress

Flowers & Herbs

Lettuce

Celery

Lettuce

Broccoli

Cress

Kale

Flowers & Herbs

Carrots

Chard

Belgian
Endive

Potatoes

figure 2

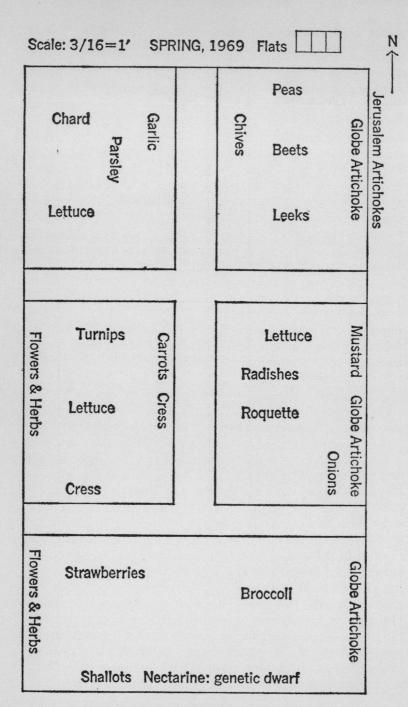

figure 3

around, as there are three seasons here for a vegetable garden; spring, summer, and fall-winter. This marine climate does not encourage plants that have high warmth requirements, such as okra and corn. But we can raise head lettuce in midsummer, globe artichokes thrive, and Belgian endive can be sprouted in winter outside, where the roots were grown. Several perennial herbs grow the year around, and we use thyme, sage, and chives as bed borders and make specimen plantings of oregano and rosemary. The annual herbs are handy as summer space-fillers in various beds, as is tarragon, which comes back from the roots each spring. We also employ various flowers (marigolds, zinnias, geraniums, pansies, heuchera) as color accents in the vegetable garden and with the feeling they and the vegetables help each other grow. In addition, we usually plant some flowers in clay pots for spotting here and there in the garden. If you live in a warm-summer area you can grow such heat lovers as corn, tomatoes, melons, okra, peppers, and lima beans, even in so small a garden as this one. Corn should be planted at the north end so it does not shade other vegetables, and this is also true for pole beans and tall tomato plants. A way of saving space in a small garden is to plant pole beans at the base of corn plants. Give the corn a 2-week head start, and the beans will use it as a support.

KRAFT MISSOURI FARM GARDEN

Room was no problem with our farm garden (figure 4), which measured about 100 feet wide and 200 long. By spacing widely, both rows and beds, we were able to give each plant a generous amount of soil to draw on for moisture—and this was vital as we had no water available for sprinkling during dry spells. The soil was heavy clay, difficult to work, but productive. We also mulched to hold moisture in the soil, an important aid to gardening in most climates of the United States. The plan here shows a typical arrangement of this garden as of midsummer. We shifted plantings of annual vegetables each year, and used some flowers and herbs as companion plants for vegetables and for an attractive appearance throughout the garden. At various times we also used dwarf iris and chrysanthemums for borders. The garden proper was divided into quarters by two wide grass walks, kept groomed with a lawn mower. With so much ground at our disposal we allowed some rows and beds to

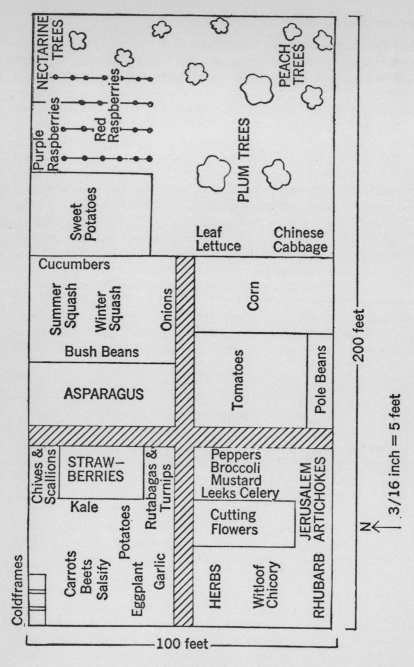

NECTARINE TREES

Purple Raspberries

Red Raspberries

PEACH TREES

PLUM TREES

Sweet Potatoes

Leaf Lettuce

Chinese Cabbage

Cucumbers

Summer Squash

Winter Squash

Onions

Corn

Bush Beans

ASPARAGUS

Tomatoes

Pole Beans

Chives & Scallions

STRAW-BERRIES

Rutabagas & Turnips

Peppers
Broccoli
Mustard
Leeks Celery

JERUSALEM ARTICHOKES

Kale

Potatoes

Cutting Flowers

Coldframes

Carrots
Beets
Salsify

Eggplant

Garlic

HERBS

Witloof Chicory

RHUBARB

200 feet

3/16 inch = 5 feet

N

100 feet

figure 4

lie fallow each season, or planted idle beds to a soil-enriching legume such as a vetch, which was turned under in the fall. Though about half the whole area was taken up with fruits, the part devoted to vegetables provided a large surplus for canning and freezing, and for many friends and neighbors.

Chapter 2

... AND THE KRAFT KITCHEN ... to plate

No matter where we are living, we run a country kitchen. It smells like a country kitchen, too, fragrant with herbs drying at times, or strawberry preserves bubbling on the range, or sourdough bread baking. The kitchen is an extension of the garden in the twin aspects of economy and good dining. The purpose of this chapter is to explain ahead of time some of the things in the kitchen that are common to many of the recipes, and to touch on a few items of cooking interest that don't fit elsewhere.

We considered saying something here about kitchen tools and utensils, but after thinking it over we decided our kitchen has so many fewer such items than most, there isn't much to say. A cook's knife and chopping board do the jobs two dozen conveniences might be mustered to do. This multi-use is repeated many times, until now, if we find we aren't using a cooking aid often and something else can serve as well, we give the other away. "Casserole" in the recipes means a 2-quart one. "Stew pan" is a 5- or 6-quart pan.

Like our kitchen equipment, our recipes are uncomplicated. Also, we have tried to avoid such terms as *roux*, which though convenient shorthand for flour and melted fat as a thickening agent is not universally understood.

Most of the recipes given make 4 servings. The diners' hunger and capacity will decide whether 4 servings will serve four of them, two of them, or six of them.

In no recipe of ours will you find such aids as bouillon cubes, packaged mixes, seasoned salts, and so on. When we cook, we cook with basic material as near to the original as we can get. To our minds, most packaged convenience is a poor trade for true flavor. There is another pitfall here—pretty soon, in the kitchen of the packaged convenience, everything may get to tasting vaguely alike. One of us had an aunt who discovered chili powder for the first time late in her fifties and was enchanted. As if to make up for what she'd been missing, she added chili powder to almost everything but the desserts until her family finally rose in hot-tongued revolt. It is an extreme case only in the choice of condiment.

On our Missouri farm we canned hundreds and hundreds of jars of jellies, preserves, jams, fruit, fruit juices, vegetables, chicken, beef, meat sauces, soups, and pickles. Our shelves of canned goods were a constant satisfaction in accomplishment and convenience, a source of delicious food ready for use at any time. This takes special kitchen equipment and meticulous care of food to be processed, along with close attention to directions. We used as our constant guide the *Kerr Home Canning Book.* You can obtain a copy of this clearly written handbook by sending 35 cents to Miss Hattie Kilgore, Director, Research & Educational Department, Kerr Glass Manufacturing Corporation, Sand Springs, Oklahoma, 74063. The booklet also has instructions on freezing foods.

A word about oven temperatures: If we say, "Bake in a 325-degree F. oven 30 minutes," for example, this means you should heat the oven to 325 degrees *before* starting the baking.

MEASUREMENTS

When dealing with garden vegetables you aren't likely to weigh them as at the supermarket, so it seemed idle to talk in terms of pounds in recipes. "Three cups broccoli," for example, is a general guide, to be judged by eye; such amounts need be only approximate. In other cases we use gardeners' terms: medium-large beets, 12 large chard leaves, 2 cucumbers 6 inches long. . . . Where there may be some question of how large medium-large, say, is, we mention size in the gardening part of the chapter that precedes the recipes.

Other measurements used are standard: Teaspoon, tablespoon, cup, or fractions of each.

In stating the amount of seasonings we are specific where it seems needful to be, but we know that one person's pinch is another person's ¼ teaspoon, and in the end everybody suits himself. For this reason we seldom specify amounts of salt and pepper.

STEAMING

For the occasional steaming we do, as for some potato and ruta-baga recipes, we find this a simple and satisfactory method:

We use a round aluminum rack or grid a little smaller than the bottom of a large stew pan. We put enough water into the pan barely to reach the bottom of the grid, arrange on the grid the vegetables to be steamed, cover the pan, and cook over enough heat to keep the water boiling gently. We add more water if necessary and test with a sharp fork for doneness once or twice during the steaming.

STANDARD INGREDIENTS

Each recipe lists its ingredients in the order they are used. Herewith, a few remarks on some of these ingredients:

STOCK. Vegetable stock and a chicken stock we call Kraft Stock* appear frequently. See Chapter 38, "Soups and Stocks," for information on these and other stocks.

BUTTER AND OILS. Most of our cooking fats are one of these or a combination of them. If you use a margarine, we suggest it be a premium grade. When tasted alternately with butter a good margarine can be very close to the flavor of butter, but the difference will show up more in a delicately flavored cooked vegetable.

Olive oil and corn oil are mentioned in the recipes. In neither case does it seem sensible to us to buy for price. Oil is a small part of the total food bill, but a cheap oil can kill some of the flavor you paid for or gardened for in another ingredient. We seldom use peanut oil, but do use flavorless oils such as soya. Since oil does not keep indefinitely, we buy it in amounts that will be used up in about a month.

VINEGARS. Our standard vinegars are cider, white, red wine, and white wine, plus some herb vinegars. There are many other interesting vinegars but we can do everything we want to do with these basic ones and with citrus juices. If kept very long at room temperature a dinner wine will become vinegar. This is an expensive way of getting wine vinegar if you do it on purpose, but a good way to salvage a leftover bit of wine.

SPICES. We use very few spices. Garden vegetables need but few. If dry mustard can be considered a spice, we mean Colman's mustard when we refer to it in a recipe. Ground ginger is an alternative. We keep poultry seasoning on hand though we seldom use it; both whole and ground cloves; cinnamon; whole nutmegs; sugared ginger; and paprika. We buy these in containers holding an ounce or so, and discard them when they lose strength. A year is a reasonable shelf life for most.

HERBS. In each recipe that calls for herbs, *fresh* herbs are meant, and the amounts are based on fresh-herb strengths, which are pretty consistent. Dried herbs are anything but consistent. As we state also in Chapter 34, "Herbs," when we use our own dried herbs at any time the fresh ones are out of season, we cut the amount to ⅙ or ⅛ as much as the same herb fresh. You can often test the strength of a dried herb accurately by merely smelling it.

MILK. Years ago when we had a farm we always had at least one cow giving milk and sometimes there were three, so we had an abundance of milk and cream. After we left the farm we settled on evaporated milk as the best substitute for our own Jersey and Guernsey milk. Evaporated milk when used undiluted gives us close to the same results in most dishes as our farm cream did, and when cut half and half with water it serves the cooking purposes our farm milk did. In fact, when we made hot chocolate on the farm we found it was better when we added some evaporated milk to it. Without this, the hot chocolate was a trifle thin in spite of no lack of fresh cream. It is a comparison not many people have the chance to make and we thought it spoke very well for evaporated milk. Whenever a recipe here calls for evaporated milk, it means *undiluted* milk just as it comes from the can, unless otherwise specified.

SOUR CREAM. Whenever we call for sour cream in a recipe we mean commercial sour cream, not cream that has turned sour or has been soured with the addition of an acid. If commercial sour cream is to be heated, it should start out at room temperature to avoid curdling. Take the amount needed from the refrigerator well ahead of time.

WINE AND SPIRITS. The wines used in our kitchen are of three kinds: dry vermouth, sherry, and red or white dinner wines that are usually left over from a meal. These are California wines in most cases. We make no distinction between wines for cooking and wines for drinking. If a wine is not worth drinking, it is no favor to the cooking either. Dry vermouth can usually be used where a white wine is called for in these recipes, but be sure the vermouth is lightly flavored; herbs and other aromatics enter into vermouth's making, and brands differ.

A few recipes call for cognac brandy. Here again we use the same bottle we serve guests. So far, we have found no California brandy we thought very close to a good imported one. Bourbon whisky, however, is an acceptable substitute for brandy in the recipes, especially a sour-mash straight bourbon.

GRATED CHEESE. When we need grated cheese we grate it at that time or not long before. It loses strength too fast if grated and then stored for weeks or months, even in the refrigerator. We use Parmesan for a fairly mild cheese flavor, and Romano for a heartier one. We haven't come across any domestic Parmesan we wanted to settle on, but there are domestic Romanos we like. For grating, we use the coarse side of the same four-sided grater we grate nutmegs and anything else on.

PEPPER. We don't make a fetish of freshly ground pepper, but it is what we nearly always use. We can't see an enormous difference between it and a shaker of pepper that hasn't been opened longer than a month or two (taste both for yourself, but be sure the two are about the same fineness of grind, for accurate comparison). However, there is a subtle difference, and garden-fresh vegetables deserve subtleties, so when you see "Pepper" among ingredients, read it as "Freshly ground pepper." As to white pepper, we see no point in complicating the seasonings shelf with it. It is merely a little stronger than black. Cut a peppercorn in two and you'll see the white part from which white pepper is made—so you get both when you grind your own.

SPECIAL INGREDIENTS

GARLIC OIL. Where oil is part of the cooking liquid in a recipe
and garlic is a flavoring, the use of this garlic-flavored oil is a
convenience and we find the flavor superior to that obtained by
cooking the garlic in the oil. For one thing, garlic is easily burned
in such cooking, and takes time to watch. For another thing, we
usually discard the garlic partway through the cooking anyway. And
though we once used a garlic press to extract garlic flavor, the press
took too much labor to clean. Here's how you make Garlic Oil:

1 cup corn oil
4 fresh garlic cloves

Choose a jar with a tight lid and pour the oil into it. Peel the
garlic cloves and cut each into 2 or 3 pieces, lengthwise. Drop
them into the oil, cap the jar, and shake well. Keep it in the pantry
for a week, shaking it a few times each day. Then remove and
discard the garlic. The oil will keep at room temperature as well as
it will without the garlic flavor added.

Until you get used to its strength, use this oil sparingly. One part
of it added to three or four of corn oil will give a noticeable garlic
flavor.

NASTURTIUM CAPERS. These are an old-fashioned stand-in for capers.
They are green nasturtium seeds pickled, and they are a splendid
flavoring addition to certain dishes. They can be used in place of
capers though the two are not quite the same flavor. Nasturtium
Capers are milder and have a slightly nut-like taste. Here is how to
make them:

Green nasturtium seeds with ¼ inch of stem left on
White vinegar

Wash the seeds, drain, and put them into a jar with a lid. Pour in
enough vinegar to cover them. Drain vinegar into a saucepan, bring
to a boil, and return it to the jar. Cap jar and store. The Nasturtium

Capers will be ready for use in about 2 weeks. We find they keep well at a room temperature of about 60 degrees F., or in the refrigerator.

PREPARING FRESH VEGETABLES AND FRUIT FOR BABY

With your own fresh vegetables and fruit, you will want to see that the youngest member of the family enjoys the good nutrition they offer.

The processing is best done in a blender. If you have an Osterizer you can order half-pint jars called Mini-Blend Containers from the John Oster Manufacturing Company, 5055 North Lysell Avenue, Milwaukee, Wisconsin, 53217. The jars are just the right size to blend a fruit or vegetable for a baby's use. This method of preparing a baby's meals makes for a wide selection of garden-fresh vegetables and fruits, and can also greatly reduce costs.

VEGETABLE MEALS

Because we are diligent gardeners, someone occasionally mistakes us for vegetarians. The nearest we come to this is when Pat, occasionally swept away by the bounty of the garden in midseason, cries, "Let's have a vegetable dinner tonight." The response is invariably: "Good idea. And I'll broil a steak to go with it."

Nevertheless there is something very satisfying about an all-vegetable meal from your own garden. The reducer feels virtuous, the vitamin counter victorious, the gardener rewarded, and the budget takes a holiday. So . . . here are some suggestions for good combinations of color, taste, and textures through the seasons:

Spring Vegetable Platter Dinner

> A *heap of Chateau Potatoes** in the center, sprinkled
> with chopped parsley.*
> *Asparagus spears at one end of the platter, sauced with
> melted butter.*
> *Young carrots the size of the spears at the other end,
> also sauced with the butter.*

FOR A SPRING LUNCHEON

> Garden-fresh Caesar Salad*
> Bowknots*
> —or—
> Asparagus Vinaigrette*
> Stuffed eggs (using Shallot Mayonnaise*)
> Bowknots*

FOR A SUMMER DINNER

> Broiled Eggplant*
> Tomato-Onion Casserole*
> Lima beans
> Chiffon Potatoes*

FOR A SUMMER LUNCHEON

> Salad Soup*

FOR AN AUTUMN DINNER

> Broccoli Bruton Sisters*
> Carrots in Honey*
> Potatoes Pat*

FOR AN AUTUMN LUNCHEON

> Borsch*

TWO WINTER DINNERS

> This dinner is from the winter garden:
> Mashed rutabagas
> Kale Anchovy*
> Fried Jerusalem Artichokes*

This dinner is from your storage cellar and home-canned shelf or freezer:

Baked Sweet Potatoes*
French Fried Onions*
Orange Beets*
Kentucky Wonder beans

And for an after-the-game supper, try Minestrone* with Sourdough Bread*. Have the soup all ready except for the pasta, and cook that after you are back home.

SOURDOUGH BREAD

We are including this word on bread—which has nothing to do with a garden unless you wish to make herb bread, which we don't —because we refer to our homemade sourdough bread in other chapters. The recipe we use is one we worked out after years of experiments that involved, as nearly as we can now estimate, between four and five thousand loaves. We think the recipe is a good one though we still make little changes in it now and then. The most recent one was to shorten the processing time by one-third.

The bread has a distinctive character and a fine natural fragrance and firm texture. A friend to whom we often give a loaf of it has passed along a number of compliments on it from foreign visitors, usually along the lines of: "They said it was the first good bread they'd had since they left France," or Italy, Switzerland, Germany. . . .

To make sourdough bread you must have a starter, which is what sourdough yeast is called. This starter is a batter, usually of flour, water, and a little sugar, which is fermenting due to the action of living cells in it. There are three ways to get some starter. You can buy a package in dried form for about a dollar at some specialty food shops or from a supplier (one is listed in Chapter 40).

Second, if a friend has some starter, borrow half a cup of it and gradually build it up with flour and water to a jarful.

Third, you can make your own. This is quite a lot more trouble but there is something pioneerish and contented about the notion of enticing wild yeasts into working for you. We usually make one of these new starters each time we move to some new part of the country, partly out of curiosity to see what the air-borne yeasts there are like, and partly for insurance in case some disaster ever overtook our regular starter. We've always mixed up the new one by feel, but in order to explain it here, we mixed a new starter and kept track of just what we did and when. If you will follow this step-by-step procedure, you should end up with an excellent sourdough starter of your own:

The whole operation, from beginning the starter to making a satisfactory run of bread, took just about two weeks, and could have been short-cut here and there. Here are the steps taken:

March 16, noon. Mixed in a 2-quart bowl, 1 cup flour, ¾ cup lukewarm water, ¼ teaspoon sugar. Set the bowl outdoors uncovered for three hours to attract air-borne yeasts. Brought it indoors, stirred it, covered bowl with sheet plastic and set it in a warm place, about 85 degrees F., out of drafts.

March 17, 9 A.M. Stirred mixture, which was bubbling from fermentation, and added ¾ cup flour, ¼ cup water, ½ teaspoon sugar. Covered with sheet plastic and set it in a warm place.

March 17, 6 P.M. Mixture thick and gluey, felt right. Stirred in 1 cup flour, ½ cup water, ½ teaspoon sugar. Covered with sheet plastic and set it in a warm place.

March 18, 1 P.M. Starter looked right, with bubbles breaking surface. Made a half batch of bread with it (only half a batch, to make it easier for the new starter to raise the dough, since the same amount of starter was being used as for a whole batch). Result was a heavy, sour, close-grained bread, too sour for our taste but liked by some fanciers of sour French bread. The crust was also off-color. A new sourdough starter is always a little wild for a while, meaning its flavor and rising power are not yet mature. To tame this new starter down, we made two dry runs next, one March 20 and the other on March 23. Each time, we proceeded as if we were going to make bread, mixing the starter in a big bowl with 1 cup of flour, ½ cup lukewarm water, and 1 rounded teaspoon of sugar, then covering the bowl with sheet plastic and putting it in a warm place for 5 or 6 hours. It rose well each time, and each time we put about a good pint of it into a quart jar, put the jar in the refrigerator, and threw the rest away.

March 27. Made a regular baking. The starter behaved well, raising the bread normally, and the crust color was exactly right—a warm golden brown. The crust color is an index to the quality of the loaf. The texture was also good—evenly raised, without large air pockets. The flavor was the only remaining sign of a new starter; though less sour than the first batch, it was still a little sourer than we would choose for our daily bread. This condition corrects itself with repeated bakings, and a few more dry runs would hurry it along. Our experience is that after 6 or 8 bakings, a new starter is turning out bread close to what an old starter makes, and after a few months you can't tell the loaves apart.

Never put anything into your starter but flour, water, and sugar, never stir it with anything but a clean spoon or fork, and it will last indefinitely. Our old one is said to be more than 80 years old (though there is a constant renewing process going on among living cells, so we don't know how old "old" really is in the case of these yeasts). Try to use your starter at least once a month, and keep it in the refrigerator, the jar covered with sheet plastic, in between uses.

SOURDOUGH BREAD

This recipe will make 7 or 8 loaves and will use nearly 5 pounds of flour.

> *1 quart jar partly full of starter*
> *2½ cups lukewarm water*
> *4 cups flour*
> *1 tablespoon sugar*

Noon: Empty the starter into a bowl as big as a dishpan. Stir in the other ingredients. This should make a thick and gluey batter that follows the spoon up. Cover bowl with sheet plastic and put it in a warm place. We use the oven, warmed with a pilot light. In 6 hours the starter should half fill the bowl.

Bowl of starter
1 teaspoon baking soda
⅓ cup sugar
4 tablespoons butter
1 tablespoon bacon drippings
2 tablespoons salt
1 cup evaporated milk
2 cups lukewarm water
12 cups flour, approximately

6 P.M.: First spoon enough starter from the bowl to refill your quart starter jar slightly more than half full. Store it in the refrigerator for your next baking.

Fold baking soda and sugar into the starter that remains in the bowl. While it rises, melt butter and bacon drippings in a saucepan. Remove from heat and stir in salt, milk, and water. Pour this mixture into the bowl and stir until well blended with starter.

Stir in flour until the dough is thick enough to knead. We do this kneading in the bowl, stopping while the bread is still slightly sticky—a point at which a regular yeast bread would not be quite finished kneading.

Turn the ball of dough upside down in the bowl, with the smooth side up, cover bowl with sheet plastic, and let dough rise overnight. The best temperature is about 60 degrees F.

Morning: Turn dough out of bowl onto floured board. Cut it into 7 or 8 pieces and form them into loaves about one-fourth the size of what you want the finished loaf to be. Put them into lightly buttered baking pans, cover with plastic, and put into a warm place to rise. We use the oven warmed with a pilot light, and the rising takes about 3 hours. The loaves should be nearly tripled in size.

Slash tops of loaves ½ inch deep with a razor blade. A cross-hatch pattern or an X is often used on round loaves, and a single slash on others.

Bake about 25 minutes at 425 degrees F., until the bread is nicely browned and is loose in the pans. Turn loaves out upside down on paper towels to cool. Store extra loaves in freezer, and the one in current use in the refrigerator, in plastic bags.

CROUTONS

We use croutons in some recipes, so we do this to have them on hand: Cut slices of sourdough bread ½ inch thick and cut the slices into ½-inch cubes. Dry them for 15 minutes in a 300-degree F. oven. Store in plastic bags in the freezer. When needed, brown them lightly in a skillet in 1 or 2 tablespoons of olive oil or butter, stirring.

VISITING GIFT BOX

When we go to see some friend who lives alone and isn't feeling well, or one who is unusually busy—perhaps getting ready to move, or meeting some deadline—we take what we've found is always a welcome little gift, a box of good things all ready to be eaten.

First we cover a small grocery carton inside and out with white shelf paper. Then we pack it with a main course, a potato dish, a salad, bread, and cookies, all in disposable containers, like this:

Main course: We often roast a Rock Cornish chicken if we find them at a good price. We stuff it with a few sprigs of herbs such as tarragon or parsley, making it easy to reheat quickly if wished. Or we pack a foil container of Beef Ragout*, or Turnip Chicken Casserole*.

Potato dish: This is usually two Herbed Baked Stuffed Potatoes*. We make a "baking dish" from a sheet of foil, for reheating.

Salad: This is a Lettuce Roll* as described in Chapter 18, and a jar of our Herbed French Dressing*.

Bread: A loaf of our Sourdough Bread*.

Cookies: We choose some of those described in Chapter 36.

As decoration and cheer we tuck in a little tussy-mussy bouquet of whatever is blooming at the time, usually surrounded with fragrant rose geranium leaves. The whole gift box costs less than a dollar out-of-pocket, though we make the servings large enough for two persons in case our friend asks a friend to share them, which usually happens. "Your gift box saved my life," we're sometimes told afterward. At least it does save time and spreads a little pleasure around.

Chapter 3

ARTICHOKES—GLOBE AND JERUSALEM

GLOBE ARTICHOKES (*Cynara scolymus*)

In the coastal area of central California where we've been living in recent years, globe artichokes love to grow, and they are also an ornament to any house grounds. The part you eat is a huge bud, and if you let it alone it will open into a spectacular purplish flower. The plant is a perennial and grows 3 or 4 feet high, spreading 4 to 6 feet in a loose form like some ferns.

The globe artichoke came from the southern Mediterranean region and its ideal climate is one almost frost-free in winter and in summer mostly cool and often foggy. If you don't have this kind of climate you may not be able to grow worthwhile globe artichokes. We didn't even try to grow them in other parts of the country, but gardeners are an adventurous lot and globe artichokes often find themselves planted in strange places.

What you usually plant is a root, or sucker, from the base of an old plant, but you can grow an artichoke from seed. A plant from seed will be a little off type but may be exceptionally good. The Shumway and Park seed houses list seed, and plants are available from three nurseries that we know of: Stribling's, Nichols, and California. Green Globe is the variety usually offered.

If you live in non-artichoke country but are determined to grow globe artichokes, plant them in the spring after frosts are over. During the growing season give them frequent mist-like top-watering. Also, protect them in winter by cutting them off a few inches above ground level, putting a flower pot upside down over this stub, then covering the flower pot with a bushel of straw, and the straw with a 2-foot mound of earth.

In a favorable growing area, half a dozen flourishing plants will supply a family table. Fall or winter is the time to plant in artichoke country, at which time you cut suckers back to stubs a few inches long, trimming away all old leaves, and set plants with the crowns (the part between root and stem) just above ground level. They will get along in most garden soils.

Suckers from your own plants will supply you with new plants, and the best practice is to replace old plants every three years. Cultivate plants frequently, give them a weekly watering, and side-dress them once or twice during the season.

The edible buds form at the tops of the stalks. Cut them off while they are still tightly closed, taking an inch or two of stalk along. Later on when the leaves turn yellow, cut the stalk off at ground level. In California the entire plant is cut back in July and then given a feeding to force growth for winter production.

You can store surplus buds in a plastic bag in the refrigerator for days but for best eating we suggest you pick the buds young and small, which rewards you with something you can't buy at the store. These baby artichokes, about an inch and a half thick, are tender little treats with a delicate flavor, and can be eaten entire for they haven't yet developed the thistly center that must be cut out of older buds.

RECIPES

To prepare a mature globe artichoke for cooking, take a sharp, heavy knife, cut off the stem along with a thin slice of the bottom, cut off up to an inch of the top, and break away the outside layer or two of leaves. With a scissors trim away the sharp tips of exposed leaves. You can then separate the leaves somewhat and dig out the center thistle, called the choke, with a spoon or a ball cutter, though it's easier to remove it after cooking. Very young artichokes have no choke and are sometimes eaten raw. They need only a little trimming.

Cooking time depends on the size of the artichoke, but 30 minutes uncovered at a brisk boil in enough water just to cover the artichokes is a general guide. Half this long is enough if you remove the choke beforehand. Small young artichokes will be done in 15 or 20 minutes, and big ones can take an hour. Pull off a leaf and eat it to see if the cooking is finished. You eat an artichoke leaf by

1. Until you have tasted your own home-grown vegetables, you cannot imagine the difference garden freshness makes in flavor, and their eye appeal is superb. *Rohm & Haas photo*

2. Broccoli is both a handsome garden plant and one of the most nourishing, as well as being delicious. This one is Green Comet, a speedy new hybrid with a center head as big as a cauliflower.

W. Atlee Burpee Co. photo

3. Carrots are easy to grow, and when garden-fresh their flavor and texture are far superior to store carrots. The variety shown here is medium long, and others range from little fellows only 2 or 3 inches long to some that grow a foot in length. *W. Atlee Burpee Co. photo*

closing your teeth on it halfway up it, and pulling it out of your mouth. Another test for doneness is to press the bottom, which will feel slightly soft when ready. This bottom is called the heart and is greatly prized.

Here are five good ways to cook globe artichokes:

ROMAN ARTICHOKES

> *4 large globe artichokes*
> *Salt*
> *Pepper*
> *1 tablespoon finely chopped oregano*
> *¼ cup corn oil*
> *¼ cup olive oil*

Trim the artichokes, press them open, and place them bottoms down in a stew pan. Sprinkle them with the salt, pepper, and oregano. Mix the oils and pour them over the artichokes. Add water enough to come about halfway up the artichokes. Cook at a brisk boil until the outer leaves are tender but not limp, about an hour, basting the artichokes several times during the cooking, with the cooking liquid.

Remove the artichokes to a serving dish and pour over them a few spoonfuls of the cooked-down liquid left in the pan. *Serves 4.*

GREEK ARTICHOKES

> *12 small young globe artichokes*
> *1 cup Vegetable Stock**
> *2 tablespoons corn oil*
> *2 tablespoons olive oil*
> *1 garlic clove*
> *1 tablespoon lemon juice*
> *1 medium-sized onion, finely chopped*
> *1 large carrot, sliced*
> *2 tablespoons chopped parsley*
> *½ teaspoon salt*

Trim the artichokes and put them into a stew pan with all the other ingredients. Cover the pan and cook at a light boil, stirring occasionally, until the artichokes are tender and the other vegetables well cooked, about 20 minutes.

Remove artichokes and keep them warm while you do this: Remove the garlic clove if wished (though it will not be objectionably strong after this cooking) and mash the vegetables in the pan. Cook this mixture down rapidly to the consistency of a medium sauce, and serve it over the artichokes. At this young stage the entire artichoke is edible. *Serves 4 to 6.*

PORTUGUESE ARTICHOKES

> 12 small young globe artichokes
> 1 tablespoon lemon juice
> 1 tablespoon Garlic Oil*
> ¼ cup olive oil
> 2 shallots, finely chopped
> 2 ripe tomatoes, chopped, or 1 cup canned tomatoes
> 2 tablespoons finely chopped parsley
> Salt

Trim artichokes and cut into quarters. Cook them for about 5 minutes in a sauccpan of briskly boiling water to cover, with the lemon juice added and the pan lid on.

Meanwhile heat the oils in a large skillet, stir in shallots and tomatoes, and simmer for a few minutes.

Drain artichokes, lay them in the skillet, and simmer uncovered for about 20 minutes or until artichokes are tender, occasionally basting them with the cooking liquid. Sprinkle with the parsley and salt during the last minute of cooking. At this young stage the entire artichoke is edible. *Serves 4.*

BRAISED ARTICHOKES

This is a simpler version of Portuguese Artichokes*.

12 small young globe artichokes
6 tablespoons corn oil
*2 tablespoons Garlic Oil**
4 tablespoons butter
2 tablespoons finely chopped parsley
White wine vinegar

Trim and quarter the artichokes. Heat the oils and melt the butter in a large skillet. Add the quartered artichokes, cover the skillet, and cook gently until the artichokes are tender, shaking the pan occasionally.

Two or three minutes before the cooking is finished, add the parsley, blending it with the liquid in the pan, and sprinkle the artichokes lightly with the vinegar. At this young stage the entire artichoke is edible. *Serves 4 to 6.*

ARTICHOKES AND EGGS

A friend of ours runs a shop selling fine foods of the southern European cuisine. He is John Coniglio, and when he described this artichoke dish for us, John did so lovingly, with gestures.

12 small young globe artichokes
¼ cup olive oil
Salt
Pepper
6 eggs, beaten

Trim artichokes and cut them into about 6 round slices each. Warm olive oil in a big skillet, add the artichoke slices, salt, and pepper. Cover the skillet and simmer until the artichokes are tender, stirring now and then. During this cooking, the artichoke slices will separate.

Pour the beaten eggs over the artichoke pieces in the skillet, cover skillet and cook until the eggs are barely set. Tip the pan and pour or spoon off a little oil. Then—and this is the art, John says—turn the contents of the skillet upside down on a warm oiled plate and immediately slide it all back into the skillet to finish cooking the other side, which will take only another minute or less. *Serves 4 to 6.*

JERUSALEM ARTICHOKES (*Helianthus tuberosus*)

The Indians liked Jerusalem artichokes, and the plant is as native American as they. Their name for it was "kaischuchpenauk." It is a perennial, gets along almost anywhere, and will even grow in partial shade although it is a species of sunflower. We raised Jerusalem artichokes in the hot Midwest, and they also thrive in the cool climate of central coastal California.

The part of the Jerusalem artichoke that you eat grows underground—tubers about as long as your finger and two or three times as thick, or thereabouts. They are light brown and look like knobby little potatoes. They taste a little like potatoes but are not floury and have an agreeable, slightly nut-like flavor. They can be used in place of water chestnuts.

As you can see, the plant isn't in the least like an artichoke nor does it owe anything to Jerusalem, but its name is something we have to live with.

If you find Jerusalem artichokes on sale in your supermarket it will be a wonder. They aren't widely known or well understood. We've occasionally seen them offered in ours for fifty cents a pound, and they were seldom worth buying—usually limp from poor storage, and tired out. To get good fresh ones, crisp and delicate, raise them yourself. Not many garden suppliers offer Jerusalem artichokes but you can order them from Burgess, who carry a strain they consider larger and sweeter than others they formerly listed, and from Nichols.

Any soil will suit Jerusalem artichokes. Spading it well before planting will please them, as it will any root crop. One plant will produce up to a pound of tubers in a season, and the tubers should be planted 3 or 4 inches deep, in the spring.

The top growth is typically sunflower—stalky and 8 feet or more high, with yellow flowers something like daisies.

The new tubers produced will provide all you need for making new plantings, but whether you make them or not, the original planting will keep right on producing each year. It may try to take over the garden, and if so, simply dig up any off-limits tubers. In fact this is the ideal plant for what someone has called the garden of neglect. Literally, you don't have to do a thing for Jerusalem artichokes once you do them the favor of planting them. Keeping down weeds with cultivation is welcome but they don't insist on even this. They'll out-weed the weeds.

Once the plants are well established, tubers can be dug as needed throughout the year. If your winters get severe, you'll probably want to dig most of the crop before the ground freezes, leaving a few to maintain the planting. Use a spading fork and start digging 2 feet or so from the base of the stalk.

We find an ideal storage method is to keep the tubers in a plastic bag in the refrigerator. They'll store pretty well in any cool place where they won't dry out.

RECIPES

Many recipes call for parboiling Jerusalem artichokes to begin with. The thing to remember is: Don't peel them beforehand. Just scrub them with a brush; after parboiling, scrape them lightly to remove what little skin they have. We parboil them much more briefly than some cooks think necessary, but garden-fresh ones cook quickly. We drop them into rapidly boiling water, give them 5 minutes, then drain and plunge them into cold water before scraping.

There are occasional exceptions to this procedure. For salads, Jerusalem artichokes are simply peeled and sliced. And when used instead of water chestnuts in an oriental dish—for which they are splendid—peel the Jerusalem artichokes, slice them, and cook them quickly. This procedure has also seemed better in the recipe we give for Fried Jerusalem Artichokes*.

BRAISED JERUSALEM ARTICHOKES

This is a simple and splendid dish in which the flavors of fresh mushrooms and Jerusalem artichokes make a happy marriage. You can parboil the artichokes a day ahead of time and hold them in the refrigerator, scraping them just before using.

> 8 medium-sized mushrooms
> 4 tablespoons butter
> 8 Jerusalem artichokes, parboiled and scraped
> 2 tablespoons Kraft Stock*
> Salt
> Pepper
> Medium sherry

Cut mushrooms into quarters, both stems and caps. Melt butter in a skillet and simmer the mushrooms in it, covered, for 5 minutes, stirring once or twice.

Slice the Jerusalem artichokes into ⅛-inch rounds, add them to the mushrooms and simmer, uncovered, for 2 or 3 minutes, shaking the skillet now and then.

Add the stock, turn up the heat and cook until the stock is absorbed, about 2 minutes, shaking skillet frequently. Season with salt and pepper and a sprinkle of sherry at the last minute. A dry or medium sherry is preferred. *Serves 4.*

JERUSALEM ARTICHOKE SAUTE

In our recipe file this one is marked "Very good." It is similar to Braised Jerusalem Artichokes* but drier and brings out the nut-like flavor more distinctly. If you don't have garden cress on hand, you can scissors some chives or parsley over the dish before serving.

> 8 Jerusalem artichokes, parboiled and scraped
> 6 large mushrooms
> 1 tablespoon butter
> 1 tablespoon olive oil

1 teaspoon *Garlic Oil**
Salt
Pepper
Garden cress

Cut the artichokes into ¼-inch slices and lay them on paper
towels to absorb moisture. Cut mushrooms into ¼-inch slices, both
stems and caps, put them into a skillet with the butter and oils, and
cook over medium-low heat for 5 minutes, stirring occasionally.

Add the artichoke slices and cook 5 minutes more.

Salt lightly just before serving, and grind a little pepper over the
dish. Garnish with sprigs of garden cress. *Serves 4.*

JERUSALEM ARTICHOKE SALAD

We've said Jerusalem artichokes can be used as water chestnuts
are, and this recipe will demonstrate it. A good combination of
lettuces here is Cos and one of the crisp butter-heads such as Deer-
tongue, Bibb, or Fordhook.

4 raw Jerusalem artichokes
¼ cup fresh lemon juice
Chives
Lettuce
*Herbed French Dressing**

Wash the freshly dug Jerusalem artichokes and peel them with a
potato peeler. Then slice them with it into very thin rounds, spread
the rounds in a shallow bowl, and pour the lemon juice over them.
Let them marinate for 15 minutes.

Chop a handful of fresh chives into a salad bowl and tear enough
lettuce into it for 4 servings. (See Chapter 18, "Lettuce," for a
suggestion on preparing salad lettuce.)

Drain the artichoke slices, reserving lemon juice for other uses
such as salad dressing, and add the artichokes to the salad bowl
contents. Pour the dressing over this, about ¼ cup, toss, and serve.
Makes 4 servings.

FRIED JERUSALEM ARTICHOKES

10 raw Jerusalem artichokes
2 tablespoons butter
Salt
Pepper
Dry white wine

Wash and peel the artichokes. Slice them into thin rounds about
the thickness of a penny. Heat butter to bubbling in a skillet and
slide in the artichoke slices.

Cook them quickly over brisk heat, stirring and turning them
with a pancake turner so that they brown lightly on both sides.

Then sprinkle them with a little salt and pepper, pour over them
2 or 3 tablespoons of the wine (a California sauterne is good here),
simmer for a few more seconds, and dish up. *Serves 4.*

JERUSALEM ARTICHOKES AND CHARD

This recipe would be included among those for cooked leafy greens
except that it is the Jerusalem artichokes that give it character even
though only two are in it. The chard stalks are not used. We often
use mustard greens, Chinese cabbage, or curled endive in place of
some of the chard.

2 Jerusalem artichokes, parboiled and scraped
1 tablespoon olive oil
20 large chard leaves
1 tablespoon butter
¼ cup dry vermouth
½ teaspoon salt
Pepper

Slice artichokes in ⅛-inch rounds. Bring olive oil to a simmer in
a large deep skillet, add artichoke slices, and cook gently, uncovered,
for a few minutes, stirring once.

Meanwhile, wash chard, trim out stalks, drain and chop the leaves coarsely. Add them to the artichokes, cover skillet, turn up heat to medium and cook until chard is limp but still bright green. Remove it and the artichokes to a serving dish and keep warm, leaving juices in the skillet.

Quickly melt butter in the skillet, add the rest of the ingredients and rapidly cook this mixture down to a thin sauce, stirring constantly. Drizzle it over the vegetables and serve at once. *Serves 4.*

(For another good Jerusalem artichoke recipe, see Jerusalem Artichoke Chicken* in Chapter 39, "Casseroles, Etc.")

Chapter 4

ASPARAGUS

ASPARAGUS (*Asparagus officinalis*)

If you are willing to wait longer for edible results you can grow asparagus from seed, but it is more usual to start with roots because even so, it takes two years to grow good plants.

If this seems too long, reflect that putting in an asparagus bed is almost like planting an apple tree—a lifetime property. Even though you may be told to renew the bed every 15 or 20 years for best production, if you don't, it will go on producing just the same. You'll sometimes find an old neglected bed in an abandoned farmhouse yard, choked with weeds and half starved, but bringing forth tender green spears every springtime as if it expected the folks home again any day now. In parts of Europe, Asia Minor, and North Africa the plant grows wild; now and then it escapes the garden in this country, via seeds, and sets up on its own in a hedgerow, all of which shows its vigor.

Asparagus is one of the old vegetables, on man's dinner table for 2,000 years and probably longer. It is related to asparagus fern, and what looks like its leaves are really thready green branches. The real leaves are the scales on the shoots, which you remove before cooking. Another peculiarity of asparagus is that plants are nearly always either male or female, and the females are the ones that grow the nice plump stalks. Since you don't need pollination to get a crop, you can dig the roots of male plants out of your bed once you identify them by their skinny shoots, and replace them with new roots you hope will grow female plants. If so, do it very early in your bed's life. Asparagus roots are rugged to dig out after they've grown for a few years.

If you live where the winters get cold enough to freeze the top two inches or more of earth, asparagus will do better for you than in milder climates.

Many varieties of asparagus have come and gone but the one you're sure to find is Mary Washington. We grew it in Missouri and recommend it to you. If you find another variety selling in your region you may still want to plant some Washington roots also as insurance. Lately a hybrid has come on the market and is said to yield heavily. It was developed in Minnesota, and Farmer Seed handles it under the name of Faribo F_1.

Asparagus likes a rich soil—manure if you can get it, compost if you can't, mixed with your garden soil at the bottom of a trench a foot wide and about a foot deep. Add enough compost or manure to bring the trench bottom to 10 inches from the surface level. Water the trench lightly and lay the roots in it 18 inches apart from center to center, with the eyes or crown up, and the roots spread. The 18 inches can be 15 if you are short of space, or 24 if you aren't. This is one time when it pays to have your soil tested to see if you need lime and fertilizer, and if you do, it should be mixed with the trench fill before the roots go in. In the absence of a test, a general rule is to include 1 pound each of a commercial fertilizer and superphosphate for every 10 feet of trench, and for acid soils include about 1 pound of hydrated lime.

After you have the roots placed, rake in about 2 inches of the earth you dug out to make the trench, and tamp it down with your feet. As the shoots appear, keep raking in earth, not quite covering the shoots, and by August or so you'll have the trench refilled.

How big a planting should you make? Two rows, each 20 feet long and about 3 feet apart, will take care of most families. This will accommodate two dozen plants comfortably. Like strawberries, asparagus roots are often sold in lots of 25, so this would plant the two rows. Instead, what we do is this:

We buy 50 roots and select the best 25 or so for the asparagus bed. Then we plant the discards in a temporary place in the garden, not taking too many pains about it. The spears they produce are what we eat while we're waiting the two years it takes to get a permanent asparagus planting into production. This is a pandering to human greed, we know, but many a new asparagus bed has been enfeebled because its owner couldn't keep his hands off it those

first and second years when it needed all the growth it could make,
to build a strong constitution for a lifetime of bearing.

Besides being beautiful, an asparagus bed is simple to care for.
Each fall cut the plants off 6 inches from the ground, burn this
brush, and spread a mulch. Leaves will do but if you have compost
to spare, it will feed the roots too.

In early spring, before any spears appear, use a pre-emergence
weed killer. Your garden center will have one, and this will save you
a lot of tiresome weeding later.

At about the time the first spears begin to appear, spread commercial fertilizer and with a rake gently work it and the compost
mulch into the soil. Spread about 1 pound of fertilizer for every 5
feet of row, scattering it in a broad band on each side of the row.
The bands should be 2 or 3 feet wide, measuring out from the center of the row. After the cutting season is over, when your asparagus
bed is in production, give it another feeding, about half as strong.

You can begin harvesting a new bed in its third season. Start
about mid-April and stop at the end of May. Each year *after* that,
you can cut all you can eat until about the end of June. The sign
to stop cutting is when spears begin to get skinny. Your eyes will
tell you when. With two thrifty 20-foot rows a family of four can
eat asparagus practically every day during the season's peak.

As to the technique of harvesting asparagus: Though we say
"cut," and this is the usual method, either with a knife or a V-notch
asparagus cutter, we prefer to snap off the spears with our fingers.
It is faster, you can't hurt the roots by accident with a cutter, and
there won't be any tough bottom bit to discard.

RECIPES

Before you can do a thing with asparagus you have to get rid
of the scales—those abortive leaves clinging tightly to the lower half
or so of the spear. If you take them off with a potato peeler you'll
waste a good deal of the spear. We remove scales by lifting the
tip of each with a paring knife and carefully skinning it off. Tedious
but rewarding.

Here we must say frankly that we aren't going to suggest many
ways to cook asparagus. Asparagus right out of the garden is too

superb to need anything but butter and a little salt to make it heavenly food. Market asparagus is something else again, of course.

In the recipes that follow, and for asparagus in a Divan*, a preliminary basic cooking is needed. It consists of tying a string around a bundle of asparagus spears, standing them in the bottom of a double boiler with an inch of boiling water in it, and then using the top of the double boiler as a lid (since the spears are often too tall to let the regular lid fit). Keep the water boiling, and cook until you can just pierce the base of a stalk with a sharp fork, about 8 to 12 minutes. This method steams the more tender tops while it is boiling the bottoms. It is a good idea to use the same size spears in any one bundle, as thinner ones cook faster.

Another and perhaps simpler way to cook asparagus is to cut an inch or two off the bottoms, lay these in a saucepan with just enough water to cover them, and lay the upper parts of the spears over them in a single layer. Cover the pan and cook at a moderate boil until the bottoms are tender but still firm. A variation of this method that we like is:

Cut an inch or two off the bottoms of the spears and split each of these pieces vertically. Then put them and the upper parts of the spears into a large saucepan with enough Vegetable Stock* to cover all the asparagus. Put a lid on the pan, bring stock to a boil, and cook gently until the asparagus is tender, about 6 or 8 minutes.

In each of these three moist-cookings of asparagus you can dish it up at once and serve it with just a little melted butter over it and a bit of salt or lemon juice. Don't overcook it and you will have asparagus at its supreme best—if it is garden-fresh asparagus.

Asparagus is also a nice addition to Garden-fresh Caesar Salad*, as given in Chapter 18, "Lettuce."

ASPARAGUS ROQUEFORT

Butter
24 cooked asparagus spears
⅓ cup crumbled Roquefort or bleu cheese
Salt
*½ cup Croutons**

Butter a casserole generously and lay half the asparagus spears in it in a single layer. Sprinkle the cheese evenly over them and arrange the rest of the spears on top of the cheese. Lightly salt the top layer, strew the croutons over it, dot the croutons with butter, and bake uncovered for 20 minutes at 375 degrees F. *Serves 4.*

ASPARAGUS VERMOUTH

> 24 cooked asparagus spears
> 3 tablespoons melted butter
> ½ garlic clove
> 2 tablespoons finely chopped parsley
> ⅓ cup dry vermouth
> Salt
> Pepper

Arrange the asparagus in a casserole in a crisscross pattern. Melt butter in a saucepan and simmer the garlic in it until the garlic is lightly brown. Discard garlic.

Sprinkle parsley over the asparagus, pour the vermouth over it, wetting each spear; pour the melted butter over it, and sprinkle with a little salt and pepper.

Bake uncovered at 375 degrees F. until the juices in the casserole have cooked down to about ¼ cup, about 20 minutes. Spoon some of this sauce over each serving. *Serves 4.*

ASPARAGUS VINAIGRETTE

> 24 cooked asparagus spears

VINAIGRETTE SAUCE

> 2 tablespoons lemon juice
> 3 tablespoons cider vinegar
> ⅓ cup olive oil
> ⅓ cup corn oil
> 1 teaspoon salt
> ⅛ teaspoon pepper
> ½ teaspoon ginger
> 1 teaspoon finely chopped parsley

1 *teaspoon finely chopped tarragon*
1 *tablespoon finely chopped chives*
1 *tablespoon chopped Nasturtium Capers**

Lay asparagus in a shallow pan or platter. Blend all the other ingredients by shaking them together in a jar. Pour this dressing over
the asparagus, cover with plastic wrap, and put into the refrigerator
to marinate and chill for 30 minutes or longer before serving.
Serves 4.

Chapter 5

BEANS—SNAP AND LIMA

SNAP BEANS (*Phaseolus vulgaris*)

If you are willing to go to the trouble of providing a support for it to climb, we think there is no snap bean like Kentucky Wonder. Another name for it is Old Homestead, and one taste of it brings back to us the sunny summer pleasures of our Missouri farm garden and the bounty of jar after jar in the stone-walled fruit cellar under the kitchen. Bush beans are simpler to look after, needing no support, and there are some good ones, but we're prejudiced in favor of Kentucky Wonder, and have been so for years in spite of some interesting new varieties in both climbers and bush that have been developed. Incidentally, if you have a fancy for producing your own dried beans (we don't), Kentucky Wonder is popular for that purpose.

Wax beans are an attractive vegetable to serve when you want their yellow color on the table but we've always preferred green snap beans. Either kind will supply you with a good amount of vitamins, though the green beans are light on B_2 and the yellow ones on A. Both are good but not wildly good sources of protein, which may surprise those who always thought all beans are bursting with protein. If it's protein you're after, eat lima beans; they outdo snap beans three to one. Soy beans are another vegetable rich in protein, and peas are well up toward the top of the protein list too. Soy beans (*Glycine max*) are natives of Asia, but snap and lima beans are natives of the American tropics.

Bush beans mature pods in 7 or 8 weeks, and pole beans take a week or two more but bear longer. Bush beans seldom grow as high as 2 feet. Pole beans shoot up to 6 or 8 feet, so plant them where they won't shade other vegetables.

Aside from Kentucky Wonder we have no favorites among pole beans, and of the bush types Tender Pod is one of the best.

Snap beans do well in a sunny spot in almost any garden soil, but don't plant till the soil has warmed up and frost danger is entirely past. Pole beans are especially touchy about this, and all beans want the longer days of summer. Planting too soon won't save you any time, and the seeds may even die in cold wet soil before they can sprout.

Before planting the seed, treat it with a nitrogen-fixing bacteria inoculant such as Legume Aid. The package directions are simple, and this will make your beans grow better, especially in soil where beans haven't been planted before.

Planting depth for beans varies from ½ inch to 2 inches, depending on soil texture and moisture. Try planting three rows at different depths and see which does best in your garden. Then you'll know for future guidance.

Snap beans grow fast and a fertilizing at planting time is usually enough. Too much nitrogen, in fact, will make them grow more leaves instead of beans.

Rough poles will support pole beans, set firmly in the ground or arranged in tepee style with 3 or 4 poles tied together at the top. Or grow the beans on a string trellis.

Keep your beans weeded well but cultivate shallowly. Better yet, spread a mulch.

For continuous production through the season, make a planting of bush beans every two weeks. If you live in the Midwest and make your first planting about May 1, you have a chance of getting nine crops of beans in this way. The first and last plantings will be chancy, but that's part of the game.

Bean diseases, if they occur, can be considered incurable. Plant resistant varieties and run a clean garden, and don't disturb the beans when the leaves are wet. Use an all-purpose dust or spray for any other problems.

Pick your beans when they are still young enough so that there is scarcely any swelling of the beans inside the pods. You'll never see beans like this at the supermarket. Older beans also are more delicious when freshly picked and cooked soon after, but by growing your own you'll have the chance to find out what a treat a tiny, tender snap bean really is. After that, nine succession plantings won't seem too many. Snap beans freeeze well and also can well, so even if you have a lot coming in at one time you can keep picking them young. Occasionally a pod will hide from you and become more mature than you want. Pick it anyway, and shell out its beans. Added to the young beans in a dish, these older ones give an extra dividend of flavor.

RECIPES

Old-fashioned cooks always used to cook string beans, as snap beans were then called, for about 3 hours and sometimes longer. This seems like cruel and inhuman treatment when you consider you can cook a snap bean in only 10 minutes, but there is something to be said for the long cooking. For one thing, our old-fashioned cook usually dealt with more mature beans and with varieties often less tender than those in today's home garden. For another thing, a long slow simmer brings out hidden flavor in a snap bean. We include one recipe for long-cooked snap beans as done by a neighbor of ours, Marietta (Mrs. R. A.) Tracy. She does them deliciously and when she has a bean-cooking day she makes enough for all her friends, including us, we're glad to say.

To prepare snap beans for cooking, wash them, break off the tips of both ends, and if beans are large, break each into 2 or 3 pieces. We cook small beans whole.

SIMPLE SNAP BEANS

This quick and easy way to prepare young snap beans right out of the garden at the last minute has always been one of the most popular with us—and with guests.

4 cups Vegetable Stock*
4 cups young snap beans
Salt
Pepper
3 tablespoons butter
Lemon juice

Bring the vegetable stock to a boil in a saucepan, drop the beans in, cover the pan, return to a boil and cook over medium heat, stirring now and then, until just tender enough to pierce with a fork, 8 to 10 minutes.

Drain, lightly salt and pepper the beans, add the butter and, while it melts, shake the pan a few times to coat all the beans with butter. Serve with a few drops of lemon juice sprinkled over the beans (or it can be used in place of the butter if calories are a consideration, in which case we suggest the addition of 1 tablespoon of olive oil). *Serves 4.*

SNAP BEANS ITALIAN STYLE

2 *cups young snap beans*
2 *cups Vegetable Stock**
2 *medium-sized onions*
2 *tablespoons olive oil*
1 *teaspoon Garlic Oil**
Salt
Pepper
2 *tablespoons finely chopped oregano*
2 *medium-sized tomatoes, chopped*
½ *cup bread crumbs*
1 *tablespoon butter*
1 *teaspoon anchovy paste*

Simmer the beans in the stock 8 to 10 minutes, covered.

Meanwhile, slice the onions thickly and cook them in the oils in a skillet over low heat until onions are slightly translucent.

Drain the beans, spread half in a casserole, then spread half the onions, then the rest of the beans, then the rest of the onions. As you make the layers, sprinkle each lightly with salt, pepper, and oregano.

Spread the tomatoes on top and over them the crumbs. Mix butter and anchovy paste with a fork and dot the crumb topping with it. Cover casserole and bake 20 minutes at 350 degrees F. Uncover and bake 10 minutes longer. *Serves 4 to 6.*

DILLED WAX BEANS

The American Indians raised and cooked beans, and this recipe
is an adaptation of one the Indians were said to use, or perhaps
still use.

> 2 strips fat bacon, cut into small squares
> 3 or 4 cups young wax beans cut into 1-inch pieces
> ½ cup Vegetable Stock*
> Salt
> Pepper
> 1 teaspoon molasses
> I tablespoon finely chopped dill
> Tarragon wine vinegar

Fry bacon lightly in a large skillet, and add beans, which should be
a little damp. Add stock, cover skillet and simmer 15 minutes, shaking skillet now and then. Season beans with the rest of the ingredients, stirring gently. Not much salt will be needed, and a scant
tablespoon of the vinegar will do. *Serves 4.*

SNAP BEAN CASSEROLE

> 3 or 4 cups fresh young snap beans
> Vegetable Stock*
> 6 tablespoons butter
> ½ pound mushrooms, coarsely chopped
> ½ cup evaporated milk
> Salt
> Pepper

Put beans into a saucepan with enough stock to cover, and simmer
with the lid on for 15 minutes or until beans are tender.

Meanwhile melt half the butter in a skillet, add mushrooms and
cook covered over brisk heat for 5 minutes, shaking skillet several
times.

Drain beans. Put them with the milk into a casserole, cover them

with the mushrooms, season with salt and pepper. Melt the rest
of the butter in the skillet and drizzle it over the beans, scraping
all the juices out of the skillet with a rubber spatula. Bake uncovered for 10 minutes at 325 degrees F. *Serves 4.*

SNAP BEANS WITH ALMONDS

4 tablespoons butter
½ cup chopped Blanched Almonds*
4 cups fresh young snap beans
Vegetable Stock*
Salt
Pepper
½ teaspoon finely chopped rosemary
1 tablespoon dry vermouth

Melt butter in a skillet, add the almonds, and cook over low heat
till almonds turn golden.

Meanwhile cook the beans with enough stock to cover them in
a saucepan with the lid on, until they are just tender, about 10
minutes.

Drain beans, dry them a little by shaking them in the pan over
high heat for a minute or so. Add them to the almonds in the
skillet, season with salt, pepper, and rosemary. Sprinkle them with
the vermouth and stir gently. *Serves 4.*

SNAP BEANS WITH HORSE-RADISH

4 cups fresh young snap beans
Vegetable Stock*
2 egg yolks
1 tablespoon melted butter
1 tablespoon freshly grated horse-radish
½ cup evaporated milk, scalded
Salt
1 teaspoon lemon juice

Put beans in a saucepan with enough stock to cover them. Simmer
them with the lid on until they are just tender, about 10 minutes.

Meanwhile put the yolks, melted butter, and horse-radish in the top of a double boiler and beat until creamy, with an egg beater. Stir in the scalded milk. Heat this sauce over simmering water in the double boiler's bottom section until it thickens.

Then drain the beans, salt them, and sprinkle them with the lemon juice. Gently add them to the sauce in the double boiler, stirring, and serve at once. *Serves 4.*

MARIETTA'S BEANS

Here is the recipe for the long-cooked beans we spoke of, in the cook's own casual words. Our word: Delicious.

Put a ham bone in water to cover. Bring to a boil. Skim a bit, and toss in about 2 pounds of green unstrung beans.

Cover the pan, lower the heat, and simmer for a long time, maybe 4 hours. The beans should be nice and soft by then.

Add about ½ cup of sugar and, if you like, some chopped onion.

Add wine vinegar, or plain vinegar, or lemon juice, about ¼ cup.

Simmer approximately another hour, and serve.

SNAP BEAN FRITTERS

This recipe came from an enthusiastic cook and gardener, Mr. Jerome Kantor, who said it is his favorite way to prepare a good snap bean, his favorite variety being Tender Pod. He added: "The batter here may be used either for deep-fat cooking or for sautéeing. In any case, drain the fritters well on paper towels after frying."

2 eggs, separated
1 tablespoon oil or melted butter
Salt
⅔ cup milk or water, or equal parts of each
1 cup sifted flour

1 or 2 tablespoons sugar (optional)
1 tablespoon lemon juice (optional)
Raw snap beans

Beat egg yolks well, add oil or butter, ¼ teaspoon salt, and the milk or water alternately with the flour, to make a smooth batter. The sugar is an optional addition, as is the lemon juice. Or a dry white wine may be used instead of lemon juice. If the fritters are to be served with drinks, sugar is probably best left out.

Next, beat egg whites and ⅛ teaspoon salt until stiff. Fold into the batter. Dip beans in batter, singly or by spoonfuls, and fry them —6 to 8 minutes in deep fat at 360 to 380 degrees F., or just until they turn a delicate brown. Time them by the color if sautéeing.

LIMA BEANS (*Phaseolus limensis*)

As with snap beans, you have a choice of pole or bush types in lima beans. We've usually chosen the bush ones because they are convenient but we have golden memories of the climbing limas grown by a Dutch neighbor in Virginia. They were the variety called Sieva or Carolina, which are small-seeded, and they simply covered a homemade fish-net trellis 8 feet high and 12 feet wide. They bore what seemed to be bushels of their plump little pods during their season and were some of the best things we ever tasted. Pole limas have a reputation for superior flavor.

Bush limas bear two or three weeks faster than pole ones, but you need a long summer to grow either. Figure on 4 months, including warm nights, from seeding to final harvest for pole limas. They are temperamental about this and some other conditions. Like snap beans they originated in the tropics but they've stayed more tropical in their weather tastes. If you have a short but hot summer you can start limas in peat pots in a cold frame or greenhouse a month before it will be warm enough outside for planting.

Not only are lima beans good for you because they are high in protein—they are also excellent sources of Vitamins B_1 and B_2, and good sources of Vitamins A and C.

Popular lima beans seem to stay in favor year after year. The bush one called Fordhook was introduced in 1907, for instance, and continues in high popularity today, amply justifying the thousand dollars its discoverer, a California commercial grower, demanded and got from seedsman W. Atlee Burpee. The bush variety Henderson is still older, having been found growing wild along a roadside in Virginia nearly 100 years ago. It is a small-seeded, so-called baby lima, and Fordhook is the large-seeded type, called potato lima. One of the tenderest is Baby Fordhook, a potato-seeded bush type. King of the Garden is a famous old pole lima still sold widely, and Prizetaker is another very good pole type, with big pods six inches long containing 3 or 4 beans twice the size of other large limas.

Lima beans like their soil a little richer than snap beans insist on, but like snap beans they'll run to leaves instead of beans if they get too much nitrogen.

Sow limas with the "eyes" facing down; the eye is the curved-in place on the bean's edge, where the root will sprout. Care for limas as you do snap beans, but since limas take longer to bear, more than one or two succession plantings are not apt to succeed.

To feel as rich as Croesus, pick some of your lima beans before they have filled out their pods completely. You'll get only a dab compared to the harvest when pods are mature, but you'll get a treat that only a home gardener can afford. Shell them out and then merely simmer these tinies in a little butter in a pan with a lettuce leaf laid over them and the pan lid on, for a few minutes until they are tender.

Aside from this extravagance, the time to pick limas is when the pods fill out. If in doubt, open one by pressing on the outward curving side. You'll quickly learn to tell at a glance when pods are ready for picking.

You can store limas a few days simply by not shelling them after they are picked, but for the best eating pick them just before you are ready to shell them for cooking, and freeze or can any surplus.

RECIPES

We're only talking about fresh lima beans here. Dried ones are good but there isn't any point in taking up limited garden space for them when you can buy good ones at the store.

In preparing fresh lima beans a preliminary cooking is often called for. We usually do this in Vegetable Stock* as with snap beans. Since limas vary greatly in size, cooking time varies. Shell the beans, rinse them, and cook briskly in a covered saucepan till tender. This will take from 10 minutes to 40, and the best way to test for tenderness is to fish a bean out and eat it.

LIMAS WITH THYME

  3 tablespoons butter
  2 shallots, finely chopped
  1 tablespoon finely chopped thyme
  3 cups fresh lima beans, cooked
  Salt
  Pepper

Melt butter in a saucepan, add shallots and simmer 3 or 4 minutes. Add the rest of the ingredients and stir gently several times until lima beans are heated through. *Serves 4.*

LIMA CASSEROLE

A white wine vinegar may be used in place of the lemon juice, and Parmesan cheese in place of Romano.

  3 cups fresh lima beans, cooked
  1 teaspoon fresh lemon juice
  Salt
  3 tablespoons butter
  ½ clove garlic
  ½ cup Romano cheese, freshly grated

Put limas into a casserole, sprinkle them with the lemon juice and salt them lightly. Melt butter in a saucepan, simmer the garlic in it a minute or so till garlic browns lightly, discard garlic and drizzle the butter over the limas.

Cover the limas with the cheese. Put casserole into a 300-degree

F. oven for 20 minutes, uncovered. Finish cooking under the broiler just long enough to turn the cheese topping golden. *Serves 4.*

SAUTEED LIMAS

> 2 *tablespoons butter*
> 1 *tablespoon corn oil*
> 6 *scallions, cut into ½-inch pieces*
> 2 *cups fresh lima beans, cooked*
> *Salt*
> *Pepper*
> 1 *tablespoon finely chopped savory*
> ¼ *cup dry white wine*

Melt butter in a skillet, add oil and scallions and simmer for about 5 minutes, until the green parts of the scallions are soft, stirring frequently. Add the beans, salt, and pepper, and heat, stirring gently, about 5 minutes longer.

Sprinkle the chopped savory into the skillet, stir briefly, and remove beans and scallions to serving dish with slotted spoon. Quickly add the wine to the juices remaining in the skillet and cook for a minute over brisk heat, tilting the skillet to blend liquids. Pour the resulting sauce over the beans and serve at once. *Serves 4.*

Chapter 6

BEETS

BEETS (*Beta vulgaris*)

The beet is another of the old plants, cultivated for about 2,000 years, but not in the improved forms we grow today, which go back only about 400 years. According to some taste-test researchers, beets are very popular with those who like them but these fans aren't numerous. If so, our friends all belong to this minority, because they all take beets every time we offer them some from our garden.

Beets are willing to grow almost anywhere in the United States and they grow faster than you might think. You can grow a beet almost the size of a tennis ball in just 8 weeks and some varieties mature about 2 weeks sooner. One of our own favorites happens to be a slowpoke but produces lots of leaves, and beet leaves are extremely high in minerals and vitamins. It is the Lutz Green Leaf and takes about 12 weeks to make its big roots. It keeps beautifully in the garden until we are ready to pull it, and stores well if you pull it to make room or to escape frost at the end of the season.

Other good varieties are Crosby's Egyptian, Early Wonder, and Detroit, which also comes in a semi-dwarf strain for closer plantings. A variety called Cylindra and one called Formanova are sausage-shaped, making them easy to cut into uniform slices. There is also a white table beet (sugar beets are white, too), and a new yellow beet. Burpee's list the yellow one as Burpee's Golden Beet. We don't know it, as it's new, but we are testing it in the garden this season.

If your soil is acid, treat it with hydrated lime, enough to whiten the ground being a rule of thumb when you prepare the beet bed. Dig the soil well and plant as early in the spring as the soil can be worked, for the first crop. Be particular about keeping the soil moist during germination of the seeds, which will take about 10 days.

You can make succession plantings, but give the last one time to mature before frost.

Beet seeds, except for a variety called Monogerm, are capsules containing more than one seed. Thin out the extra seedlings with a scissors at ground level.

As the little plants grow, thin to 6 inches apart. You can transplant thinnings; water them first so they'll pull out easily. Keep beets growing fast to keep them tender, and side-dress them when they are 6 or 8 inches high. We dig compost into the soil when seeding beets, a bucketful to 5 feet of row, and also give them a mulch of it later.

You can harvest beets young—in fact, the thinnings are a delicacy, cooked whole, both tops and young roots. By planting a late crop in a cold-winter climate you'll have some beets to store for the winter. Do so by leaving an inch of the stem on, washing the beets carefully without removing small roots, and putting them in layers on a shelf or in a box. People used to store them in boxes of sand but this is not practical for most of us, nor is an outdoor pit in which root vegetables are laid on a bed of sand, then covered with straw, and then with earth and sod.

RECIPES

Beets are the outstanding ingredient of that wonderful soup Borsch*, and the recipe will be found in Chapter 38. The recipes that follow here are all for beet roots, beet leaves being covered in Chapter 17, "The Leafy Greens."

Most recipes call for a pre-cooking of beet roots. You do it this way: Wash the beets and cut off all but an inch of the tops. Don't peel the beets or remove any rootlets at this time; doing so will make them bleed. Put the beets into a saucepan of boiling water, enough to cover them. Put the lid on and boil briskly until the beets are slightly soft to the touch. This will take from 20 minutes to an hour, depending on the size of the beets. Garden-fresh beets cook a little faster than those that have been stored. When the beets are done, drain them and slip the skins off. Cut away small roots and the stub of stalk.

You can also bake a beet. It takes about 3 hours, however. A quicker way is to steam it in the oven by wrapping it in foil. It will take about 1½ hours at 325 degrees F. for a medium-size beet.

ORANGE BEETS

This is a recipe we worked out as a substitute for the popular Harvard beets, which we like but which we found do not accompany some red dinner wines well. This recipe not only does not give an off flavor to the wine but is more delicate than Harvard beets and rated an "Excellent" in our personal grading of recipes.

> 2 tablespoons butter
> ½ teaspoon sugar
> 2 large beets, cooked and peeled
> Salt
> Orange

Melt butter in a saucepan, add sugar and the beets cut into ½-inch cubes. Simmer until beets are heated through. Salt lightly.

Cut 8 very thin slices from the unpeeled orange. Cut each slice into eight segments, add them to the beets and stir gently while simmering for another minute. *Serves 4.*

BEETS AND NASTURTIUM CAPERS

You can make this dish with regular capers but Nasturtium Capers* are milder and, we think, more interesting.

> 2 large beets, cooked and peeled
> 2 tablespoons olive oil
> 4 tablespoons finely chopped Nasturtium Capers*
> Salt
> 2 tablespoons dry red wine

Cut beets into ½-inch cubes. Put oil and Nasturtium Capers in saucepan, add the beets, and simmer until beets are heated through.

One minute before serving, salt lightly, sprinkle wine over beets, and simmer, shaking pan. *Serves 4.*

BEETS AND SOUR CRREAM

The dill gives this recipe an interesting character. Fresh dill is best, though dry dill keeps well and will work here. If you don't care for dill, tarragon, preferably fresh, is very good in this dish.

> *4 medium-large beets, cooked and peeled*
> *Butter*
> *½ cup sour cream*
> *¼ teaspoon lemon juice*
> *1 tablespoon finely chopped dill*
> *Salt*
> *Pepper*

Cut beets into ½-inch cubes and put them into a buttered casserole. Stir into the sour cream the rest of the ingredients and spread this mixture over the beets. Bake 15 minutes at 300 degrees F., or just until the sour cream begins to bubble. *Serves 4.*

RICH BEETS

This is such a full-flavored dish that the servings should not be very large. The beets can be grated ahead of time and held in the refrigerator. They tend to stick to the skillet, so we suggest using a Teflon one. We often use dry vermouth as a cooking wine but for this dish a sauterne or Riesling is better.

> *4 raw, medium-sized beets*
> *2 tablespoons butter*
> *1 teaspoon lime juice*
> *¼ teaspoon sugar*
> *Salt*
> *⅓ cup dry white wine*
> *⅓ cup sour cream*
> *1 orange rind*

Wash beets, peel them with a potato peeler, and grate them. Melt butter in a medium-sized skillet, add lime juice, and swirl to blend. Put grated beets in the skillet, cover it and simmer for 20 minutes.

Dissolve the sugar and a pinch of salt in the wine. Stir this into the beets, cover skillet again and simmer 5 more minutes.

Stir the sour cream into the beets and simmer, uncovered, for 1 or 2 minutes. Just before serving, squeeze sections of orange rind over the beets to spray them with the aromatic oil (the zest). To do so, hold the pieces 3 or 4 inches above the surface of the beets, skin side down, and squeeze quickly. *Serves 4.*

BEET AND CABBAGE SAUTE

By cooking the beets ahead of time this becomes a fast dish you can put together in about 10 minutes while a steak is broiling. And it is a good partner for a steak, say with Potatoes Pat*, also quickly prepared.

4 tablespoons butter
4 cups shredded Savoy cabbage
2 tablespoons dry vermouth
2 large beets, cooked and peeled
Salt
Pepper
¼ teaspoon grated nutmeg
½ teaspoon finely chopped fresh rosemary
2 teaspoons lemon juice

Melt butter in a saucepan, add cabbage and vermouth, and cook for 5 minutes over brisk heat, stirring now and then. Cover pan, turn heat to low, and cook another 3 minutes, while cutting the beets into ½-inch cubes.

Add beets and the rest of the ingredients to the cabbage and cook, covered, another 2 minutes, stirring once or twice. *Serves 4.*

Chapter 7

BELGIAN ENDIVE

BELGIAN ENDIVE (*Cichorium intybus*)

It was our pride to tell dinner guests at our Missouri farm that the prime Black Angus beefsteak they were eating cost us only 15 cents a pound to raise. If pressed, we had to admit we didn't charge the steers for our time in taking care of them, nor did we charge them rent for the barn, so maybe the 15 cents was low. If you raise Belgian endive in your garden you'll find yourself in something of the same situation. On the market it costs 2 dollars a pound or more, and you can raise it for less than a dime a pound. As a garden vegetable, Belgian endive puts its growers into the virtuoso class; very few people ever attempt it, so those who do are marvels to their friends.

There isn't anything hard about raising this plant, however. The stumbling block for those who don't try it is the time and patience involved, and a few extra pains one must go to. You start out by planting witloof chicory seed in the spring. This grows into leafy plants about a foot high and looking like a cooking green (which they are; the leaves are bitter, but a few included with chard are agreeable).

These plants are then cut down in the fall, and from their roots grow during the winter the sprouts called Belgian endive. Incidentally, you could roast the roots instead of sprouting them, then grind them and you'd have the chicory that is blended with coffee. In the South they use a different variety, Magdeburg, but there is little difference in taste.

Witloof chicory is a strong-growing plant without temperamental likes and dislikes, so you can grow it in any ordinary garden soil that will let the roots develop. They grow to about the size of carrots, 8 inches or so in length. Plant seeds only after the soil is warm in late spring. If you sow it too early, the plants will try to form seed and the roots will be worthless.

Twenty-five feet of row will give you enough good roots to do something with. If your winter climate is mild and you plan to sprout the roots right where they are growing, plant short rows to make a squarish bed that you can later enclose with boards to form a sand box.

When plants are about 3 inches high, thin to 6 inches apart. You can transplant these thinnings.

Plants need 4 months to make good roots, so give them a mid-season side-dressing. Moisture is not critical. It takes a good deal of dry weather to daunt chicory, and it makes a dense leafy growth that doesn't give weeds much chance.

To sprout chicory in the garden, in a mild-winter climate, do this at the end of the season, say in mid-November: Cut the plants down to an inch or so above ground level. Box in the bed with boards, cover the stubs of the plants with 2 inches of earth and then with 6 inches of sand. In 6 or 8 weeks some early sprouts will begin to break surface, and this will go on for a month or more; we harvest for about 3 months, and some roots sprout more than once.

To harvest the sprouts, or Belgian endives, dig down and cut them where they join the root.

In colder climates, dig the roots before the ground freezes, trim off all but ½ inch of the tops and cut a little off the ends of the longer roots to make all roots about the same length. They can be stored like carrots in a cool place till you want to sprout them. When you do, stand a dozen or so of them in earth up to their tops, and cover them with 8 inches of sand, or light soil, or sawdust. A nail keg is good for this purpose. Water the planting and keep it at a temperature between 50 and 60 degrees F., ideally. The sprouts should break surface in about a month. With enough roots on hand you can make succession plantings all winter.

RECIPES

To prepare a Belgian endive for use, cut off any bit of root remaining and wash the sprout under running water. We usually peel off the outside layer of leaves for easier cleaning.

The imported Belgian endives are often cooked for two hours or more because they seem to take to it, but we cannot recommend this for garden-fresh ones. We've tried both ways, and much prefer a briefer cooking of this crisp and distinctive little garden delicacy.

In the recipes we specify one endive per serving. This assumes that you are using endives 5 or 6 inches long and about an inch wide. An endive's size depends on the size of the root that sprouts it. We grow large and robust roots by giving them room to develop and a sunny location, and as we were writing this chapter we took time out to dig an endive that was showing above the sand. While cutting it we also cut the two just behind it in the row, since they were about ready to break surface, and all three were enormous by Belgian endive standards, 8 and 9 inches long and an inch and a half wide, weighing a quarter-pound each. They would cost 50 cents each at current rates.

BRAISED BELGIAN ENDIVE I

> *4 Belgian endives*
> *Salt*
> *4 tablespoons butter*
> *¼ cup dry white wine*
> *1 tablespoon lemon juice*

Lay endives in a casserole and add the other ingredients. Cover casserole and bake for 60 minutes in a 300-degree F. oven. *Serves 4.*

BRAISED BELGIAN ENDIVE II

> *2 tablespoons butter*
> *4 shallots, finely chopped*
> *8 mushrooms, quartered*
> *4 Belgian endives*
> *½ cup Kraft Stock**
> *Salt*
> *Pepper*
> *½ teaspoon sugar*
> *1 tablespoon finely chopped parsley*

Put everything but the parsley into a casserole, preferably an enameled metal one. Cover it and bake in a 325-degree F. oven until the liquids are nearly absorbed. This should take about 40 minutes.

Remove casserole from oven and sprinkle the parsley into it, stirring gently. Serve at once. *Serves 4.*

BELGIAN ENDIVE PARMESAN

> 4 Belgian endives
> Salt
> Pepper
> 4 tablespoons butter
> 2 shallots, finely chopped
> Lemon juice
> ½ cup grated Parmesan cheese

Put endives into a casserole and sprinkle with salt and pepper. Add the butter, strewing it over the surface, cover casserole and bake for 30 minutes at 300 degrees F.

Remove casserole from oven and sprinkle in the shallots and a few drops of lemon juice. Spread the grated cheese over the endives, turn oven temperature up to 375 degrees F., and bake uncovered for 20 minutes. *Serves 4.*

BELGIAN ENDIVES WITH ORANGE SAUCE

This dish goes beautifully with chicken. The orange serves to offset the slightly bitter taste of the endives.

> 2 cups Vegetable Stock*
> 4 Belgian endives
> 1 tablespoon butter
> Juice of ½ orange, about 3 tablespoons
> 2 tablespoons dry white wine
> Salt
> Pepper

Bring the stock to a boil in a saucepan. Put endives into it, cover, return to a boil and cook briskly for 10 minutes. Drain and set endives aside, keeping them warm.

Melt the butter in the saucepan and add the rest of the ingredients. Simmer briefly, then put the endives into the pan and simmer for 5 minutes, covered, shaking the pan several times to coat endives with the sauce. Pour the remaining sauce over the endives on the serving dish. *Serves 4.*

BELGIAN ENDIVE SAUTE

Canned or frozen corn, your own if possible, must be used here because fresh corn is long gone from the garden when Belgian endives are sprouting.

> 1 *tablespoon corn oil*
> 1 *teaspoon Garlic Oil**
> 1 *tablespoon butter*
> 4 *large mushrooms, thickly sliced*
> 4 *Belgian endives, cut into 1-inch lengths*
> 2 *cups whole corn kernels*
> ½ *cup Vegetable Stock**
> *Salt*
> *Pepper*
> ¼ *teaspoon sugar*
> 2 *tablespoons finely chopped parsley*
> 2 *ripe olives (Greek, preferably), coarsely chopped*

Heat oils and butter in a skillet, add mushroom slices and simmer for 5 minutes. Add endives and simmer 10 minutes longer. Stir in corn and simmer 15 minutes more. If frozen corn is used, thaw it first.

Meanwhile, put the rest of the ingredients into a saucepan. If you are using corn you have canned, substitute the juice for the stock. Bring to a boil and simmer until the liquid amounts to about ¼ cup and the sauce has slightly thickened. Top the endive dish with the sauce when it comes to the table. *Serves 4.*

BELGIAN ENDIVES WITH SOUR CREAM

4 Belgian endives
Vegetable Stock*
2 tablespoons butter
Salt
Pepper
¼ cup sour cream
1 tablespoon lemon juice
12 stalks chives

Put endives into saucepan with enough stock to cover them, cover saucepan and bring stock to a boil. Cook over medium heat for 10 minutes and drain.

Put butter into the saucepan, season with salt and pepper, simmer on low heat for 15 minutes.

Stir sour cream and lemon juice together. Add this to the endives and simmer for a minute, stirring gently to coat endives with the cream. Transfer to serving dish and chop the chives over the endives with a scissors, cutting them into ¼-inch pieces. *Serves 4.*

BELGIAN ENDIVE AND BROCCOLI

As you may have noticed, many of our recipes that combine two or more vegetables are based on those growing in the garden at the same time. In the case of this recipe, this will hold true for gardeners in mild-winter climates such as our present coastal one, where we sprout Belgian endive and grow broccoli at the same period. In other climates, frozen broccoli can be used here.

1 tablespoon olive oil
1 tablespoon corn oil
3 cups broccoli
2 large or 4 small Belgian endives
2 tablespoons dry vermouth
Salt
Pepper

Heat oils in a large skillet and add the broccoli, which should be slightly damp. Cover skillet and cook for 10 minutes over medium heat.

Cut endives into ½-inch lengths, add them to the skillet and cook for 10 minutes, shaking skillet now and then. Test broccoli stems with a fork, and if tender-crisp, sprinkle with vermouth, salt, and pepper, stir briefly and gently, and remove from heat. *Serves 4.*

Chapter 8

THE CABBAGE FAMILY

Because they are related and take the same general culture, and also because there is a relationship in taste, we'll take up these five plants in this chapter: Broccoli, Brussels sprouts, cabbage, kale, and kohlrabi.

BROCCOLI (*Brassica oleracea italica*)

Sprouting, or Italian, broccoli, as the usual garden broccoli is called, is one of the handsomest plants in the garden, along with being stunningly high on vitamins and having the respectable protein percentage of 3.3. If broccoli didn't exist, we'd probably grow cauliflower in our garden, but as it is, we grow only broccoli. It objects to heat and drought but is not as finicky as cauliflower, and it bears bonuses of tender side sprouts for three months or longer after presenting you with a fine big central cluster up to 8 inches across. The plant grows from 2 to 4 feet tall.

Like the other Brassicas, broccoli's ancestor was probably a cabbage that grew wild along some coasts of Europe. The cabbages have been popular with man for so long that only such old-timers as the onions can rival their long history.

Two good varieties of broccoli that have been on the market for years are De Cicco and Calabrese. De Cicco matures earlier, in 65 days from transplanting. An improved selection from it, Greenbud, is 5 days earlier than this, and a new hybrid called Green Comet actually matures center heads as big as cauliflowers in as little as 40 days from transplanting in favorable localities. Another quick grower is Spartan Early, developed at Michigan State University. A slower (about 75 days) but very good variety developed in Massachusetts is Waltham 29.

You can usually buy broccoli plants at nurseries but you'll have a much wider choice of varieties by planting seed.

Broccoli does well in ordinary good garden soil with plenty of humus in it. Dig in extra compost, and pick a place in the garden where no Brassicas grew the year before. You can seed broccoli where it is to grow, or start plants 6 weeks ahead of time in a flat and transplant to the garden. Figure on transplanting an early bed of broccoli at the time your last spring frost is barely over. In the Midwest and East we rushed this date, knowing we could protect the little plants with straw or cardboard boxes if frost threatened.

For the fall crop, just figure backward from the average date of your first fall frost, giving the plants time to mature by that time.

Broccoli is apt to do poorly in hot weather. However, the United States Department of Agriculture has reported spring-set plants as doing well in the hot District of Columbia latitude until past midsummer. We suggest you do a little experimenting in your own garden with two varieties, one new and one old, and perhaps with two others the next year. It will tell you more than any amount of advice from other places.

Broccoli can take a little frost, we've found, so if the fall crop survives a light frost, it will go on bearing until a black frost kills it, which may not be for a month or more.

An all-purpose dust will keep broccoli protected from most troubles, along with a powdering of 5 percent chlordane around each transplant when you set it in the garden. We repeat the treatment two or three times. If you plant seeds directly in the garden, sprinkle chlordane along the row and work it into the soil before seeding.

The central sprout of broccoli develops first and should be cut while its many buds are still tightly closed. There are hundreds of these buds and they open into small yellow flowers if given the chance. Cut the sprout with several inches of stem attached. The stem is perfectly edible and so are the leaves—which are in fact the most nutritious part of the plant.

Cutting the central sprout makes the plant grow side sprouts strongly. These grow from the axils of the leaves. They aren't as big as the central sprout, but altogether can amount to about as much.

You can store broccoli in the refrigerator for days if necessary, but not all the plants mature at the same time and this helps spread the harvest. Another good way to handle this is to start cutting sprouts a week or two before the planting is due to mature. Only a gardener can get such broccoli, and it is delicious.

RECIPES

You will often find instructions in recipes to peel broccoli stems before cooking, or to stand the sprouts in water. Don't do it with garden-fresh broccoli. It will stay tender even when stored in the refrigerator for a few days, and there is no comparison to the woody-stemmed broccoli sold in stores.

We usually cook broccoli simply. Fresh, it needs a minimum of handling and seasoning, though it will accept more elaborate preparation if you desire this.

It was once the practice to boil broccoli for about 30 minutes. Fifteen minutes is the time more often used today, and sometimes as little as 5 minutes. Our frequent practice is to blanch broccoli before proceeding with the rest of the recipe. We put it into a saucepan of cold water, bring the water just to a boil and immediately drain the broccoli and rinse it briefly. So treated, it finishes its cooking very quickly and keeps its bright green color. Because broccoli sprouts vary in size from the large central head to the smallest of the side sprouts, most of the recipes suggest testing for tenderness rather than relying on the clock for timing.

Also because of this variation in size of sprouts, we have given quantities in terms of cups. This implies some guesswork and measurement by eye on the cook's part, but this is not a critical point.

SIMPLE BROCCOLI

This is an especially good way to cook the small side sprouts, of which you always have such a lot after the big central one is harvested.

> 2 tablespoons butter
> 1 tablespoon olive oil
> 4 cups broccoli, blanched
> Salt
> Pepper
> Sugar
> Dry vermouth

Melt butter in a skillet, add olive oil and broccoli, cover the skillet and cook over medium heat for a few minutes, shaking the pan occasionally, till broccoli stalks can be easily pierced with a sharp fork. Season with salt, pepper, and a pinch of sugar, then sprinkle the broccoli with vermouth and serve at once. *Serves 4.*

BROCCOLI SAUTÉ

Greek olives may be used in place of the Italian ones here, and, as a reluctant third choice, canned ripe olives.

> 3 tablespoons butter
> ½ clove garlic
> 4 cups young, raw broccoli
> ½ cup stoned and coarsely chopped Italian olives
> 1 tablespoon lemon juice
> Salt
> Pepper

Melt butter in a skillet and simmer the garlic in it until garlic browns lightly. Discard garlic. Put broccoli into the skillet and cook over medium heat, shaking the pan frequently, until the broccoli stems are just tender enough to pierce with a sharp fork. Add the olives, stirring while simmering for about 1 minute. Season with the lemon juice, salt, and pepper and serve at once. *Serves 4.*

BROCCOLI TARRAGON

2 *tablespoons butter*
1 *tablespoon olive oil*
1 *teaspoon Garlic Oil**
4 *shallots, finely chopped*
4 *cups broccoli, blanched*
2 *tablespoons tarragon wine vinegar*
Salt
Pepper

Melt butter in a skillet, add oils and chopped shallots and cook for a minute or two over low heat.

Increase heat to medium, add broccoli, cover skillet and cook for 5 minutes, shaking skillet several times.

Season with the vinegar, salt and pepper, stir lightly, and dish up. *Serves 4.*

FESTIVE BROCCOLI

2 *tablespoons butter*
4 *cups broccoli, blanched*
Salt
¼ *cup Shallot Mayonnaise**

Melt butter in a skillet and simmer the broccoli in it over low heat, covered, until tender. Salt very lightly, transfer to serving dish, and top with the Shallot Mayonnaise. *Serves 4.*

BROCCOLI DILL

2 *tablespoons butter*
4 *cups young, raw broccoli*
1 *tablespoon finely chopped dill*
Salt
Pepper
1 *teaspoon lemon juice*
¼ *cup sour cream*

Melt butter in a skillet, add broccoli, cover skillet and cook over low heat till tender. Sprinkle with the dill, salt, and pepper. Stir gently.

Mix lemon juice into the sour cream and add it to the broccoli. Toss broccoli lightly with a pancake turner to coat each sprout with the sour cream while warming the cream. *Serves 4.*

BROCCOLI IN MILK

> *1 tablespoon butter*
> *¼ cup evaporated milk*
> *4 cups broccoli, blanched*
> *4 large mushrooms, sliced*
> *1 clove garlic*
> *Salt*
> *Pepper*
> *Romano cheese, grated*

Melt butter in a saucepan. Pour in the milk, add the broccoli, cover the pan and cook over low heat for 5 minutes.

Add mushrooms and garlic, cover pan and continue cooking until the broccoli is tender, a few minutes.

Discard garlic. Season vegetables with salt and pepper, stir gently, remove to serving dish and sprinkle lightly with the grated cheese. *Serves 4.*

BROCCOLI BRUTON SISTERS

The Bruton sisters, Misses Margaret and Helen of Monterey, California, took a trip and loaned us their home once when we needed to be in Monterey for three months. They are artists and we enjoyed their house and studio. We named this dish for them because we invented it while we were living in that creative air.

> *3 tablespoons butter*
> *1 tablespoon corn oil*
> *1 teaspoon Garlic Oil**

    3 *shallots, finely chopped*
    4 *large mushrooms*
    2 *tablespoons flour*
    ½ *cup grated Romano cheese*
    ½ *cup Kraft Stock**
    ¼ *cup evaporated milk*
    ¼ *cup dry white wine*
    4 *cups broccoli, blanched*

Melt 1 tablespoon of the butter in a skillet. Add oils and shallots and simmer 2 minutes.

Chop mushroom stems. Add them and mushroom caps to the skillet, cover skillet and simmer for 5 minutes, turning the caps over halfway through this cooking.

Remove caps and add the rest of the butter to the skillet, then stir in the flour and half the cheese. Remove skillet from heat and stir in stock, milk, and wine until blended. Return skillet to heat and simmer until the sauce thickens.

Arrange broccoli in casserole, pour sauce over it and top with mushroom caps and the rest of the cheese. Bake, covered, for 20 minutes at 375 degrees F. Remove lid and glaze under broiler for a few minutes until cheese browns lightly. *Serves 4.*

BRUSSELS SPROUTS (*Brassica oleracea gemmifera*)

Brussels sprouts look like cabbage heads about the size of Ping-pong balls. They have a mild cabbage flavor and are interesting little vegetables to serve. People who wouldn't dream of serving cabbage to guests usually regard Brussels sprouts as perfectly suitable.

The sprouts, which are buds, grow from the axils of the leaves, eventually creating a club-shaped plant. The lower sprouts form first and become the large end of the club by the time the sprouts highest up on the stem are developing. This structure is topped with a bowl-shaped garland of leaves.

As you might suspect, Brussels sprouts are named for the Belgian city Brussels, because some of the first plantings were in its vicinity.

Long Island Improved and Catskill were leading varieties for years and are still popular, but a new one called Jade Cross is the best. It is a hybrid, growing about 2 feet tall.

You care for Brussels sprouts the same way you do broccoli. A spring crop is usually omitted, though, and only a fall crop raised. This is partly due to the long growing season (about 3 months from transplanting) and partly to the plant's partiality to cool weather. A little frost even improves the crop.

If your winter isn't severe, you can keep on picking sprouts until Christmas. Or lift the plant and transfer it to a cold frame and it will stay alive while you harvest sprouts as needed.

To harvest a Brussels sprout, hold it with two fingers and give it a little twist. Pick lower sprouts first, and don't let them grow as big as golf balls or they'll be tough. The time to start picking is when lower leaves turn yellow, or a little before. Each time you pick a sprout, remove the leaf below it, breaking it from the stalk. This makes the plant form more leaves and thus more sprouts. One good plant will give you up to 100 sprouts.

RECIPES

Brussels sprouts are often parboiled, whole, and then finished in some way—served with a sauce, or simply with butter, or merely with a sprinkle of lemon juice or a herbed vinegar. We do the parboiling in Vegetable Stock* after trimming the sprouts, like this:

Peel away the outside layer of leaves to expose the bright green ones underneath. Make an X-cut in the bottom of each stem about ¼ inch deep. This speeds cooking. Wash and drain the sprouts, and cook them at a brisk boil, covered, for 10 minutes.

BRUSSELS SPROUTS WITH ALMONDS

40 trimmed Brussels sprouts
*3 cups Vegetable Stock***
3 tablespoons butter
*¼ cup slivered Blanched Almonds***
Salt
Pepper
1 tablespoon lemon juice
1 tablespoon cognac

Put Brussels sprouts and stock in a saucepan; put lid on pan and bring to a boil. Turn heat down and simmer until tender but still crisp, about 10 minutes. Drain, remove sprouts to serving dish and keep them warm.

Melt butter, add almonds, and cook gently with a little stirring till almonds turn golden. Add salt, pepper, and lemon juice, simmer briefly. Add cognac, stirring to blend for a few seconds, then pour over the Brussels sprouts and serve at once. *Serves 4.*

BRUSSELS SPROUTS CASSEROLE

> 40 *trimmed Brussels sprouts*
> 1½ *cups Vegetable Stock**
> 2 *tablespoons butter*
> ½ *teaspoon salt*
> ¼ *teaspoon pepper*
> ½ *teaspoon grated nutmeg*
> ½ *cup sour cream*

Put all ingredients except sour cream into a casserole. Cover it and cook in a 350-degree F. oven for 30 minutes. Check it after 20 minutes and add more stock if needed. Small sprouts may take less than 30 minutes to cook tender-crisp.

Remove casserole when done, stir a tablespoon of the juices into the sour cream, then gently stir this mixture into the casserole. *Serves 4.*

CABBAGE (*Brassica oleracea capitata*)

Cabbage is called one of the most important home garden crops, and perhaps it is, but we have never cared about taking up space in a small garden with it. Cabbage is always available at the store, its price is reasonable, and it keeps so well that there is little advantage in freshly harvested cabbage.

If you want to grow cabbage anyway, we suggest you plant red cabbage, or a midget cabbage, or Savoy cabbage. None of these is often found in markets.

When choosing a variety of cabbage, check its resistance to yellows, a fungus disease, if this is troublesome in your area. Golden Acre is resistant, as are Wisconsin Hollander, Marion Market, and Globe. Early varieties mature in about 2 months from transplanting. Late ones can take over 100 days, but grow larger.

Little Leaguer is a midget that makes a head in 60 days, about the size of a softball and weighing a pound. It takes little space in the garden and can be harvested over a longer period than some others.

Of the few red varieties offered, Red Acre is fairly fast, about 10 weeks. Two late-season good ones are Red Danish and Mammoth Red Rock.

Savoy varieties are also few but they include a hybrid, Savoy King. It matures in 3 months and heads weigh 3 or 4 pounds.

You grow cabbage the same way you do broccoli, and look after it the same.

To harvest cabbage, simply cut its stalk just below its base. Early or midseason cabbage sometimes grows too fast and the heads crack open. It doesn't hurt the cabbage as long as you use it right away.

When cold weather comes, you can store surplus cabbages by pulling them up by the roots, putting them in a box in the basement or garage, and covering it with burlap if necessary for protection from temperature changes. Well-stored cabbage will keep for several months.

RECIPES

Cabbage has suffered in reputation because people used to insist on cooking the life out of it, and you could smell it a block away. If you shred cabbage, it cooks tender in a few minutes in a liquid or in butter. Remember too that cabbage is delicious raw, as in coleslaw.

The stem of a cabbage is cut out before cooking and discarded, including the central core it forms inside the head.

BRAISED SAVOY CABBAGE

1 tablespoon bacon drippings
1 tablespoon corn oil

    4 shallots, finely chopped
    3 cups shredded Savoy cabbage
    ½ cup Kraft Stock*
    ½ cup dry white wine
    1 tablespoon tarragon wine vinegar
    ¼ teaspoon grated nutmeg
    Salt
    Pepper
    2 tablespoons butter
    ½ cup Processed Chestnuts*

Melt bacon drippings in a large saucepan, add oil and shallots
and simmer a few minutes. Then add all the other ingredients
except butter and chestnuts, cover saucepan and cook over low
heat for 12 to 15 minutes. Remove from heat.

    Melt butter in a skillet. Cut chestnuts into slices as thick as a
nickel and simmer them in the butter, stirring till they brown lightly.
Drain into the skillet the juices from the saucepan, simmer a few
minutes until this sauce slightly thickens, then pour it over the
cabbage and toss lightly. *Serves 4.*

BLEU CABBAGE

    ½ head Savoy cabbage, shredded
    ½ cup water
    2 tablespoons butter
    2 tablespoons flour
    Kraft Stock*
    Salt
    Pepper
    4 tablespoons crumbled bleu cheese

Put cabbage and water into large saucepan, cover and bring to a
boil. Cook over brisk heat until cabbage is tender-crisp, about 5
minutes, shaking the pan frequently. Remove from heat and drain
into a measuring cup the liquid remaining.

    Melt butter in a small skillet. Stir in flour. Add to the liquid in
the cup enough Kraft Stock to make 1 cup, and stir this into the
butter-flour mixture to make a sauce. Simmer, stirring, until it

thickens, then season with salt and pepper. Add bleu cheese and stir over low heat until well blended. Pour the sauce over the cabbage, stirring, over low heat, and serve at once. *Serves 4.*

RED CABBAGE IN CIDER

> *1 small red cabbage, shredded*
> *4 scallions, chopped*
> *4 tablespoons butter*
> *Salt*
> *Pepper*
> *½ teaspoon nutmeg*
> *2 tablespoons flour*
> *1 tablespoon lemon juice*
> *Cider*

On a double sheet of aluminum foil spread the cabbage and over it the scallions. Dot with 2 tablespoons of the butter and season with salt, pepper, and the nutmeg. Make a package, sealing the edges of the foil by crimping and folding, put package into a shallow baking pan, and cook in a 350-degree F. oven for 20 minutes.

Meanwhile melt the other 2 tablespoons of butter in a large skillet, stir in the flour and cook briefly over low heat. When the vegetables in the foil are done, drain the accumulated juices into a measuring cup, add the lemon juice and enough cider to make 1 cup. Stir this into the butter-flour mixture in the skillet over medium heat until it thickens. Then stir the vegetables from the foil into this sauce, and transfer to serving dish. *Serves 4.*

SWEET-SOUR CABBAGE

> *1 tablespoon corn oil*
> *1 tablespoon olive oil*
> *2 medium-sized onions, thinly sliced*
> *1 small head green cabbage, coarsely sliced*
> *2 tomatoes, cut into quarters*
> *2 green peppers, cut into ¼-inch rings*

1 teaspoon sugar
2 tablespoons Herb Vinegar* (thyme)
Salt
Pepper

Heat oils until they shimmer, add onions and cook over low heat until they are translucent, shaking pan now and then. Add cabbage, cover the pan and cook over medium heat, stirring once or twice, until cabbage is tender-crisp, about 5 minutes.

Add tomatoes and peppers and cook covered for another 10 minutes. Stir, and cook 10 minutes uncovered. Dissolve sugar in the vinegar and sprinkle it over the vegetables. Season with salt and pepper, stir well, and serve at once. *Serves 4.*

KALE (*Brassica oleracea acephala*)

"Acephala" means without a head. Kale is a cabbage that you harvest leaf by leaf. We grew a good deal of it in the Midwest because it takes cold so well that we could leave it out in the garden all winter and depend on it for leafy greens. This is a tremendous advantage, especially when you consider that kale is very high on vitamins.

Another name for kale is borecole. The word kale itself is an old variation of "cole," which is a synonym for Brassica. That ancient ancestral plant, from which all cabbage-type plants came, probably looked strikingly like today's kale.

Kale is associated with Scotch tastes, one variety being called Scotch Curled, and columns on some abbeys in Scotland and other parts of the British Isles were decorated with stylized kale leaves.

Scotch Curled is a good variety, and a compact version of it is Dwarf Blue Scotch. Dwarf Siberian is another good one.

Kale takes the same general care as broccoli but less of it. You can plant it directly where it is to grow, or transplant it.

To harvest kale, clip off the lower leaves as needed. You can cut the whole plant, of course, but it will probably stop producing. We tried an experiment with old plants, cutting off the final top cluster of leaves after all the others had been gradually harvested;

the result was a small new growth of tender young leaves both at the top and above each joint where an earlier leaf had been. Growth was so slow, however, that the experiment was more interesting than useful.

Kale leaves become tough as they mature, so pick them young.

RECIPES

Even young kale leaves need a little softening up with a precooking before being used in most recipes. You can do this by steaming or by parboiling. We bring Vegetable Stock* to a boil, drop the washed, stemmed, and coarsely chopped kale leaves into it, and simmer for about 5 minutes after the stock returns to a boil. One cup of stock is enough to parboil 4 cups of kale.

Like all leafy greens, kale cooks down, though not as much as some do. A cup of cooked kale specified in a recipe translates into about 3 cups of kale fresh from the garden, coarsely chopped.

BRAISED KALE

> 2 slices bacon, cut into ½-inch squares
> 2 tablespoons butter
> 3 cups coarsely chopped kale, parboiled
> ¼ cup Vegetable Stock*
> Salt
> Pepper
> ¼ teaspoon grated nutmeg

Fry the bacon squares in a skillet and drain all but 1 tablespoon of the drippings. Add butter and melt it. Add kale and stock, cover skillet, and cook over medium-low heat until kale is heated through and the liquid is cooked down somewhat. Season with salt and pepper, stirring. Transfer to serving dish and sprinkle with the nutmeg. *Serves 4.*

KALE ANCHOVY

> 2 *tablespoons olive oil*
> 2 *teaspoons Garlic Oil**
> 1 *teaspoon anchovy paste*
> 3 *cups coarsely chopped kale, parboiled*
> *Salt*
> *Pepper*
> 1 *tablespoon lemon juice*

Put the oils into a saucepan and blend the anchovy paste with them. A rubber spatula is a good tool for this purpose. Stir in the kale, cover pan, and cook over medium-low heat until kale is heated through. Season with salt and pepper, sprinkle with the lemon juice, stir lightly and dish up. *Serves 4.*

KALE CASSEROLE

> 4 *strips lean bacon, cut into ½-inch squares*
> 1 *tablespoon butter*
> 1 *clove garlic*
> 2 *cups chopped raw kale*
> 1 *bay leaf*
> 2 *medium-sized potatoes, peeled and thickly sliced*
> *Salt*
> *Pepper*
> ½ *cup Kraft Stock**
> *Romano cheese, grated*

Put bacon, butter, and garlic clove cut in two, into a skillet and cook over low heat. Remove garlic when it browns (or reserve it to add to the casserole; it will not be objectionably strong when cooking is completed).

Stir kale into the skillet, cover, and cook for 5 minutes.

Line the bottom of a deep casserole with contents of skillet, lay the bay leaf on them and then the potato slices. Season with salt and pepper and add the stock. Sprinkle enough grated cheese over to cover the potatoes. Put lid on casserole and cook for 40 minutes in a 300-degree F. oven. Remove lid and cook for 20 minutes more. Discard bay leaf before serving. *Serves 4.*

WINTER'S NIGHT KALE

This is a hearty dish, easily prepared, and makes a good accompaniment to beef or pork. If scallions are not on hand, use an onion.

1 tablespoon butter
6 scallions, chopped
½ cup Vegetable Stock*
3 cups coarsely chopped kale, parboiled
1 tablespoon finely chopped marjoram
Salt
Pepper

Melt butter in a saucepan and simmer the scallions in it for 5 minutes, stirring a few times. Add stock, tilting the pan to blend. Turn up heat and cook until the liquid thickens slightly.

Stir in kale and cook until it is heated through. Season with the marjoram, salt, and pepper a minute or two before the cooking is finished, stirring and lifting. *Serves 4.*

KOHLRABI (*Brassica caulorapa*)

Judging by comments of visitors to our garden, Kohlrabi is a surprise. We don't know why more gardeners don't grow it, for kohlrabi is an agreeable plant, easy to look after, takes up little space, and is ranked by some lovers of good food as the best Brassica in existence (on the score of taste; kale and broccoli are more nutritious).

Kohlrabi is also an attractive plant and one that excites curiosity when its lower stem begins to enlarge near ground level into what becomes a bulb-like swelling, the part you eat.

Kohlrabi apparently originated in the Mediterranean region. It grows well where broccoli does.

Two varieties are commonly offered—Early White Vienna and Early Purple Vienna. The white one is a bit smaller, its flesh is white and it matures in 55 days. The other is purple-skinned, has greenish flesh, and matures in 60 days.

Cultural needs are about the same as for broccoli. Keep kohlrabi growing fast to keep it prime. You can seed it where it will stay, or transplant. Succession plantings every two weeks are a good idea, since it matures fast and there is only one harvest per plant, but don't plan on growing kohlrabi in midsummer; it prefers cooler weather, so is a spring and fall vegetable.

Kohlrabi is ready to harvest when the bulb is 2 inches wide, about the size of a small apple. Cut the stem just below the bulb, and tear off the leaves. You can cook the smallest leaves, which grow out of the very top of the bulb, but we find them a little tough. Kohlrabi is said to contain a trace of arsenic, also a normal component of the human body.

RECIPES

Like some of the other Brassicas, kohlrabi is often parboiled and then prepared further, though it can be served simply parboiled until barely tender, with a little butter or lemon juice. If sliced thinly it is also good raw and can be included in a salad as if it were a radish.

To parboil it, cut a slice off the top, then pare the bulb with a potato peeler, slice it thickly and cook in rapidly boiling water or Vegetable Stock* till tender, about 10 minutes with the pan covered.

Cooked in this way, kohlrabi combines well with Mornay Sauce* and with Pekin Sauce*. Plan on getting 4 servings from 3 kohlrabi bulbs, and simply dress the cooked slices with one of the sauces at the time of serving.

KOHLRABI WITH HORSERADISH

3 kohlrabis, pared, sliced, and parboiled
½ cup Vegetable Stock*
1 teaspoon freshly grated horse-radish
1 teaspoon lemon juice
½ cup sour cream
Salt

Arrange kohlrabi slices in a warm serving dish and keep them warm while preparing the sauce:

Put stock in a saucepan and quickly cook it down over high heat, uncovered, to ¼ cup. Turn heat to low, add the rest of the ingredients and stir until blended. Pour this over the warm kohlrabi and serve at once. *Serves 4.*

Chapter 9

CARROTS

CARROTS (*Daucus carota sativa*)

Last spring we were getting ready to plant lettuce where a bed of carrots had been growing, and as we were yanking out a huge carrot that had wintered over, a neighbor dropped by. "Are you throwing that lovely carrot *away?*" she cried. She bore it off, cuddling it. Later she reported that even though its core was woody, as we told her it would be, the rest was glorious eating. "So carroty," she said.

If you wonder what she meant, taste in succession a raw, garden-fresh carrot and the best carrot you can find at the store. In spite of their being pretty good keepers, stored carrots suffer disastrously in flavor. If your winter temperatures don't get much below freezing you can do as we do—"store" your carrots right where they are growing, pulling them from the garden as you need them.

Carrots are good for you, quite high on Vitamin A. Carotene, a substance the liver turns into this vitamin, is named for the carrot. Vitamin A helps keep you young and is good for your skin and your eyesight.

Carrot foliage is pretty enough to recommend it as a border for a flower bed or along a walk, though some leaf stalks flop over and have to be clipped for neatness. You can eat carrot foliage, though we've never wanted to.

Nearly all carrots take about 2 months to mature, so the main reason for choosing a particular variety is not so much speedy growth or later maturity as it is the type of root. Unless your soil is loose and light enough to let a deep-rooted carrot develop, choose a short-rooted one. If in doubt, plant both types and you'll learn a lot about your soil in one season.

Chantenay, Nantes, and Oxheart are good short-rooted carrots, ranging from 4 to 7 inches long. There is a midget Chantenay that grows only 3 inches long and is about 1½ inches wide at the shoulder. Another midget carrot, popular in France, is called Red Apple and is listed by Breck's. Imperator is a tapering, long-rooted carrot of good quality, about 9 inches long. Waltham Hicolor is a vigorous variety that grows to a foot long. There are also several hybrid carrots now available. Good hybrid vegetables are usually fast and lusty growers, though not always superior to non-hybrids in some locations.

Carrots appreciate deeply dug soil, and if your soil is heavy, they will be happier with some peat moss, sand, or compost worked into it. Plant as early in the spring as the soil can be handled, and make a planting every 3 weeks for a continuous supply. Some gardeners soak the seed in water first because it germinates slowly. Some carrots, however, germinate in a week, which is as fast as any reasonable gardener could ask, and the slowest ones don't take much more than 2 weeks unless the temperature stays in the 40s and 50s, which is a little cool for germination.

You want carrots to grow quickly, so don't let the soil dry out. Start thinning them when they are 2 or 3 inches high or they won't grow well. You need not do all the thinning at once, but end up finally with 2 or 3 inches between plants. When thinning, water the row first and pull the surplus carrots carefully. They will be big enough to cook, and young carrots are a treat. You can transplant very young carrots, but growth from seed is almost as fast. We only do it with very late plantings.

Starting with the thinnings, you can harvest carrots all season, and in mild climates all year. In the cold winters of the Midwest we stored late carrots in two ways: For use in the near future we threw a thick straw mulch over a short row of mature carrots when the first hard frost was expected; and before frost came, we transplanted all the rest of the growing carrots side by side in a cold frame that was well banked with earth. In there they stayed alive and fresh as long as the temperature did not sink close to zero. Cellar storage consists of clipping off all but an inch of stalk, then putting the carrots in boxes or in sand. They will keep until spring. Carrots also freeze well.

Clean carrots by washing and paring, or clean them under running water with a stiff brush or one of those dish cleaners that look like a knitted plastic ball.

Garden-fresh carrots cook more quickly than store ones. Twenty minutes is about normal for store carrots to cook tender in boiling water, whether they are small whole carrots or thickly sliced or quartered large ones, but freshly dug ones take about half this time. They are ready when a sharp fork goes through them with slight pressure. You don't want them mushy.

FRENCH CARROTS

The origin of this recipe and its name are not known to us, but it is a good one, and we have adapted it for freshly dug carrots.

    4 large carrots, sliced into ½-inch rounds
    4 cups Vegetable Stock*
    4 tablespoons butter
    4 medium-large onions, sliced
    3 tablespoons flour
    Salt
    Pepper
    ½ teaspoon sugar

Put carrots and stock into a saucepan, put lid on pan, and boil for 5 minutes. Drain, reserving 1 cup of stock, and set carrots aside to stay warm.

Melt the butter in the saucepan and cook the onion slices in it over low heat for 3 or 4 minutes, shaking pan now and then. Sprinkle flour over onions and stir lightly to blend. Add the cup of reserved stock and stir well, off the heat, until blended.

Put carrots and seasonings into pan. Cover pan and cook over medium-low heat, stirring once or twice, for 5 minutes. *Serves 4.*

CARROTS WITH SHERRY

Use half-grown carrots you thin from a row for this dish. A sweet
white table wine can be used in place of the sherry. We use a sweet
California sherry, usually Almaden's or Charles Krug's cream sherry.

16 young carrots, sliced in half lengthwise
6 tablespoons butter, melted
Salt
½ teaspoon grated nutmeg
½ cup cream sherry

Arrange carrots in an enameled metal casserole. Add the other ingredients in the order listed, cover casserole and bake at 325 degrees F. 20 to 30 minutes, or until carrots are tender. A glass or pottery casserole will take a little longer. Serves 4.

CARROTS IN HONEY

2 tablespoons butter
24 young finger-size carrots
Salt
1 tablespoon honey
½ cup Kraft Stock*

Melt butter in a large skillet. Add the rest of the ingredients, cover
the skillet and cook over medium-low heat until almost all the
liquid is absorbed and the carrots are tender. During this cooking,
shake the skillet from time to time to roll the carrots and glaze each
with the cooked-down juices. Serves 4.

CARROT CASSEROLE

Again, half-grown carrots are perfect here.

12 young carrots
12 scallions, cut into 2-inch lengths

2 *tablespoons butter, melted*
1 *teaspoon honey*
Salt
Pepper
2 *tablespoons cream*
1 *tablespoon finely chopped parsley*

Arrange carrots in two layers, crisscross fashion, in a casserole. Strew scallions over the carrots, and pour in the melted butter and honey. Season with salt and pepper, cover casserole tightly, and cook 20 minutes at 325 degrees F.

Test carrots with a fork. If tender, remove casserole and reduce oven temperature to 275 degrees F. Warm the cream slightly and pour it into the casserole, tilting casserole to blend the cream with the cooked-out juices. Return casserole to the oven for 5 minutes, uncovered. Sprinkle with parsley just before serving. *Serves 4.*

Chapter 10
CELERY AND CELERIAC

CELERY (*Apium graveolens dulce*)

We urge you to grow celery in your garden—even if you only have room for a single plant. Celery is so useful in adding flavor to other dishes that even one plant is worthwhile, for in an instant you can clip off a few leaves from it or strip off one stalk—which is often all you need. And garden-fresh celery will open your eyes to how brimful of crisp flavor celery can be. Another point: Celery takes an eternity to mature, about 6 months from seeding, but you can get a stalk or leaf for flavoring from time to time all through the growing season.

Celeries with "Pascal" in their names are good performers and are usually available. Summer Pascal is an early celery, maturing 115 days after transplanting. Another good 115-day celery is Golden Self-Blanching, and Golden Plume is a home-garden early one. "Fordhook" is another name element in celery varieties, and always indicates some original connection with the large and old seed house W. Atlee Burpee Company. They currently are carrying one called Burpee's Fordhook, a 130-day celery. Two other late ones that can do well in home gardens are Green Light and Giant Pascal.

By the way, don't plant the celery seed used for flavoring. It will grow, certainly, if it isn't too old or badly stored, but what a growth! One spring when we completely forgot to get celery seed for planting and were already behindhand, we thought we might as well see if some of the celery seed we used in cooking would be willing to move to the garden. It was willing enough, but it turned out to be a specialist. It grew plants that quickly bolted and produced great bouquets of flowers determined to set a vast lot of seed, but the stalks were all tough and leggy, and without much flavor.

Celery can be grown in mild-winter climates by seeding in September, but elsewhere it is planted to mature in summer or fall. For this, plant seed *early*, 8 or 10 weeks before plants will go to the garden. They can go there a little before your last spring frost is due. If that date is April 10, you can start setting celery plants out about April 1 if the soil is workable.

For stockier plants, transplant them once before they go to the garden.

Celery likes soil rich and well drained, and appreciates frequent waterings and shallow cultivation.

If you want to blanch celery, the simplest way is to tie brown paper from a grocery bag around the stalks for 10 days. We prefer the natural green color, though blanching is supposed to make celery grow a larger heart also.

For flavoring, even thinnings or the discards when transplanting are of kitchen interest, and you can harvest the others starting when they are half grown. Cut plants at ground level and leave the roots to add humus to the soil.

Even in cold climates celery can be stored in the garden for a while by banking it with soil and covering with a foot or two of leaves. In the Midwest we transplanted it to a cold frame in late fall, standing the bunches side by side, and they stayed alive and in good condition. You can also do this in a box of moist earth in a cool cellar.

RECIPES

More celery is eaten raw than cooked, probably, and except in soups and stews the only way we knew celery when we were children was uncooked—as a salad vegetable or served raw with a meal, sometimes with a stuffing of cream cheese. But celery welcomes cooking, as in the recipes that follow. The leaves can be used as well as the stalks, if you wish. To avoid confusion in the recipes, we say "bunch" when we mean the whole plant, and "stalk" for one stem.

Garden-fresh celery is almost 100 percent usable, since the outer stalks are not bruised from shipping, and its cooking time is briefer. For example, if you cut an outer stalk of garden celery on the bias, in slices about ¼ inch thick, it will cook fork-tender in rapidly boiling stock or water in 4 minutes. Cut from a more tender inside stalk, the slices will take only 3 minutes. Larger pieces, say pieces of stalk 2 inches in length, will take no more than twice as long to cook. Gentler cooking will take longer, as will drier cooking.

SIMMERED CELERY

The potato water here is that in which peeled potatoes have been cooked. It will keep for 3 or 4 days in the refrigerator.

> *6 stalks celery, cut on the bias in ¼-inch slices*
> *Milk*
> *1 cup potato water*
> *2 tablespoons butter*
> *Salt*
> *Pepper*
> *¼ cup grated Romano cheese*

Marinate celery for 30 minutes in enough milk to cover it. Then drain, put celery in a saucepan with the potato water and butter, cover pan, bring just to a boil and simmer for 8 minutes, stirring once or twice.

Remove lid, season with salt and pepper, sprinkle cheese over, and simmer 5 more minutes. *Serves 4.*

BRAISED CELERY

This roundly flavored casserole is a splendid accompaniment to beef.

> *4 celery hearts, cut in half lengthwise*
> *8 finger-sized carrots, cut in half lengthwise*
> *4 cups Vegetable Stock**
> *4 scallions, chopped*
> *3 sprigs parsley*
> *1 sprig thyme*
> *1 sprig rosemary*
> *Bay leaf*

1 *clove garlic*
Salt
Pepper
¼ *cup crumbled pork sausage*

Cook celery and carrots in covered saucepan in enough stock to cover them, for 5 minutes. Drain and reserve stock.

Lay the carrots in a deep casserole, sprinkle scallions over them, and arrange celery on top.

Wrap herbs, bay leaf, and garlic in a 6-inch square of white muslin, tie it shut and tuck this bouquet garni in among the celery. Add to casserole salt, pepper, and sausage, and enough stock nearly to cover the contents. Cook covered for 45 minutes in a 375-degree F. oven. Remove and discard bouquet garni. Drain off any liquid left in casserole and cook it down rapidly in a saucepan. Sauce the dish with this before serving. *Serves 4.*

BAKED CELERY

2 *tablespoons finely chopped parsley*
2 *tablespoons finely chopped basil*
¾ *cup dry white wine*
½ *cup Kraft Stock**
Salt
Pepper
2 *bunches celery, cut into 2-inch lengths*
*Vegetable Stock**
6 *tablespoons butter*
2 *shallots, finely chopped*
½ *cup bread crumbs, toasted*

In a saucepan simmer the parsley and basil in the wine for 10 minutes. Add the Kraft Stock, salt, and pepper, and cook another 2 or 3 minutes.

Put celery in another saucepan with enough Vegetable Stock to cover it, put lid on pan and boil for 6 minutes. Drain.

Butter a casserole generously with half the butter. Put celery into it, sprinkle with the chopped shallots, and add the contents of the other saucepan. Sprinkle the crumbs over the top and dot with the rest of the butter. Bake uncovered for 20 minutes at 400 degrees F. *Serves 4.*

CHESTNUT CELERY

This dish has a subtle flavor that goes well with broiled breast of chicken. Apple cider can be used in place of the wine.

> *12 Processed Chestnuts**
> *4 tablespoons butter*
> *6 stalks celery, cut on the bias in ¼-inch slices*
> *Salt*
> *½ cup dry white wine*

Slice chestnuts into halves or thirds, cutting to expose the most inner surface. Melt butter and simmer chestnuts in it for 2 or 3 minutes.

Put celery into a casserole, add salt and wine, and chestnuts with the butter they were cooked in. Cover casserole and bake for 45 minutes at 300 degrees F. Inspect it halfway through and add more wine if needed. *Serves 4.*

PIQUANT CELERY

A nice dish that keeps the celery crisp. Nasturtium Capers* are less assertive than regular capers and contribute an agreeable texture.

> *8 stalks celery, cut on the bias in ⅛-inch slices*
> *Vegetable Stock**
> *2 tablespoons olive oil*
> *1 tablespoon finely chopped Nasturtium Capers**
> *Salt*
> *Pepper*
> *Tarragon wine vinegar*

Drop celery into boiling Vegetable Stock in a saucepan, return to a boil, and drain. Add olive oil and Nasturtium Capers. Stir well, cover pan, reduce heat, and simmer for 3 or 4 minutes. Season with salt, pepper, and a sprinkling of the vinegar. Stir well and serve at once. *Serves 4.*

CELERY ITALIAN

We have been cooking this dish for years, ever since we invented it during a big celery season in our garden, and it rates an "Excellent" in our files. The longer cooking is to effect a blending of flavors.

2 *tablespoons butter*
½ *clove garlic*
4 *stalks celery, cut on the bias in ¼-inch slices*
1 *cup chopped tomatoes*
Salt
Pepper
2 *teaspoons chopped oregano*
1 *tablespoon finely chopped Nasturtium Capers**
½ *teaspoon dry mustard*
½ *teaspoon sugar*
1 *teaspoon tarragon vinegar*

Melt butter in a skillet and brown the garlic lightly in it. Discard garlic, add celery and simmer for 2 or 3 minutes. Add the rest of the ingredients, stir well, cover skillet, and cook over medium-low heat for about 25 minutes. *Serves 4.*

CELERIAC (*Apium graveolens rapaceum*)

Like many homely things, celeriac is dependable and good. You don't see it often in the stores but it is well worth raising if you aren't terribly short of garden space. It is also called knob celery because of the knobby or club-like root, which is the part you eat. It tastes like celery flavored with English walnuts, with a rooty undertone.

Two good varieties are Giant Prague and Alabaster.

Plant and care for celeriac exactly as you do celery. It takes just as long to grow, and like celery, you can use it before it is mature. Celeriac roots grow to 4 inches thick or more, but you can start using them when they are half this thick. To store them, dig the roots when cold weather approaches, cut off all but an inch of the tops, and put them in a cool place. They will keep for months.

RECIPES

Most recipes for celeriac start with parboiling it. A freshly dug whole root, 3 inches thick and unpeeled, takes about an hour and a half of boiling, with the lid on the pan. Peel it after it cools, trimming away the knob-like buds on its surface also.

Or peel it to start with, slice or cube it, and boil for 10 to 30 minutes till tender, in a covered saucepan with just enough water to cover the pieces. Twenty minutes is average. Old celeriac needs less time. The water that is left from this cooking is a mild vegetable stock. You can also boil it in Vegetable Stock* to begin with.

Celeriac can also be steamed in about the same time as by boiling. By wrapping a peeled celeriac in foil you can steam it in the oven. It takes a small one about an hour at 350 degrees F.

After any of these preliminary cookings, celeriac will keep well in the refrigerator for several days.

FRIED CELERIAC

4 tablespoons butter
Flour
Fine, dry bread crumbs
8 slices parboiled celeriac, ½ inch thick
2 egg whites, slightly beaten
Salt

Melt butter in large skillet.

Sift flour over surface of a sheet of waxed paper and spread crumbs evenly over another sheet. Coat slices of celeriac with flour on both sides, dip each into the egg whites, then into the crumbs.

Lay slices in the skillet and cook over medium heat until golden. Turn slices and cook the other sides. Salt lightly. *Serves 4.*

STUFFED CELERIAC

4 small celeriacs, parboiled
4 scallions, finely chopped
4 mushrooms, finely chopped
2 tablespoons corn oil
1 large tomato, chopped
Salt
Pepper
½ cup Croutons*
3 tablespoons butter
½ clove garlic

Scoop out centers of the celeriacs with a ball cutter and reserve for another use. Stand celeriac shells in a baking dish and put them into a 300-degree F. oven to warm while you prepare the stuffing:

Simmer scallions and mushrooms in the oil for 2 minutes. Add tomato, salt, and pepper, and simmer 2 more minutes. Remove from heat, stir well, fill celeriac shells with this mixture and top with the croutons.

Melt butter, simmer garlic in it till garlic browns lightly. Discard garlic, dribble butter over stuffed celeriac shells and return them to the oven for 10 minutes. *Serves 4.*

CHINESE CELERIAC

Whether or not the Chinese would disown this recipe, it is a good one. The celeriac should be freshly dug for best results.

1 raw celeriac about 3 inches thick
⅓ cup corn oil
2 eggs, beaten
1 tablespoon soy sauce
Pekin Sauce*

Peel celeriac, cut it into finger-sized pieces and cut the pieces into very thin slices. Heat 3 tablespoons of the oil in a skillet and cook the slices in this over medium heat for 2 or 3 minutes.

Remove from heat. Add celeriac to the beaten eggs and soy sauce in a bowl and stir well.

Heat the rest of the oil in the skillet and drop tablespoonfuls of the celeriac-egg mixture into it. Cook over medium heat until these little pancakes are nicely brown, turning them once. Serve with Pekin Sauce. *Serves 4.*

CELERIAC CASSEROLE

> 1 *large celeriac, parboiled and cut into ½-inch slices*
> 3 *tablespoons butter*
> 3 *tablespoons flour*
> ½ *cup grated Romano cheese*
> ½ *cup Kraft Stock**
> ½ *cup Vegetable Stock**
> 2 *tablespoons dry vermouth*
> *Salt*
> *Pepper*
> 2 *tablespoons finely chopped parsley*
> 1 *tablespoon finely chopped oregano*

Arrange slices of celeriac in a shallow baking dish and make the sauce:

Melt butter, stir in flour and cook over low heat for 1 minute, stirring. Stir in half the grated cheese. Add all other ingredients, turn up heat, and stir until sauce thickens.

Pour sauce over celeriac slices, sprinkle the rest of the cheese over, and cook uncovered for 30 minutes in a 350-degree F. oven. Finish by browning under broiler. *Serves 4.*

Chapter 11

CORN

CORN (*Zea mays rugosa*)

One of the compensations for living in a climate where the summers are blistering is the delicious corn you can grow. Even in some smaller gardens we had in such climates we never begrudged corn the space it takes, and when space was no problem we planted corn enough to supply friends and have a surplus to be canned and frozen. In recent years there has been interesting work done on dwarf sweet corns so that small gardens can also grow their own. We've grown some and can recommend it. The ears are also dwarfed, and are more manageable at the table than are some of the big ears.

Corn is native to the Americas and has been in existence so long that fossil evidence of it has been found in Peru. It was one of the vegetables American Indians cherished, and field corn—which is today's corn of agriculture and commerce—is also called Indian corn. When you say "corn," a European is apt to think you mean this field corn or any of several grains such as barley or wheat. Sweet corn is largely an American enthusiasm.

Golden Bantam corn is not as big a producer as some others but we think it has never been equaled for flavor. It is a superb corn, with exactly eight rows of tender, delectable, deep yellow kernels to each little 6-inch ear. And we prefer yellow corn to white corn. Golden Bantam stalks grow 5 or 6 feet tall and make an attractive and well-behaved planting.

If you have space, plant varieties of corn maturing at different times. It is the simplest way to spread the corn season. Include a hybrid or two; they are usually more vigorous and thrifty growers. Here, in order of maturity, are four good yellow corns ripening during a month's time: Early Sunglow (hybrid), Spancross (hybrid), Golden Bantam, Burbank Hybrid.

Here, in order of maturity, are three good white corns, ripening over a span of about two weeks: Burpee's Snowcross (hybrid), Stowell's Evergreen Hybrid, Silver Queen.

There are also a few varieties of corn with both white and yellow kernels on the same ear. Honey and Cream Hybrid is one, and Butter and Sugar another.

Dwarf sweet corns include Miniature Hybrid (yellow), White Midget, and Golden Midget.

Plant sweet corn where it will get at least 6 hours of sun a day, and don't plant it until all danger of frost is over.

Hybrid corns are heavy feeders, and all corns need well-drained soil. Make a block planting rather than a single file. Corn pollen is carried by gravity and the wind from the tassels on top to the silks of the ears, and in a solitary row of corn the pollen may all blow away and no kernels will form. For insurance, we always clip off a few ripe tassels and shake them over the young silks, even though we plant in blocks.

You can transplant seedlings, but they grow so slowly that you may as well plant seed.

Cultivate corn shallowly, or still better, mulch it. Suckers sprout from the bases of plants but they do no harm. At one time it was thought best to pull them, but experiments have shown it doesn't help the plant and may hurt it.

Corn earworms are sometimes a nuisance, and though you can attack them with sprays, a simple treatment that has often worked for us is to half fill an eye dropper with mineral oil and squirt it into the silk at the very tip of the ear as soon as the silk wilts.

Each good corn plant will give you 2 or 3 ears, and you can start eating them several days before the ears are quite mature and for several days after. The sign of a mature ear is dried silk. To make sure, pull back a husk and see if the kernels are plump, tender, and milky. Ideally, pick it at this point and within a few minutes of cooking. If the harvest overwhelms you, freeze or can the surplus. Storing ears in the refrigerator in plastic bags is a better-than-nothing alternative, better than anything you can buy at the store but a long cut below just-picked ears.

4. Cress is so easy to grow, you can raise it on a window sill. In the garden it makes a fast growth, and it can be an attractive edging for a flower bed. W. *Atlee Burpee Co. photo*

5. Peas fresh from the garden are a delight—sweet, crisp, and with a flavor so good you must taste it to believe it. A bush variety, such as that shown here, grows from 1 to 2 feet high. W. *Atlee Burpee Co. photo*

6. Certainly one of the handsomest of the leafy greens, chard is also one of the heaviest yielders over a long harvesting season. It is easy to grow and has almost no problems.   *W. Atlee Burpee Co. photo*

Incidentally, don't save the kernels of any hybrid corn for planting, unless you want to experiment. The second generation will be an assortment of varieties, probably none of them much good. We went into this at some length in another book (*Garden to Order*, Doubleday & Company, Inc., 1963), and it is true of any modern hybrid seed no matter what the plant is.

RECIPES

We cook most of our fresh corn by roasting it, usually in the oven and sometimes over coals. We were once happy to see that Nero Wolfe, Rex Stout's fictional connoisseur of good food agreed with us, saying that sweet corn cooked in water is edible, but "roasted in the husk in the hottest possible oven for forty minutes, shucked at the table, and buttered and salted, nothing else, it is ambrosia." (From *Murder Is Corny*, Viking, 1964.) Our procedure is slightly different but the general idea is the same.

When we roast the corn over coals we shuck it first (pull off the husks that cover the ear, and remove the silk), lay the ears on the grill, then turn ears from time to time until cooked all around. This takes 10 minutes, more or less, depending on how hot the coals are. We then butter the ears by rolling them in melted butter in a very hot platter, and salt them lightly.

When we roast corn in the oven we remove all but the inner layers of husks, peel them back to remove the silk, then smooth them down over the ear again and twist the ends or tie them with string. They then go into a 375-degree F. oven for about 15 minutes. They come out with the husks crisp and the kernels partly steamed and partly roasted. We strip off the remaining husks and roll the ears in melted butter in a hot platter that is also the serving dish.

MR. ODIORNE'S CORN PANCAKES

This recipe was given us by a friend, Ben Cassell, who said that a friend of his cooked these toothsome morsels each sweet-corn season in southern California. The proportions of ingredients are based on one ear of corn, and should be multiplied by the number of persons to be served. Note that the milk from the kernels is the only part of the corn used. Sometimes this corn milk is a little hard to press out without its squirting, and an experienced gardener and cook passed along this way of taming such corn: Blanch the ears first, by plunging them into boiling water for a minute.

> 1 ear corn
> 1 teaspoon flour
> ¼ teaspoon baking powder
>
> 1 egg, separated
> Milk
> Melted butter
> Salt
> Pepper

Slit each row of kernels with a sharp knife and squeeze out the corn milk by drawing the back of the knife blade down the ear as you hold it upright in a bowl. Stir in flour and baking powder. Beat yolk and stir it in. Add just enough milk to make a thin batter.

Beat egg white fairly stiff but not dry, fold it into the batter, and drop batter by spoonfuls onto hot griddle. Turn pancakes when puffed and lightly browned, cook briefly on other side, and serve at once topped with melted butter, salt, and pepper.

CORN AND SQUASH CASSEROLE

> 4 medium-sized zucchini squashes
> 4 large mushrooms
> 4 ears corn
> 1 cup Vegetable Stock*
> 3 tablespoons butter
> 3 tablespoons flour
> ½ cup evaporated milk
> Salt
> Pepper
> ¼ teaspoon allspice
> 3 tablespoons finely chopped parsley
> 1 tablespoon finely chopped basil

Cut squashes and mushrooms into ¼-inch slices and put into a casserole. Add the kernels of corn, cut from the ears, and half the stock. Cover casserole and bake for 20 minutes at 350 degrees F.

Meanwhile, make the sauce by melting butter, stirring in flour, adding the rest of the stock and the milk. Cook over medium heat until thick, stirring constantly. Remove from heat and stir in the rest of the ingredients.

Remove casserole from oven, stir gently and top with the sauce. Return casserole to oven and bake for 20 more minutes, uncovered. *Serves 4.*

SKILLET CORN

> *4 strips bacon, cut into small squares*
> *6 ears corn*
> *¼ cup cider*
> *4 scallions, chopped*
> *2 large mushrooms, sliced*
> *Salt*
> *Pepper*
> *1 tablespoon finely chopped tarragon*

Cook bacon over low heat in a skillet. Add the kernels of corn, cut from the ears, plus any corn milk you can press out. Stir in cider, cover skillet and cook over medium heat for 20 minutes. Add the rest of the ingredients, turn up heat and cook uncovered for 10 more minutes, stirring frequently as the liquid thickens. *Serves 4.*

Chapter 12

CRESS

CRESS (*Lepidium sativum*)

Don't despair if you haven't a brook running through your garden and can't grow water cress. There is a garden cress so good that every time we give some away it creates another customer for the seed. This is an upland, or dry-land, cress, often called peppergrass, but far better than the sorts we knew years ago. It is a curled-leaf variation. Most seed houses carry a strain of it, and Burpee's have an especially good one they call Curlycress. It grows in a hurry and likes cool weather. We grow it most of the year in coastal California. In most areas it is a spring and fall crop.

Unless you want a great deal of cress at one picking you may want to do as we do—make an edging around other beds with it. This is also a splendid little plant to use as an edger for a flower bed. It grows less than a foot high.

You can start using curled cress three weeks after seeding. Don't pull plants up; just clip off branches, and the plants will keep on growing. The leaves look like a delicate curled parsley, though occasionally a plant or two will revert to the broad-leaf type.

RECIPES

The chief use for curled cress is as a salad plant, and it also makes an appealing and delicious garnish, better than parsley, and if used in place of lettuce in sandwiches it will add flavor and crispness without excessive moisture. If you have a lot of cress and want to try cooking it, here are two recipes.

CREOLE CRESS

This is an old French colonial dish, also used for lettuce.

6 strips bacon, cut into thirds
6 scallions, chopped
1 large tomato, peeled and sliced
Salt
½ teaspoon finely chopped candied ginger
¼ cup Vegetable Stock*
4 cups coarsely chopped cress

Simmer bacon in a skillet for a few minutes, add scallions and simmer until they become a little soft. Add the rest of the ingredients except the cress, and cook over medium heat for 10 minutes, stirring.

Add cress to skillet, put the lid on, and simmer 5 minutes. Stir for another minute to blend and finish cooking. *Serves 4.*

CREAMED CRESS

This is a delicate dish and only if you raise cress in quantity can you entertain the idea of cooking it.

3 tablespoons butter
6 cups coarsely chopped cress
Salt
3 tablespoons whipping cream

Melt the butter in a large skillet. Stir in cress, cover, and cook over low heat for 10 minutes, stirring frequently. Salt lightly, dribble the cream over cress, stir briefly, and dish up at once. *Serves 4.*

Chapter 13

CUCUMBER

CUCUMBER (*Cucumis sativus*)

There are many good old cucumber varieties, but it is the newer hybrids that put cucumbers back into gardens from which plant diseases had routed them earlier this century. When we bought our Missouri farm after World War II everybody in the countryside told us we were wasting our time planting cucumbers, but when the hybrids we planted produced bushels and bushels of perfect fruits, every garden had cucumbers again the very next year.

The cucumber is a member of the cucurbit family, which also embraces melons and squashes. Cucurbits are often called the vine crops, and they all take the same care. All are tender plants, easily destroyed by frost. Most want a warm summer, but not an extreme one, and all do best in full sun. The cucumber originated in some warm climate, possibly in the East Indies, and is a very ancient vegetable. There are several good hybrids, and new ones keep appearing.

Two good hybrids are Burpee's M & M, and Challenger. Triumph is a neater grower than some. Burpless is being offered as an answer to cucumber lovers with whom cucumbers disagree. A fifth hybrid, Gemini, produces far more female flowers than male ones, the advantage being that you get more cucumbers, as only female flowers form fruits. To make sure you have *some* male flowers for pollinating, it is well to grow another variety also.

Black Diamond and Early Fortune are two good older open-pollinated (non-hybrid) varieties, and the little cucumber called Lemon is delicious and sweet. A variety seldom seen but worth a trial by more gardeners is a cucumber from the Orient called China, or Japan. Harris carries it, Burpee's do not list it but they carry a strain of it, and Stokes carry two. The fruits grow as long as 20 inches but remain about 2 inches thick, and the vines are more tolerant toward poor growing conditions than some varieties.

Among the pickling cucumbers, good ones are Ohio MR 17 (the MR stands for "mosaic-resistant"), West India Gherkin, and Chicago Pickling. These are all small-fruited. A home-garden hybrid pickler is Triple Purpose, suitable for picking at different stages for different-sized pickles. Lemon cucumber is also used for pickling.

Fertile, light, and well-drained soil is ideal for cucumbers, and they dearly love its enrichment with manure. We used manure when we had it on the farm, but we now use compost and the cucumbers don't seem to know the difference. Plant after all danger of frost is past, though you can get a head start by seeding under a Hotkap (trade name for a protective paper cover) about 10 days ahead. Cucumbers are natural climbers, and will go up a fence if planted alongside it.

All the cucurbits bear over a long period, so succession plantings are usually not needed except as insurance against failure of the earlier planting, perhaps. In climates with very hot summers, though, an early spring planting and a late summer one are often worthwhile, as we discovered on the Mississippi Gulf Coast.

Give young plants a few weeks to grow before you thin them, so that if some die you won't be left short. Two or three plants per hill are enough, and in a row they should be at least 2 feet apart. Keep weeds down while the plants are small, and then mulch them. Side-dress them after they have been growing about 6 weeks.

Weekly deep watering is helpful, and we try to give more than that, as cucurbits need a lot of water to form their juicy fruits. A cucumber is about 95 percent water. Ridge earth around a hill of them to form a basin and it will keep water from running off.

When growing a cucumber up a fence, pinch off the center stem when it reaches the top, and let the side stems grow out on each side; they are the ones that will bear the fruit.

Cucurbits have a name for being attacked by all sorts of troubles but we've had them go right through the summer without a care. One way to keep them healthy is to burn old plants at the end of the season and to rotate plantings each year. With garden sanitation and an all-purpose dust, along with planting resistant varieties, you should have little trouble raising cucumbers. Do not, by the way, ever use sulphur as a fungicide on cucumbers or any other cucurbits. It is harder on them than a disease.

Early in the season, plants often insist on producing either all male or all female blossoms. If there is a great abundance of female ones, do this: When a male one appears (you can tell it by its thin stem) snip it off when it is so full of ripe pollen that some will dust off on your finger tip. Then touch the sticky stigmas in the centers of the female blossoms with this pollen, to make them set fruit. This is also the answer when a lack of bees slows down natural pollination. Small or poorly shaped fruit is a sign of poor pollination. Incidentally, don't pay any attention to tales of poor flavor in cucurbits being caused by cucumbers pollinating melons or squash, or the other way around. It doesn't make a bit of difference in flavor. All it affects is the seed, which won't grow the true variety if planted.

Cucumbers are ready to eat from when they are about 3 inches long to when they become their variety's mature size. And you can pickle any size or eat fresh most pickling cucumbers when they are young. Old cucumbers turn yellowish and are then too seedy to use except for pickling. You'll get more and better cucumbers from a vine if you keep the fruit picked and never let any of it grow oversize. However, if you plant hybrid varieties and your climate favors cucumbers, half a dozen vines may overwhelm you with their production. You can store a surplus in the refrigerator for several days in that case.

RECIPES

Though they lose their fine crispness when cooked, cucumbers have an interesting, piquant flavor in cooked dishes. We are a house divided on cooking cucumbers, so we don't cook many. A friend recommends simmering cubed cucumbers in water till tender, draining, and then reheating with fresh chopped tomatoes that have been stewed briefly in their own juice. A touch of chopped oregano would join well with this dish.

If you pick cucumbers while they are young, you need not peel them. And instructions in some recipes on removing seeds do not apply to garden-fresh cucumbers that have been harvested when they should be.

For a winter treat, wrap individual servings of sliced cucumbers in foil during the cucumber season, and freeze them. To serve the slices, unwrap them, and without thawing them, put them into individual sauce dishes and pour heavy cream mixed with a few drops of lemon juice over them. Serve at once. They will still be frozen enough to have a crispness resembling freshly sliced cucumbers.

CUCUMBERS SUPREME

2 medium-sized carrots, cut into thin strips
4 tablespoons butter
1 teaspoon sugar
4 zucchini squash, quartered and cut into 2-inch pieces
2 cucumbers, cut into ½-inch slices
Salt
2 teaspoons finely chopped thyme

Cook carrot strips in butter and sugar in a covered saucepan over low heat for 5 minutes. Add the rest of the ingredients and cook covered until tender, about 15 minutes, occasionally shaking pan. Serves 4.

CUCUMBERS IN SOUR CREAM

3 cucumbers, quartered and cut into 1-inch pieces
3 cups Vegetable Stock*
2 tablespoons finely chopped tarragon
1 teaspoon lemon juice
Salt
Pepper
1 cup sour cream

Put cucumbers and stock in a saucepan. Bring to a boil, turn heat down, and simmer, covered, until barely tender, 5 to 7 minutes. Drain, put cucumbers into a baking dish and add tarragon, lemon juice, salt, and pepper. Spread sour cream over the top and bake uncovered for about 10 minutes in a 350-degree F. oven. The sour cream should be heated through when the dish is served. *Serves 4.*

CUCUMBERS CHINESE

We were given this recipe by a friend who received it from a Chinese friend of hers. Two slight variations can be made: A soya oil in place of butter, and Kraft Stock* in place of the consommé. Also, young garden-fresh cucumbers need no peeling.

4 medium-sized cucumbers
4 tablespoons butter
½ cup beef consommé
Salt
Pepper

Peel cucumbers and slice them into ½-inch rounds. Melt butter in a skillet and simmer cucumbers until they are translucent.

Bring consommé to a boil in a saucepan and transfer cucumbers to it. Cover pan and cook over low heat, shaking pan occasionally, until cucumbers are just tender-crisp. Season lightly with salt and pepper and serve at once. *Serves 4.*

Chapter 14

EGGPLANT

EGGPLANT (*Solanum melongena esculentum*)

An eggplant bearing its fruits looks too good to be true. The plants are nicely compact, about 2 feet tall, with gray-green leaves, and the great glossy purple fruits can run to several pounds each. This is another of those vegetables that look at home as an ornamental planted among the flowers—and in fact the name "eggplant" has passed over into decorators' language to specify a rich purple color.

One plant can produce as many as half a dozen or more fruits, and strong varieties, usually among the new hybrids, hold their fruits off the ground despite the size. Variations of standard-type eggplants include Morden Midget, which bears medium-small fruits on small plants, and one that grows fruits the size and shape of large cucumbers.

We grow eggplants whenever we are living in a warm-summer climate, seeding them in flats indoors 2 months ahead of time and then transplanting to a bed with rich soil and where we hadn't grown eggplant, peppers, or tomatoes the year before. Eggplants start bearing in about 10 weeks from transplanting. You gain no time by transplanting to the garden before the weather warms up; the plants will just mope instead of growing.

They usually ripen their big fruits one at a time, which allows you to space the harvest nicely. Pick them when they are dark and glossy, or a little sooner if you like. Old ones develop seeds.

RECIPES

Some people peel eggplants, some don't. Those who peel them may feel the skin isn't quite edible. We doubt this but we peel them anyway. With a garden-fresh eggplant you can do so with a potato peeler, but older ones take thicker peeling with a sharp knife.

Many recipes call for drawing moisture out of a cut-up eggplant by sprinkling it with salt before cooking. We don't, and you won't find any of our recipes needing it. It may be that garden-fresh eggplant makes the difference, though we suspect the reason is lodged in long habit, and for purposes that may no longer be valid.

Eggplant is not at all a substitute for meat as is sometimes claimed, and in fact has less protein and vitamins than dandelion greens, but it is extraordinarily good to eat, a gift to the palate.

BAKED EGGPLANT

> 1 *large eggplant*
> 6 *tablespoons olive oil*
> 2 *tablespoons Garlic Oil**
> ¼ *teaspoon salt*
> *Pepper*
> 1 *tablespoon finely chopped parsley*
> 1 *tablespoon finely chopped basil*

Peel eggplant and slice into ½-inch rounds. Arrange them in one layer in a shallow pan that can go into the oven. Combine the rest of the ingredients and brush this mixture over the eggplant slices. Turn them and brush the other sides. Set them aside for 30 minutes, repeating the brushings halfway through. You should have enough left to baste the slices once during cooking.

Put pan in a 350-degree F. oven and bake for about 40 minutes, turning slices after 25 minutes and basting them. *Serves 4.*

RATATOUILLE

This traditional dish is a kind of assorted-vegetable hash, but we include it in this chapter because we find that eggplant is the indispensable element in it. The dish is also good when cold.

> 3 *onions, chopped*
> ¼ *cup olive oil*

    3 *green peppers, chopped*
    6 *zucchini squashes, cut into ½-inch cubes*
    1 *eggplant, peeled and cut into ½-inch cubes*
    6 *tomatoes, chopped*
    1 *clove garlic*
    ¼ *cup finely chopped parsley*
    1 *teaspoon salt*
    ½ *teaspoon pepper*
    1 *teaspoon sugar*
    Grated Parmesan cheese

Simmer onions in the oil in a stew pan until they are translucent. Add green peppers and cook over low heat 5 minutes. Add squash, turn heat up to medium, and cook for 15 minutes. Add eggplant, tomatoes, and garlic, cover pan, turn heat to low when boiling begins, and cook gently for about an hour and a half. (We often shorten this time, though the longer cooking is to blend flavors more thoroughly.)

Season with parsley, salt, pepper, and sugar. Cook covered 20 minutes longer, remove garlic, sprinkle the dish with the cheese when serving. *Serves 4 to 6.*

FRENCH-FRIED EGGPLANT

When we need bread crumbs, as here, we make them from our own bread by drying slices in the oven and then running them through a blender. This makes crumbs nearly as fine-grained as corn meal. Garden-fresh eggplant done by this recipe is very crisp on the outside and melting inside.

    1 *large eggplant, peeled*
    Flour
    1 *egg white, slightly beaten*
    Fine, dry bread crumbs
    Salt

Make a brick shape of the eggplant by cutting slabs off the top, bottom, and four sides. Cut the brick into pieces like large French-fried potatoes. Roll them first in flour, then in egg white, then in crumbs, coating them thoroughly each time.

Bring the fat in a French-fryer to 350 degrees F., and cook about 4 eggplant pieces at a time, until golden brown. Drain on crumpled paper towels, sprinkle with salt, and keep warm until all are done. *Serves 4.*

EGGPLANT IN MILK

1 *large eggplant*
Milk
¼ *cup corn oil*
Salt

Pare the eggplant and cut four slices ½-inch thick each. Lay these in a shallow pan with enough milk to cover them. Let them steep for 30 minutes, turning the slices several times.

Drain off the milk, reserving it for some future use as in a sauce or soup. Heat the oil in a large skillet and cook the eggplant slices in it over medium-low heat, covered, until light brown on the bottoms, about 10 minutes. Turn slices and brown the other sides. Salt lightly and serve at once. *Serves 4.*

EGGPLANT CASSEROLE

⅓ *cup corn oil*
¼ *cup olive oil*
2 *tablespoons Garlic Oil**
1 *large eggplant, peeled and cut into ½-inch cubes*
2 *tomatoes, chopped*
3 *tablespoons finely chopped parsley*
1 *tablespoon finely chopped basil*
½ *teaspoon salt*
¼ *teaspoon pepper*
¼ *cup grated Romano cheese*
¼ *cup fresh, coarse bread crumbs*

Heat the oils in a skillet and cook the eggplant in it over brisk heat for 5 minutes, stirring.

With a slotted spoon transfer eggplant to casserole. Put into skillet all the rest of the ingredients except cheese and crumbs, and cook over medium heat for 5 minutes, stirring. Pour this mixture over eggplant in casserole.

Mix cheese and crumbs together and sprinkle over vegetables in casserole. Bake for 40 minutes at 350 degrees F. *Serves 4.*

EGGPLANT AND MUSHROOMS

Garden-fresh eggplant does not absorb as much melted butter as older eggplant, but since the size of the slices varies, you may need to add butter in the second step of this recipe.

4 tablespoons butter
4 slices eggplant, ½ inch thick
½ clove garlic
6 large mushrooms, sliced
1 tablespoon finely chopped marjoram
¼ teaspoon salt
Pepper
½ teaspoon anchovy paste
2 tablespoons dry vermouth
2 tablespoons medium sherry
¼ cup grated Parmesan cheese

Melt butter in skillet, cook eggplant 5 minutes on each side over medium heat. Set slices aside.

Put garlic and mushroom slices in skillet, add more butter if necessary, cover skillet and cook over low heat for about 5 minutes. Remove and discard garlic, turn off heat, and stir in all the rest of the ingredients except cheese.

Lay 2 slices of eggplant in a casserole and cover with half the contents of skillet. Repeat with the other two slices of eggplant and rest of skillet's contents. Sprinkle cheese over the top and bake 30 minutes at 350 degrees F. *Serves 4.*

Chapter 15

FLORENCE FENNEL

FLORENCE FENNEL (*Foeniculum vulgare dulce*)

You may not care greatly for Florence fennel at first, but give it a chance. The flavor is something like tarragon and the plants are beautiful and ferny looking. It is also called finocchio, and has an elegant Italian air about it. It is a different plant from the herb called fennel, grown for flavoring purposes, but different only to the extent of being a separate variety of fennel. You can also eat the stems of the flavoring fennel, and flavor with the seeds of the eating fennel, just to make matters more confusing. And fennel-flower, also a flavoring agent, is completely unrelated to the other two.

Most seed houses carry Florence fennel, usually listing it in their herb collections. The plant grows about 2½ feet tall and wide when in rich soil in full sun. It looks rather bushy, and if you like to combine flowers and vegetables in a bed, as we do, this plant is a good choice. It matures in 3 months, so you can plan on its sharing the flower bed all summer if you plant it in late spring.

RECIPES

In colonial days, we are told, fennel seeds were coated with sugar and eaten during long sermons in church. What we usually eat nowadays is the bulb-like base of the stalk. It looks something like a kohlrabi base, and is crisp, greenish-white, and faintly sweet. It can be cut up raw in a salad, or cooked. The root of the plant is also edible, by the way, and can be cooked like a carrot, but it is usually ignored, perhaps overwhelmed by the more attractive bulb.

Though the flavor of Florence fennel is distinctive, you will find it can be drowned by some other flavors in a mixed dish. We found this out when we put together a casserole of fennel, carrots, onions, and some slices of smoked pork shoulder. The result was tasty enough but the fennel was lost in the crowd.

To prepare Florence fennel for cooking, merely wash it and trim away the stalks that rise from the bulbous base.

BRAISED FENNEL

This delicately flavored dish goes well with chicken.

2 large Florence fennel bulbs, split in half
Salt
Pepper
2 tablespoons olive oil
Tarragon vinegar
2 tablespoons dry vermouth
2 tablespoons Kraft Stock*
Lettuce leaves

Arrange the fennel in a casserole, salt it lightly and grind a little pepper over it. Dribble in the oil and sprinkle a small amount of the vinegar over it. Add the vermouth and stock, cover the fennel with 2 or 3 layers of lettuce leaves, put lid on casserole, and bake for 30 minutes at 375 degrees F. During the last 15 minutes of this baking, remove the casserole lid and the lettuce leaves, discarding the lettuce. *Serves 4.*

FENNEL CASSEROLE

If you haven't recently roasted a chicken you can use Kraft Stock* in place of the pan juices called for here.

4 slices bacon
2 large carrots, thickly sliced
*2 cups Vegetable Stock**
2 Florence fennel bulbs, quartered
4 shallots, sliced
½ bay leaf
1 sprig thyme
6 peppercorns
¼ cup pan juices from roast chicken
Salt

Line a casserole with the bacon. Parboil carrots in Vegetable Stock till barely fork-tender. Drain, and put carrots, fennel, and shallots into casserole.

Tie bay leaf, thyme, and peppercorns in a 6-inch square of muslin to make a bouquet garni, and tuck it into casserole. Add pan juices, salt lightly, cover casserole and cook in a 325-degree F. oven for 1 hour. Remove bouquet garni before serving. *Serves 4.*

Chapter 16

HORSE-RADISH

HORSE-RADISH (*Armoracia rusticana*)

If you have never grated a horse-radish root right out of the garden, you have a thrill in store. Horse-radish is worse than onions for bringing tears to the eyes, and whenever we want some grated, we try to wait for a horse-radish lover to visit, and get him to do it. It is always "him," it seems.

Horse-radish is a perennial that will grow in any soil, but it is not one you can plant in a corner of the garden and forget. The roots will grow woody in time, so it is best to make new plantings each year or two. You can do so with finger-sized roots from your own bed in the spring. Roots for planting aren't cheap, 2 or 3 dollars a dozen, but once you plant them you'll grow roots enough for an army. This is a plant that wants a chilly winter, so don't try it in mild-winter places.

You can store roots in a cellar during the winter but we have merely let them stay in the ground until we needed some. This is one of the best reasons for growing your own horse-radish, as dug roots can lose their strength and flavor in a hurry. And to be at its best, horse-radish should be freshly grated. Roots dug in the summer aren't prime, so do your horse-radish eating in winter, spring, and fall.

Old United States Pharmacopoeias credited horse-radish with being a stimulant as well as a seasoning, and with being good for dyspepsia and rheumatism, among other things.

RECIPES

HORSE-RADISH SAUCES

Wash horse-radish roots and peel them like potatoes before grating. We like the sauce strong, so we simply mix the grated root with white vinegar or lemon juice (cider vinegar turns it dark, though the flavor isn't affected). You can reduce the strength of the sauce by mixing grated turnip with it.

Cream is sometimes mixed with grated horse-radish. If you want to try it, stir 1 part of grated horse-radish into 3 parts of thick cream and add a little lemon juice and salt. This is usually intended for serving at once, and for a fancier effect, use whipped cream.

We sometimes add horse-radish to Béchamel Sauce* or to some other. Since in that case the lemon juice or vinegar isn't always wanted, a convenient way to add horse-radish to a sauce without grating it fresh each time is to keep some horse-radish butter on hand. You make it by working 1 tablespoon of grated horse-radish into 3 tablespoons of butter with a fork. It keeps well for weeks in the refrigerator.

Chapter 17

THE LEAFY GREENS

We give a good deal of garden space to leafy green vegetables for cooking. Years ago we ate all of them raw, in salads, but we got over that phase, and now cook them. Leafy greens are loaded with vitamins and minerals and are so good for you that a list of their boons could go on and on.

Spinach is often the only thing that comes to a person's mind when you say "leafy greens" to him, but there are many others. They include beet and turnip tops, lettuce, the leaves of witloof chicory, chard, mustard greens, endives, tampala, and such Brassicas as collards, kale, and Chinese cabbage.

Most leafy greens take the same general garden care, meaning plenty of sun, enough moisture to keep them growing fast, and a side-dressing of fertilizer midway in their growth for the same purpose. The culture of beets for both roots and leaves is covered in the chapter on beets, and you grow chard the same way; culture of turnips for roots and leaves is in the chapter on turnips; lettuce is also covered separately; witloof chicory culture is covered in the chapter on Belgian endive; Brassica culture is in the chapter on cabbages; and you care for the other leafy greens as you do for lettuce.

For growing in hot weather these greens are recommended: New Zealand spinach, collards, Malabar spinach, and tampala. The first two are available nearly everywhere, and Burpee's handle the last two.

Chard, also called Swiss chard, is a beautiful plant and is one of the best producers of leafy greens. It also grows a wide white stalk which is edible. There is a red-stalked chard, attractive to see, but we think the flavor inferior to the other. Harvest chard by cutting or pulling off outside leaves at their bases. This keeps the plant producing for months. We harvest most leafy greens a few leaves at a time for the same reason.

Tampala should also be mentioned here. If you have not grown it you may find it as good as a farm neighbor of ours did. We started her on it and she deserted spinach for it because tampala was so much easier to grow in quantity for her four ravenous children. The plant was found in China years ago. You can harvest tampala when the plants are only 6 inches high. If you let them grow tall, use the side shoots when they grow to 3 inches long.

RECIPES

Leafy greens are so alike in how they can be cooked that you can use one in place of another in almost any recipe. We usually cook two or three kinds together for a more interesting flavor. Garden-fresh greens cook in two-thirds the time market ones take, and are so filled with their own delicate flavor that even the simplest cooking—5 or 6 minutes in a little melted butter or oil in a covered saucepan over medium heat—turns out an exceptional dish.

In case of chard, the stalk should be trimmed out and started cooking 5 minutes ahead of the leaves, or you can make a separate dish of stalks. Some people compare them to asparagus, though we would not go this far.

The Burpee seed company introduced tampala to American gardeners, and Mrs. David Burpee, wife of the company president, says of it: "The young stems have a slightly astringent flavor, and the leaves are delicately flavored. The combination is delicious." She cooks the stems a little longer than the leaves, in the manner described for chard stalks and leaves.

CHARD WITH HOMINY

We don't make our own hominy but the canned product does nicely here. And kale makes a very good substitute for chard in this recipe, which is based on an American Indian one.

4 *strips bacon, cut into squares*
1 *(1-pound) can hominy, drained*
12 *large chard leaves, coarsely chopped*
Salt
Pepper

Fry bacon in a skillet, stir in hominy, and cook over medium heat for 20 minutes, stirring now and then.

Spread chard over hominy, cover skillet, and cook without stirring for 5 more minutes. Season with salt and pepper, stir well, and serve. *Serves 4.*

CHARD STALKS CASSEROLE

This is a nice dish and very little trouble to make. The bacon and broccoli combine well with the blandness of the chard stalks, and the stalks contribute a crisp texture.

15 *chard stalks, cut into 1-inch pieces*
3 *cups broccoli*
4 *cups Vegetable Stock**
4 *strips bacon, cut into ½-inch squares*
4 *tablespoons butter*
½ *teaspoon salt*
½ *teaspoon grated nutmeg*
½ *teaspoon sugar*
½ *cup dry white wine*

Put chard and broccoli in the stock, cover pan, bring to a boil, and cook for 3 minutes. Drain, put vegetables into casserole, and sprinkle bacon squares over them.

Melt butter, add rest of ingredients to it, and cook over high heat for 1 minute, tipping the pan to blend the mixture. Pour this sauce over contents of casserole, cover casserole, and bake for 30 minutes in a 325-degree F. oven. *Serves 4.*

ELEGANT CHARD

2 tablespoons corn oil
8 cups chopped chard leaves
2 tablespoons dry vermouth
¼ cup Blanched Almonds*, slivered
1 tablespoon olive oil
1 tablespoon soy sauce
Salt
Pepper

Heat corn oil in large skillet, add chard, cover and cook over medium heat for 3 minutes. Then sprinkle vermouth over chard, stir well, and cook covered for another 3 minutes.

Meanwhile, simmer almonds in the olive oil and soy sauce until almonds are just golden brown.

Turn heat off under chard, add almonds, salt, and pepper, toss like a salad and serve at once. *Serves 4.*

SAUCED GREENS

We suggest 6 cups of chard or endive and 2 cups of mingled mustard greens and turnip tops for this dish.

8 cups chopped mixed greens
1 tablespoon butter
1 tablespoon bacon drippings
½ clove garlic
2 tablespoons flour
1 cup Vegetable Stock*
1 tablespoon red wine vinegar
½ teaspoon sugar
Salt
Pepper
¼ cup chopped chives

In a large saucepan cook the greens over medium heat for 5 minutes, using no liquid except the water that clings to the greens after they are washed. Stir now and then while cooking.

Meanwhile make the sauce: Melt butter and bacon drippings and simmer garlic in this until garlic browns lightly. Remove and discard garlic. Stir in flour and cook over low heat until it bubbles. Add the rest of the ingredients except chives, increase the heat to medium, and stir until sauce thickens. Remove from heat, stir in the chives. Pour over cooked greens and bring to the table. *Serves 4.*

CHARD AND ONIONS

> 2 *tablespoons olive oil*
> 2 *teaspoons Garlic Oil**
> 2 *red onions, sliced*
> 6 *cups chopped chard leaves*
> 2 *teaspoons tarragon vinegar*
> *Salt*
> *Pepper*
> 2 *tablespoons Parsley Butter**

Heat the oils in a large skillet, add onions, and cook for 10 minutes over medium-low heat. Add chard, cover skillet, and cook over low heat for 5 minutes, shaking skillet now and then.

Sprinkle chard with vinegar, salt, and pepper. Stir to mingle chard and onions. Dot surface with the Parsley Butter and simmer uncovered just until the butter melts. *Serves 4.*

DRESSED GREENS

No special combination is called for here. We use whatever the garden provides at the time.

2 *tablespoons olive oil*
8 *scallions, chopped into ¼-inch pieces*
8 *cups chopped mixed greens*
¼ *cup Herbed French Dressing**

Heat olive oil and simmer scallions for a few minutes until they are slightly soft. Add greens, cover, and simmer for 5 minutes, stirring a few times. Remove to serving dish and sprinkle with the dressing. *Serves 4.*

Chapter 18

LETTUCE

LETTUCE (*Lactuca sativa*)

Lettuce grows every month of the year where we now live, but even in the Midwest we managed to make the season last about 8 months. We did so by seeding early in cold frames (and in open ground, taking a chance on weather), and by moving the season's last lettuces bodily to the cold frame again in late fall, where they stayed close-packed and alive until we used them. In midsummer we grew loose-leaf varieties in partial shade.

We usually have at least four varieties of lettuce growing at the same time and in succession plantings. Aside from adding interest to the garden and to salads, the diversification keeps possible predators from doing much harm, since any one predator is partial to certain varieties or certain stages of growth. Lettuce doesn't have many troubles, but birds, rabbits, and deer can mow a bed, and snails can be a nuisance at times.

Lettuce comes in four types: *Loose-leaf,* such as Simpson, Grand Rapids, and Salad Bowl; *butter-head,* such as Bibb, Fordhook, and Boston; *crisp-head,* such as Fulton, Great Lakes, and Imperial; and *Cos,* also known as romaine and available in closely related varieties such as Paris White, Valmaine, and Parris Island.

The loose-leaf is the most foolproof lettuce, easy to grow, and undemanding, fast and more tolerant of summer heat than heading types. All the others balk at hot summers, and so are for spring and fall growing in hot-summer areas. (They'll grow in hot weather, but they won't form heads, or flourish as well as loose-leaf types, and they try to go to seed. Cos, for example, poked along in our warm Midwest summers, but in the Pacific coast's marine climate it nearly paces the speedy loose-leaf Simpson.

You can seed lettuce directly in the garden, but we usually seed it in a flat and then transplant an entire bed of it at once. It is easier to protect and care for little plants in a flat. When set out in the garden, the plants can be covered with plastic berry boxes for the first week, to give them filtered shade along with good air circulation, and to keep the birds away.

If you are running a tiny garden, try harvesting the outer leaves of lettuce instead of the whole plant. You'll get more lettuce that way—it works best with loose-leaf types—and another way to make a plant work harder is to leave half an inch of stem sticking out of the ground when you harvest the whole lettuce. This stem will then sprout a second growth.

LETTUCE ROLL

We often take along some garden lettuce when we visit friends, and we've worked out a way of wrapping it that you may want to try.

After washing the lettuce leaf by leaf and shaking it partly dry, we tear off a 3-towel strip from a roll of paper towels and cover it with a layer of lettuce leaves. We make 2 or 3 more such layers on 2 or 3 more strips of towels, one on top of the other. We cover the top one with a strip of the towels and then roll the whole thing into a cylinder about 4 inches thick.

Then in the center of a strip of clear plastic wrap a few inches longer than the 3-towel strips, we lay sprigs of herbs in a simple design to cover a space about 8 inches square. We usually use basil, thyme, chives with a bud or blossom, and marjoram.

Then we wrap the cylinder of lettuce in this plastic sheet by rolling the cylinder over it, starting at one end. We finish by tying the plastic at both ends of the roll with ribbon. The herbs come out looking like a botanical print in the round.

RECIPES

Lettuce is eaten raw close to 100 percent of the time, and is the perfect salad green, as we all know. But it can be cooked, and very successfully. It is also handy for adding a whisper of moisture to another dish during cooking: Lay a few leaves on top and discard them when the cooking is finished.

We recommend Herbed French Dressing* for salads. Among the recipes that follow, there is an old one for Wilted Lettuce*, a new one for the same, our own version of Caesar salad, and two recipes for cooked lettuce. We don't cook lettuce very often, but that is because we usually need it for salads and we don't go in for cooked salads. However, cooking it is a way to get some return from lettuce that has grown old before you can get to it, or has even bolted to seed. The upper stems of bolted lettuce stay crisp and juicy for some time. Cut them into 2-inch pieces, simmer them in a little olive oil in a covered saucepan for 5 minutes or less, and serve them topped with sour cream and chopped chives.

WILTED LETTUCE I

This recipe is at least 60 years old and probably older. Most wilted lettuce recipes call for less wilting than this one, and you may want to omit the final step.

DRESSING

> 3 tablespoons ham or bacon drippings
> ½ teaspoon dry mustard
> Salt
> Pepper
> 1 egg, beaten
> ½ cup cider vinegar
>
> Lettuce enough for 4 servings, torn apart

Melt drippings in a stew pan. Add mustard, salt, and pepper.

Stir beaten egg into the vinegar, and slowly add this to the mixture in the stew pan, stirring constantly over low heat. When it simmers, add all the lettuce at once, and mix thoroughly by tossing and stirring for 2 minutes. Cover pan and keep it on very low heat for 2 minutes. Serve at once. *Serves 4.*

WILTED LETTUCE II

Any vinegar will do here. We usually combine cider vinegar and white wine vinegar half and half.

DRESSING

> 6 tablespoons drippings from sausage or bacon
> 2 tablespoons vinegar
> ¼ teaspoon salt
> ¼ teaspoon dry mustard
> 1 tablespoon finely chopped basil
> 1 teaspoon sugar
>
> Lettuce enough for 4 servings, torn apart

Melt drippings in a saucepan, add all the other ingredients except lettuce, stirring over medium heat until blended. Pour this dressing, bubbling hot, over the lettuce in a bowl. Toss, and serve at once. *Serves 4.*

GARDEN-FRESH CAESAR SALAD

We make a Caesar salad work for its living. In addition to the usual eggs, croutons, and lettuce, we include cold chicken or ham cut in thin narrow strips, and also whatever the garden offers— cherry tomatoes, asparagus cooked tender-crisp and cooled, Belgian endive, cress, chives, cucumbers, raw Jerusalem artichokes peeled and thinly sliced, peppers, celery. . . . In this way we can produce a salad that is a good, quick luncheon all by itself, highly useful when you find at eleven o'clock that you are going to have visitors at noon.

First: make the dressing (this amount serves 4):

CAESAR SALAD DRESSING

> 1 tablespoon wine vinegar
> 3 tablespoons olive oil

1 tablespoon Garlic Oil*
¼ teaspoon dry mustard
½ teaspoon anchovy paste
⅛ teaspoon salt
⅛ teaspoon pepper

Put all ingredients into a small jar, cap it, and shake well. When ready to serve: Put enough lettuce and other vegetables for 4 servings in a salad bowl. Coddle 2 eggs by putting them in a pan with 2 cups of water, bringing it to a boil, removing from heat, and keeping the eggs in it for 2 minutes with lid on. Break eggs over lettuce, add dressing, and toss.

Last: Just before serving, add 1 cup Croutons* browned lightly in 2 tablespoons olive oil, 2 cups of thin strips of chicken or ham, and ¼ cup grated Romano cheese. Toss once more, fill individual bowls with the salad, and arrange on top of each a few strips of the chicken or ham, and a sprinkle of the grated cheese. *Serves 4.*

BRAISED LETTUCE

"Do you know how the French cook lettuce?" a friend asked us, and proceeded to describe the method given here. It is a good way to prepare garden lettuce when it is coming in so fast that some heads mature before you can use them in salads. Ordinarily we do not soak vegetables before cooking. A butter-head lettuce such as Bibb would be the one to use here. The number of heads needed would depend on the size of the casserole. Ours measures 8 inches across, and 6 or 8 heads of Bibb fit snugly, depending on their size, so the recipe is based on that quantity.

6 or 8 heads Bibb lettuce
3 tablespoons butter
Lemon juice
Salt
Pepper
Grated nutmeg

Discard the outside 2 or 3 layers of leaves from each head of lettuce. Immerse heads in cold water for 2 hours. Without draining them, pack heads tightly, stems down, in an enameled iron casserole. Put the lid on casserole and cook on top of the stove over high heat for 10 minutes.

Remove from heat, dot lettuces with the butter and sprinkle them lightly with the rest of the ingredients. Put lid back on and bake for 45 minutes in a 325-degree F. oven. *Serves 4.*

CREOLE LETTUCE

6 slices bacon, cut into squares
½ clove garlic
6 scallions, chopped
½ teaspoon salt
¼ teaspoon ginger
1 tomato, sliced
1 cup tomato juice
2 heads lettuce, quartered

Fry bacon in a skillet, simmering garlic in it. Discard garlic, add scallions and cook over low heat for 2 or 3 minutes.

Add all other ingredients except lettuce, turn heat to medium high, and cook for 10 minutes, stirring gently 2 or 3 times.

Lay lettuce in skillet, put the lid on, and cook for 5 minutes, turning lettuce quarters once, halfway through. *Serves 4.*

Chapter 19

MELONS

CANTALOUPE (*Cucumis melo*)

WATERMELON (*Citrullus vulgaris*)

Most home gardens won't accommodate melon vines, which sprawl all over the place, and the fruits are too heavy for trellis culture, but we include melons here because they are interesting to grow and you may be willing to give them half the garden. And we can't deny it—a cantaloupe well grown, picked at its peak of perfection from your own garden and eaten at once, is a delight you will never experience with store-bought melons. It takes 3 months to grow a cantaloupe, and watermelons take nearly as long.

There are several hybrid cantaloupes, and we think they are a good home-garden choice. The earliest, and a very superior melon, is the Burpee Hybrid. Harper Hybrid, developed in Canada, is nearly as early, and one called Mainerock is earlier. Saticoy is a good mid-season hybrid.

Among the non-hybrids, a good and strictly home-garden cantaloupe is Delicious 51, developed at Cornell University. Hearts of Gold is grown in home gardens, and so is Netted Gem, the variety known commercially as Rocky Ford.

Besides cantaloupes there are casaba and honeydew melons, and crenshaws, to name three that are grown in home gardens. However, the first two are pretty well confined to warm parts of California, though a University of New Hampshire development called Sungold Casaba looks promising. The best crenshaw melon we know of is a hybrid offered by Burpee's, which grows to the weight of a medium-sized watermelon.

Watermelons come in different shapes (round, oval, and long), in different colors (grayish green, dark green, striped), and different weights (5 to 50 pounds). Sugar Baby and New Hampshire Midget are two little ones, and a good new big one is Charleston Gray. Northern Sweet, developed at the Minnesota Experiment Station, ripens in about 10 weeks from planting, which is fast for a watermelon of its weight, up to 12 pounds. Among the hybrids, Burpee's Fordhook is also a 10-week watermelon of about the same size. Dixie Queen Hybrid takes a week longer but grows a bigger melon, 30 pounds or so. There are some seedless watermelons on the market, hybrids, but for a home garden their drawback is that you must grow still another watermelon to pollinate them.

The preserving type of watermelon, known as citron (but not the same as the citron that is candied, which is the rind of a citrus fruit, *Citrus medica*), is handled by a few houses. One is Olds.

Cantaloupes and watermelons belong to the cucumber family, and all cucurbits take much the same care. Follow the suggestions given for cucumbers, but space melon hills 6 feet apart. You must let melons grow on the ground, but you can limit their spread somewhat by pinching off the tip of a vine when it has grown to 6 joints long. This pinching back makes it put out lateral vines, which you can also pinch back later, after they have set some fruit.

Cantaloupes are a little fussy about moisture, and will resent too much rain or humidity. If your area is somewhat humid and cool, try a small hybrid called Sweetie. Breck's and Park's list it.

Watermelons like their soil mildly acid.

When is a cantaloupe ripe? Some people can tell by smelling them. A rule that works most of the time is: Touch the stem. If it parts easily (slips) from the melon, the melon is ready. A cantaloupe's sugar reaches its greatest point at this stage, and soon after picking starts to decline. A cantaloupe picked green will not get any sweeter, but honeydew melons go on ripening after being picked.

The merit of a home-grown cantaloupe is its peak-of-perfection flavor, so that storage in the usual sense is pointless. We have held a surplus few in the refrigerator briefly, well wrapped in plastic, as their aroma is penetrating, but for longer storage, freezing is best. Cut balls with a ball cutter, and freeze. When you use them, don't let them thaw completely. Mint flavor joins well with cantaloupe, and our friend Jerome Kantor serves frozen cantaloupe balls with this sauce:

Cold Mint Sauce

*Boil ½ cup sugar dissolved in ½ cup water for 5 minutes.
Pour it over 3 or 4 tablespoons finely chopped mint leaves.
Strain when cool, and add the juice of 1 lemon and 1 orange.*

To tell when a watermelon is ripe, thump it with your knuckles.
A dull hollow sound means "yes." There is a 65-day variety, Golden
Midget, with a rind that turns yellow when ready for harvest. Park's
list it.

Watermelons stand up well in storage for a few weeks, especially
in a cool place. Though it is a type of stunt storage, you can coat a
watermelon with paraffin to make it keep longer. A variety called
Winter or Christmas is best for this, having a hard rind. It also
makes an interesting little project for a young gardener, especially
if he has grown the watermelon himself.

Chapter 20

OKRA

OKRA (*Hibiscus esculentus*)

Okra deserves a larger public than it has. As a plant it is attractive, with handsome flowers something like those of its relative, the ornamental hibiscus. Okra's showy leaves sometimes become a foot wide, and the pods are good to look at as well as to eat. Even half a dozen of these plants tucked into a flower border will be a pleasure to the eye as well as furnishing flavor and nutrition.

Gumbo is another name for okra, and in South America they call it quimbombo. It is a tropical crop and mainly grown in the South but it will grow wherever the summer is hot enough. If you can grow corn you can grow okra. About other conditions okra is not in the least fussy, having no troubles to speak of, and getting along in any garden soil.

It starts producing pods in about 2 months and continues to do so for weeks. Plants average 4 feet high but there are dwarfs that don't get much higher than 2 feet. Clemson Spineless and Emerald are good tall ones, and Dwarf Green Long Pod is a well-known dwarf. In okra, "dwarf" refers to the plant, not to the pod.

The temptation is to let the pods grow large—and Emerald grows 9-inch ones—but the time to harvest is when pods are 2 or 3 inches long. They are more tender then, and if you let them grow as large as they wish, the plant will soon stop producing.

RECIPES

Okra is probably more used in soups than in any other dish, as its mucilaginous property helps give body to a soup and its flavor combines agreeably with other vegetables. This is also true of its use in stews and gumbos.

Trim off both ends of the pods before cooking them. Pods are usually sliced into rounds, but very young and tender pods can be cooked whole.

We give four recipes here; another in which okra is an essential ingredient, Chicken Gumbo*, will be found in Chapter 39, "Casseroles, Etc."

OKRA AND TOMATOES

¼ pound pork sausage
2 cups ⅛-inch rounds okra
1 green pepper, cut into ¼-inch rings
2 tomatoes, coarsely chopped
2 tablespoons finely chopped parsley
1 clove garlic
Salt
Pepper

Break up sausage with a fork and cook in a skillet over medium-low heat until lightly browned. Stir in okra and cook for 5 minutes.

Add green pepper, tomatoes, parsley, and garlic, cover skillet and simmer 1 hour, stirring now and then.

Remove and discard garlic, season with salt and pepper. If more than about 2 tablespoons of liquid remain, thicken by cooking it down separately, and sauce the dish with it. *Serves 4.*

BRAISED OKRA

This is a simple but splendid dish. Okra and leeks have an affinity for each other, as this recipe will show.

4 tablespoons corn oil
*1 tablespoon Garlic Oil**
*¼ cup Kraft Stock**
3 cups ¼-inch rounds okra
Salt
Pepper
1 leek, thinly sliced

Heat oils and stock in a skillet. Add okra, cover, and cook for 10 minutes over medium heat. Season with salt and pepper, stir in the leek, cover and simmer 10 more minutes, shaking skillet now and then. *Serves 4.*

BASIL OKRA

2 tablespoons butter
3 cups ¼-inch rounds okra
Lettuce leaves
4 mushrooms, finely chopped
2 tablespoons finely chopped basil
1 tablespoon finely chopped parsley
Salt
Pepper

Heat butter in a saucepan, add okra and lay enough lettuce leaves over it to cover okra completely. Cook over medium heat for 5 minutes.

Discard lettuce, add chopped mushrooms and cook for 10 minutes, stirring now and then, till okra is lightly browning. Add basil, parsley, salt, and pepper, stir lightly during 1 more minute of cooking, and dish up. *Serves 4.*

MRS. PARK'S FRIED OKRA

This is a recipe used by Mrs. William J. Park, wife of the president of George W. Park Seed Company, which is located in the South (South Carolina), where okra is especially appreciated. Three or four cups of okra would be needed to serve 4 persons.

"Pick young tender okra and remove a small portion from each end of the pod. Slice pods horizontally into small pieces about ½ inch wide. Soak in salty water, then roll in corn meal. Fry in deep fat until golden brown."

Note: Pre-soaking okra as done here reduces its mucilaginous content.

Chapter 21

THE ONION FAMILY

In this chapter we deal with six members of the onion family (or genus, to be botanically exact), in this order: Shallots, the family's little aristocrats; scallions, also called green, spring, and bunching onions; chives; garlic; leeks; and the familiar globe onions.

During World War II there was a serious shortage of many foods in England, as any reader of Angela Thirkell knows very well. Oranges were one of the scarcer items, which is easy to understand, but the story is that English housewives were far more distressed by the shortage of onions. So were the Old Testament Israelites in the wilderness. We sympathize with such feelings, and not because we use very many onions either. It is because onions are so valuable to just about everybody who enjoys food, as a flavoring agent and as a partner to other ingredients of a dish. Many good cooks class the onion family as our most important seasoning after salt, and mention its versatility—from the sweet, mild chive on up through patrician shallots and leeks, to garlic's firm authority.

Onions of any sort are easy to raise in a home garden if the climate suits them. That is, they aren't temperamental about soil and aren't greatly bothered by pests or diseases, but they are a cool-weather crop, and are sensitive to day-length. Plant them in spring. Some will do all right also when planted in fall in the warm-winter zones, but certain bulb-forming varieties need longer days than wintertime provides. Ordinary garden care plus some extra fertilizing and attention to weeding will please all of them.

But you may be thinking: Why raise onions in the garden when good onions are always available in the store? They aren't always so good, but even if they were, there are reasons to consider raising your own. In the case of globe onions, raising your own is the only way you are likely to taste some choice Bermudas, Sweet Spanish, and good hybrids. As to store scallions, they suffer from storage and shipping. Shallots, chives, and leeks are seldom found in markets. And garlic must be fairly fresh to be at its best, with a hard, solid feel and a pinkish blush showing through the papery skin.

SHALLOTS (*Allium ascalonicum*)

Shallots look something like garlic cloves with papery brown or gray skins. They are hideously expensive on the market, 2 dollars or more a pound when they are to be had at all. If you can get them, buy enough to plant a dozen. Plant them with the blunt ends down, and cover them with 1 inch of soil. Plant them in the spring, and try them in several locations, as they are choosy about where they grow. If you can't buy them locally, Hemlock Hill Herb Farm and Nichols Garden Nursery are two houses that handle them.

Like garlic, one point of growing your own shallots is to get them fresh. When they grow old in long storage they lose some moisture and may burn during cooking. Harvest them in the fall when the tops die down. Dry them by braiding the tops and hanging in an airy place. Like globe onions, they will keep for months.

RECIPES

We consider shallots as mainly a seasoning even though they are also a food. If you taste a raw shallot all by itself, you won't care for it. They can be as strong as garlic. But something happens when they are cooked or blended, and they become mild and delightful. A little dab of shallot does wonders for a lot of dishes.

Shallots are peeled before cooking; the skin is like the brittle tissue-paper skin of garlic, and shallots need no more peeling than garlic. They are usually chopped finely for use in a dish, preferably on a board, with a French cook's knife. Some dishes call for a dozen or more shallots, but such recipes find no place in our files. A dozen shallots go a long way in our kitchen and do much good to many things. Scallions are a good substitute for shallots if you must have a lot of them.

As a rule we add shallots to a dish as late in the preparation as possible, or we keep the heat low. Like onions and garlic, they scorch easily.

You will find recipes for two sauces made with shallots in Chapter 37: Shallot Mayonnaise* and Shallot Sauce*.

SCALLIONS (*Allium cepa*)

Scallions are easy to grow, willing to get along under conditions that don't suit globe onions at all, though the two are the same species. A little bed or border of scallions is one of the handiest things in the kitchen garden.

You can get scallions by harvesting globe onions before they form bulbs, or by planting true scallions, which never form large bulbs and which are variously called bunching onions, multiplier onions, perennial onions, Egyptian onions, and, on the market, spring or green onions.

To grow a scallion, you can plant a bulb (or, more accurately, a bulbil), a plant, or a seed. Bulbs are the most likely to succeed. Scallions take from 2 to 4 months to reach maturity, but you can use them at any stage. If you grow them from seed, sow it thickly and in a month or so the thinnings will start providing the kitchen with small scallions.

Unless your climate is severe, scallions will live through the winter. In Missouri, where 15 degrees below zero could be expected, we carried scallions through the winter by covering the row with a thick mulch.

Some varieties, such as Beltsville Bunching, are perennial, but we've found it is a good idea to make a fresh planting each year anyway. Two other good varieties are Evergreen Long White and White Spanish. Southport White Globe is often used as a scallion when pulled young.

RECIPES

Both the green tops and white stems of scallions are used in most of our dishes, and in the garden we often harvest just a bit of the green tops for a touch of flavoring. When we call for scallions in a recipe, we mean the entire scallion unless we say differently.

As a substitute for shallots, scallions do very well. They are also an agreeable substitute for globe onions in many dishes, being milder.

Because scallions are so important to one simple dish we like, we are giving the recipe here instead of under the other vegetable concerned, broccoli.

SCALLIONS AND BROCCOLI

Be sure to use olive oil here.

> 2 *tablespoons butter*
> 2 *tablespoons olive oil*
> 4 *cups broccoli*
> 4 *scallions, chopped*
> *Salt*
> *Pepper*

Heat butter and oil in skillet. Add the broccoli, which should be slightly damp from being washed. Cover skillet and cook for 5 minutes over medium-high heat or until broccoli stems are barely fork-tender, shaking skillet now and then.

Add scallions, reduce heat to medium-low, and cook, covered, 5 more minutes, shaking skillet occasionally. Season with salt and pepper. *Serves 4.*

CHIVES (*Allium schoenoprasum*)

Even a flagpole sitter could raise chives, for they'll grow happily in a flower pot and they take no more attention than a little watering now and then, by you or the rain. This is one vegetable you must raise if you want it, for chives are seldom sold in stores, except in pots to be grown at home.

For some reason the story has got about that chives will grow only from bulbs or plants. They will grow faster to usable size from them, but they'll grow quite well from seed. And once you get them started, you are in business, as they are perennials. We've given away clumps of chives to friends until the total must run into the thousands of plants, and at this very moment chives are crowding each other in borders around our vegetable beds, and a couple of clumps among the flowers are beseeching us to divide them so they can overwhelm the terrace.

You harvest only the stems of chives, which are really the leaves and are little tubes. If you allow them to, chives will throw up flower stalks. The flowers are pretty little things, the shape of clover blossoms and an attractive lavender-rose color.

Though everybody says "chives," a single plant is called a chive. The ch is pronounced as in "chief," not as in "chivalry." The name comes from the Latin for onion, *caepa*.

The tops of chives die down in late fall but you can transplant some clumps to pots before this happens, and bring them indoors for a constant supply all winter.

In early spring, preferably, lift the clumps in the garden, pull them apart into small clumps of 15 or 20 bulbs each, and plant these small clumps a foot apart. If you don't divide chives the stems grow weak and puny.

Harvest chives with a pair of scissors, cutting stems low.

RECIPES

Chives are mainly a flavoring agent, so we offer no recipes especially for them. We use them in salads, omelets, and wherever a sprightly touch of onion flavor is good. They won't stand much cooking, so add them late, almost as a garnish before dishing up in most cases.

GARLIC (*Allium sativum*)

In our opinion not nearly enough home gardeners raise garlic. It is easy to grow, attractive enough for an ornamental foliage plant, and there is nothing like fresh garlic for the kitchen. All you do is to plant a clove, one of the 10 or so segments that make up the bulb, and the garlic does the rest. Plant it with the pointed end up, about 1 inch deep. Each planted clove will grow into a bulb in about 3 months, giving you a tenfold return, and since not many people need a great lot of garlic, you could do as we do—plant a few cloves here and there about the garden or flower beds, or make a border of garlic, instead of devoting an entire bed to it.

If we run out of our garden garlic, we go to an Italian market we know, because Italian people treat garlic with respect. Even so, the market's garlic isn't always prime, and when this is so, the proprietor hates to see us. "If you just have to have some," he told us the last time we were in, "take it—but I refuse to sell it to you." We took it, and the cloves we didn't need for current use, we planted.

You can clip off a few inches of the leaves during the growing season if you want a hint of garlic and have no cloves of it on hand. But the real harvest comes when the leaves yellow and die down. At that time, dig the bulbs and wash off the earth. Dry the bulbs in the sun or by hanging them by their leaves in an airy place. A good way to store them is to braid the leaves of several bulbs together and hang them where they'll be cool and dry but won't freeze. Or cut off the leaves and keep the bulbs in a basket.

Don't wait long to harvest your bulbs, especially if the season is wet. The papery skin may decay, making the bulbs keep less well. An early harvesting won't hurt garlic; the bulb will just be smaller than an older one, and also milder.

Many older civilizations believed that garlic was good for a long list of ailments, including snakebite, bronchitis, and earache. It is still highly regarded by many people today for health-giving purposes.

RECIPES

Like chives, garlic is a flavoring agent, so we give no recipes for it alone. You'll notice we usually suggest, in recipes where garlic is used, that it be cooked gently and then discarded before the dish is finished. The gentle cooking is needed because garlic burns easily. The discarding is a matter of choice. A way around this is to use Garlic Oil* when you can. The recipe for making it can be found in Chapter 2.

LEEKS (*Allium porrum*)

Leeks are another vegetable you seldom find in home gardens, and we don't know why. Perhaps it is because they are so leisurely about growing to maturity. They take about 4 months. But you can start them early, in flats or a cold frame, and you don't have to wait until they are all through growing before you use them. We've harvested leeks 8 weeks after they were set out.

A well-grown leek allowed to reach maturity is a thick stem up to 2 inches wide and 4 to 6 inches long, with strap leaves above and no bulb below, except for a slight swelling at the very base. Market gardeners usually whiten the stem by banking it with earth. We never saw much point in this. A home-garden leek is far more tender and crisp than any you'll buy, if you can find them at all. Another point—banking with earth sifts earth in between the leaves, making more of a chore in the kitchen.

And speaking of leek leaves, though you'll usually be told to discard them in cooking, there is no reason to do so with young garden leeks. Their flavor is mild, as is the stem's flavor, and they can be used as you use scallion tops.

There are several varieties of leeks, but not a great deal of difference between them. Broad London is a good one, and so are Swiss Special and Giant Musselburgh. Elephant is a faster grower than some others, and Unique is noted for its long stems, which run to 8 inches.

Most leeks stand cold weather pretty well. In the Midwest we tried leaving some in the garden all winter, mulching them with straw, and they stood it. They also transplanted well to a storage cold frame for winter use.

Harvest a leek by cutting off the roots at the base of the stem. Leave the roots in the soil to add humus.

RECIPES

You can use leeks in any dish in place of onions, and if onions are too strong for you, leeks will be a welcome replacement.

Leeks are also a nice addition to salads because of their mildness. Slice them into rounds as thick as a half dollar and marinate the slices in the salad dressing for 30 minutes before you toss the salad.

Thinly sliced in this way, leeks also combine well with sliced mushrooms when both are braised in butter, and we include a recipe for this dish.

LEEK CASSEROLE

3 large leeks
⅓ cup dry vermouth
⅓ cup Vegetable Stock*
Bay leaf
Salt
Pepper
2 tablespoons olive oil

Cut stems of leeks into 2-inch chunks. Coarsely chop enough of the green tops to fill 1 cup. Put both into an enameled metal casserole and add the rest of the ingredients. Cover casserole and bake for 30 minutes in a 375-degree oven. *Serves 4.*

LEEKS AND MUSHROOMS

Both the mushrooms and leeks should be sliced about ⅛ inch thick for this recipe.

2 tablespoons butter
2 tablespoons corn oil
2 tablespoons Kraft Stock*
3 cups sliced mushrooms
1½ cups sliced leeks
Salt
Pepper
2 tablespoons finely chopped parsley

Melt butter in a saucepan and add oil and stock. Bring to a simmer, add mushrooms and leeks, cover and cook over low heat for 10 minutes, stirring several times.

Add salt, pepper, and parsley, stir well and dish up. *Serves 4.*

For another use of leeks, see Vichyssoise* in Chapter 38, "Soups and Stocks."

GLOBE ONIONS (Allium cepa)

Raising globe onions from seed is an adventure. We have had seed flourish one year and sulk the next year under the same conditions so far as we could see. This experience is duplicated by many other home gardeners. Still, we continue to plant onion seed because we can get so great a number of varieties in seed, and probably because every gardener is a gambler at heart.

The other two ways of raising globe onions—which we'll call just "onions" hereafter for simplicity—are the same as for scallions: from bulbs or from plants. To give you some idea of what your garden onions will cost from each method, here are the figures:

Seed: A packet contains about 750 seeds (about 400 for hybrids) and costs from 25 to 50 cents.

Bulbs: A pound contains about 200 bulbs and costs from 75 cents to a dollar or so.

Plants: Plants are sold by the bunch, averaging about 75 plants and costing from 75 cents to $1.75.

Seeds give you by far the widest choice of varieties, including some good new hybrids. Burpee's and Stokes have the widest selections we know of, offering about 40 varieties between them.

If you buy bulbs (usually called "sets"), you'll be offered yellow onions or white onions, the variety usually unspecified but usually Ebenezer, a good onion with a flattened globe shape.

Onion plants aren't offered by every seed house, but are offered in several varieties by some. Shumway and Field, for example, offer eight varieties between them.

The Bermuda and the Sweet Spanish onions are still some of the best ever developed, and should be seeded early, indoors, to give them time enough to develop during their growing season. In warm-winter areas seed them outside in the fall or spring. They can also be bought as plants ready to be set out.

Hybrid varieties of onions are well worth trying, and their vigor may enable you to grow onions from seed if you haven't been able to grow them before.

In order to become large, onions need long days—in other words, all the summer day-length they can get. They grow best in the Northern states, but they are a home-garden crop anywhere except in the desert.

The U. S. Department of Agriculture has recommended certain varieties for home-garden use in broad sections of the country. Since not all the varieties recommended are easily available to home gardeners, we have screened those that are, and give them here, with U.S.D.A. comments:

South: The Yellow Bermuda, a large, very mild, flat onion, is recommended for spring harvest (fall planting). It has a short storage life.

Middle Latitudes: Sweet Spanish and the hybrids Fiesta, Bronze, and El Capitan are large, mild, globular onions suited for growing here. They store fairly well.

Northeast and Midwest: Southport White Globe, Southport Yellow Globe, Ebenezer, Early Yellow Globe, Yellow Globe Danvers, and the hybrid Abundance are all firm-fleshed, long-storage onions for main crops.

Northern: Early Harvest is a hybrid adapted to all Northern regions.

Even if you are growing onions for storing a winter's supply, you can start harvesting some as scallions when they are young. In this way you can thin the row and also supply your table. When the onions you allow to remain in the garden have matured, about three-fourths of the top growth will turn yellow and droop. Bend over the rest of the tops, and a few days later pull up the bulbs and spread them on the ground in the sunshine to dry. Put them under cover in an airy place such as a garage if it rains during this time. When the tops are as dry as straw, cut them to an inch or two long with a scissors and store uncovered in a cool dry place where they won't freeze. We have usually used net sacks hung from a garage or basement ceiling. The onions to store are those with *thin necks.* Thick-necked ones are planning to sprout soon, so use them up.

RECIPES

Here's a tip on freezer storage for onions: Cut them in different ways for various uses—sliced, cubed, in rings, finely chopped—and store each kind in small plastic bags in the freezer. This is a great convenience, and we are indebted to Mr. Jerome Kantor for it, who added that it is a way not only to spread the onion harvest but also to avoid "onion tears and smelly hands" each time you need onions in a recipe. It also saves time.

FRENCH-FRIED ONIONS

> 2 large Spanish onions, cut into rings ½ inch thick
> Milk
> Flour
> Salt

Put onion rings in a bowl with enough milk to cover them. Steep them for about 1 hour, then drain and dry onion rings lightly on paper towels. (The milk can be reserved for use in a cream soup or a sauce.)

Thoroughly coat onion rings with flour. Cook a few at a time in a French-fryer at 350 degrees F. until rings are golden brown. Drain them on paper towels, sprinkle with salt, and keep them warm until all are cooked. *Serves 4.*

STUFFED ONIONS

> 4 medium-large onions
> 4 medium-large mushrooms, chopped
> 2 tablespoons butter
> 2 tablespoons evaporated milk
> Salt
> Pepper
> Bread crumbs

Cut a thin slice off the bottom of each onion so it can stand, then put them in water to cover, bring to a boil, and cook over medium heat for 5 minutes. Drain.

Meanwhile, simmer mushrooms in the butter for 5 minutes, add milk and simmer another 2 or 3 minutes.

Scoop out the centers of onions, leaving walls 2 layers thick. Chop this pulp, mix it with the mushrooms, season with salt and pepper. Stuff onion shells with this mixture, sprinkle with the crumbs, and bake for about 30 minutes at 325 degrees F. *Serves 4.*

BAKED ONIONS

The onions here are the immature bulbs that result from the last thinning of the rows. They are tender, and will average perhaps ¾ inch wide. Save the surplus tops for other uses.

2 cups whole small onions
2 cups Vegetable Stock*
1 cup 1-inch pieces green tops
Butter
½ cup sour cream
¼ cup dry white wine
1 tablespoon finely chopped parsley
Salt
Pepper

Put onions in a saucepan with stock, bring to a boil and cook for 10 minutes, covered. During the last minute of boiling, add the green tops. Drain, put into a buttered casserole, and make this sauce:

Mix sour cream and wine in saucepan. Bring to a simmer, stir in parsley, salt, and pepper and cook for 2 or 3 minutes over low heat.

Pour sauce over the onions and bake for 20 minutes at 300 degrees F. *Serves 4.*

ONION CASSEROLE

> 4 tablespoons olive oil
> 2 medium-large onions, cut into ¼-inch rings
> 4 large mushrooms, cut into ⅛-inch slices
> 2 green peppers, cut into ¼-inch strips
> 1 tablespoon finely chopped Nasturtium Capers*
> 2 tomatoes, chopped
> Salt
> Pepper
> 1 egg, beaten

Heat oil to shimmering in a skillet, add onions, mushrooms, and green peppers, cover and cook for 10 minutes over medium heat, stirring now and then.

Remove skillet from heat, stir in the rest of the ingredients in the order listed, transfer contents of skillet to a casserole, and bake for 30 minutes at 300 degrees F. *Serves 4.*

BRAISED ONIONS

Claret is a good wine to use in cooking this dish. We usually use the California version called Cabernet Sauvignon.

> 8 strips bacon
> 4 large onions, split in half vertically
> 1 cup Kraft Stock*
> Salt
> Pepper
> ¼ cup dry red wine

Fry bacon and drain. Cut strips into squares and cover the bottom of a large low baking dish with them. Arrange onion halves, cut sides down, on the bacon. Add stock, salt, and pepper, cover casserole, and bake for about 40 minutes in a 325-degree F. oven, or until stock is nearly absorbed.

Sprinkle the wine over the onions and finish baking, uncovered, for about 10 minutes. *Serves 4.*

Chapter 22

PARSNIPS

PARSNIPS (*Pastinaca sativa*)

The parsnip is a much overlooked vegetable. We can recall only one true parsnip lover, and he was an artist who lived in the mountains all by himself, so he didn't have much influence. Some cookbooks simply ignore parsnips.

The parsnip came into what popularity it has enjoyed in the Middle Ages, though it was known before that, and there is still something medieval and uncompromising about parsnips. They have a like-me-or-leave-me character—a definite flavor you can never forget.

Garden-fresh parsnips have the great advantage of youth. You can harvest some early, before the center core forms. Like any root crop they want deeply dug soil, and they like it fertile, so dig in compost. The seed must be fresh, and even so, it takes 2 or 3 weeks to sprout. Water the row well before you drop the seed, cover it *very* lightly, firm the row with your feet after planting, and finish with a ½-inch layer of peat moss on top as a mulch. If you have a short summer season, plant soon after the last frost, as parsnips take 3 or 4 months to mature. In the South it is too warm in midsummer for parsnips, so there they are a spring or fall crop.

Parsnips are one of the vegetables you can leave in the ground all winter. Freezing doesn't bother them, and even improves the flavor. In the Midwest we dug them during thaws, but we mulched them for protection from the heaving that results from too much freeze-and-thaw.

All-American is a good variety, and Harris' Model is known for smoothness and whiteness. Guernsey and Hollow Crown are good older varieties.

RECIPES

Parsnips are usually given a preliminary cooking with moist heat, and are then taken a step farther. However, you can French-fry young raw ones. In England they serve steamed parsnips with mayonnaise when cold and call it poor man's lobster salad. Our Shallot Mayonnaise* is very suitable here, though we don't say you'll think you're eating lobster.

You can parboil an unpeeled garden-fresh parsnip tender in briskly boiling water in 10 minutes if it is medium-sized—about 1 inch wide at the shoulder. Here's a good way to peel it after it is cool enough to handle: Run a razor blade from shoulder to tip, cutting barely through the skin, then hold the loosened edge of skin against the cutting board and roll the parsnip away from it.

Old parsnips form cores that are often too woody to eat. You can slit the cooked parsnip lengthwise down to the core and lift it out whole, or slice the parsnip into ½-inch rounds and poke the core out of each.

PARSNIPS AND WALNUTS

6 medium-sized parsnips, parboiled
3 tablespoons butter
⅓ cup coarsely chopped English walnuts
Salt
2 tablespoons cream sherry

Slice parsnips ¼ inch thick. Melt butter in a skillet and simmer parsnip slices in it, lifting and turning a few times with a turner until they are lightly brown, about 10 minutes. Add walnuts and cook over low heat 5 minutes longer. Salt very lightly, sprinkle with the sherry, and remove from heat. *Serves 4.*

NESTED PARSNIPS

We use Monterey Jack cheese for this dish. Swiss would do, or any cheese moderately mild but with character.

4 cups chopped chard leaves
3 cups Vegetable Stock*
4 medium-sized parsnips, parboiled
Salt
Pepper
2 tablespoons butter, melted
¼ pound Monterey Jack cheese, sliced ¼ inch thick

Drop chard into boiling stock, let it return to a boil, and drain at once. Lay chard in a casserole as a bed for the parsnips.

Cut parsnips in half lengthwise and cut each half in equal pieces crosswise. Arrange them on the chard, season with the salt and pepper, pour melted butter over, and cover with the cheese. Bake uncovered for about 20 minutes in a 300-degree F. oven, until cheese is well melted. *Serves 4.*

CREAMED PARSNIPS

6 medium-sized parsnips, parboiled
4 tablespoons butter
½ cup evaporated milk
Salt
Pepper

Cut parsnips into ⅛-inch rounds. Melt butter in a saucepan, add parsnips, cook over medium-low heat for 5 minutes, shaking pan now and then.

Add milk, cover pan, lower heat and cook gently until milk is absorbed, about 4 or 5 minutes. Season lightly with salt and moderately with pepper just before serving. *Serves 4.*

Chapter 23

PEAS

PEAS (*Pisum sativum*)

Fresh garden peas are a delight, much better than you'd imagine peas could be if you have tasted only non-garden-fresh ones. Like sweet corn, peas must be captured from the garden just before they go to the kitchen if you want them at their peak of flavor. Another thing about peas—they are one of those good things that are also good for you. They are an energy food with more calories than white potatoes, they are high (between 6 and 7 percent) on protein, and they're loaded with vitamins, including the anti-sterility vitamin E. Like so many vegetables, peas are ancient. They go all the way back to the Bronze Age.

Peas are a cool-weather crop, needing to be planted early enough to mature before it gets really hot. In the South they are also often planted in the fall, and by planting them in the later summer in climates like that of the Midwest you may with a little luck get a good late crop.

The easy way to get an extended harvest of peas is to plant an early variety, a midseason one, and a late one all at the same time. We do so whenever we have the space to spare. An early variety will mature in 8 weeks, a late one in 10 or 11 weeks, and a midseason one somewhere between.

As with other legumes it is a good idea to treat the seed with a product such as Nitragin before you plant, which speeds up growth.

Pea pods come in three types: Those whose seeds are wrinkled when dried, those whose seeds are smooth when dried, and those whose pods are edible. The wrinkled peas are a little sweeter than the smooth ones, but cannot be planted quite as early. The edible-podded, also called sugar peas and snow peas, are wonderfully crisp and good. For years we didn't bother to grow them, and then one day a friend served us some from her garden and we were instant converts.

Pea plants come in two types: Bush and climber. You'll get more peas from the climbers, but the bushes take less attention. Climbers grow from 3 to 6 feet high, and supports should be set up at planting time. Bush peas grow from 1 to 2 feet high.

All peas profit from fast growth and like well-drained soil. Good tall varieties are Fordhook Wonder and Alderman. Good bush ones are Little Marvel and Sparkle. Good edible-podded ones are Mammoth Melting Sugar, a climber, and Dwarf Gray Sugar, a 30-inch bush with red flowers.

Harvest edible-podded peas as soon as you can see a slight swelling of the peas inside the pod. We give the others time to grow more, but we don't let them get as large as they want to. Young peas are sweeter and more tender. A few pods always hide, though, and grow too large, so when it happens to you, you'll quickly see what we mean if you are wondering how large "too large" is.

RECIPES

Peas right out of the garden will cook in stock or water in about 10 minutes at a brisk boil, covered. This is also true of edible-podded peas, and is a slightly longer cooking time than store-bought peas take. Five minutes will be enough, however, if you prefer slightly undercooked peas or if you are going to simmer them in a sauce, say, for a few minutes.

The traditional French approach to peas involves lettuce as a moistening and flavoring agent; some form of onions; butter; herbs; and sugar. We include among our recipes one based on this combination.

For a delicious use of peas as an indispensable part of another dish, see Arroz con Pollo* in Chapter 39.

FRENCH PEAS

You can use water or Kraft Stock* in place of the wine in this recipe. We prefer the wine, and sometimes use dry vermouth.

6 lettuce leaves
1 tablespoon chopped tarragon
2 scallions, cut into ¼-inch pieces
2 cups shelled peas
¼ teaspoon sugar
4 tablespoons butter, melted
2 tablespoons dry white wine
Salt
Pepper

Make a bed of the lettuce in a saucepan. Add the other ingredients in the order listed, except salt and pepper. Cover saucepan and cook over medium-high heat for 10 minutes, shaking pan now and then. Season with salt and pepper and dish up. The lettuce is usually discarded. *Serves 4.*

CASSEROLE OF PEAS

You can use regular capers here, but the flavor of Nasturtium Capers* is milder and goes a little better with peas.

1 cup coarsely chopped lettuce
Butter
2 tablespoons Vegetable Stock*
2 cups shelled peas
1 cup Mornay Sauce*
1 tablespoon finely chopped Nasturtium Capers*
3 tablespoons grated Parmesan cheese

Make a bed of the lettuce in a generously buttered casserole. Add stock and peas, cover casserole and bake 30 minutes at 375 degrees F.
Mix the Mornay Sauce with the capers. Pour this over the peas

and dust the cheese over the top. Bake another 10 minutes, uncovered, until cheese is bubbling. *Serves 4.*

SAUCED SUGAR PEAS

> 3 *slices bacon, diced*
> 2 *tablespoons flour*
> ¾ *cup Kraft Stock**
> ¾ *cup Vegetable Stock**
> 2 *teaspoons finely chopped tarragon*
> 1 *tablespoon finely chopped parsley*
> 3 *scallions, chopped into ¼-inch pieces*
> 2 *cups ½-inch pieces edible-podded peas*
> *Salt*
> *Pepper*

Cook bacon in a skillet. Drain drippings, return 2 tablespoons of
them to skillet and stir in flour. Cook over low heat until flour
browns lightly. Add both stocks, stirring constantly over medium
heat until sauce begins to thicken.

Add the other ingredients except salt and pepper, cover skillet
and cook for 10 or 12 minutes, stirring now and then. Remove
from heat, season with salt and pepper. *Serves 4.*

GREEN AND GOLD

This is an early-summer recipe, timed for when you'll have both
peas and young carrots in the garden. If the carrots are not much
bigger around than a pencil, you can scrub about a dozen or so
and use them whole. Otherwise, cut them into cubes.

> 1 *cup ¼-inch cubes young carrots*
> 2 *or 3 tablespoons water*
> 2 *cups shelled peas*
> 2 *tablespoons melted butter*
> ¼ *teaspoon sugar*
> *Salt*
> *Pepper*

Put carrots and water into saucepan, cover and cook over medium heat for 4 or 5 minutes, shaking pan a few times. The water should cook away almost entirely.

Add all the rest of the ingredients, cover pan again, and cook about 5 minutes longer, shaking pan several times. When the dish is ready, a sharp fork will pierce a carrot cube with slight pressure. *Serves 4.*

Chapter 24

PEPPERS

PEPPERS (*Capsicum frutescens grossum*)

The pepper plant is such an attractive one, it can go into a flower border as nicely as in a kitchen garden. When we lived on the Mississippi Gulf Coast we had an ornamental of the Tabernaemontana genus that looked something like a pepper plant and many visitors assumed it was, because we often used pepper plants in this way.

Remember that the pepper demands a warm summer, and that there is no use setting out plants until the weather is pleasant. In Missouri, where the last spring frost could be expected in mid-April, we set pepper plants in the garden in May. To get these plants, we seeded the peppers at least 2 months ahead of time, in March, in a cold frame banked with earth, or in a flat in the cellar if it was a particularly cold spring. Pepper seedlings are susceptible to damping-off, so treat the seeds with a fungicide such as Thiram.

When we say "peppers" here we mean sweet peppers. The hot peppers are also attractive garden plants but we don't grow them and not many families would have any use for the number of hot peppers they'd get from even 1 or 2 plants. As to sweet peppers, figure on 3 or 4 plants for each member of the family, or more if you want a surplus for canning.

You can plan on picking the first peppers about 10 weeks after you set plants in the garden. The fruits then ripen in succession until frost kills the plant, and 8 or 10 peppers per plant is a good yield for large sweet peppers.

To produce these big fleshy fruits, peppers need plenty of moisture. If you can water well once a week, fine. We've had good results by depending on the rain and on a heavy mulch of straw or grass clippings, or even of the garden weeds chopped off with a hoe and nestled around the bases of the plants.

The pepper is another of the native Americans—South America in its case. It is also another of the vegetables modern breeders have worked on successfully. This means you can get some good hybrids, mainly of the blocky-shaped peppers, if you grow your own plants. Peppers are a little temperamental about where they want to grow, so it is a good idea to try out different varieties.

Most sweet peppers are green in color, turning red when mature though perfectly edible while green. A few varieties change from green to yellow when mature. As to shape, there are four main kinds:

(1) *Blocky* (Pennwonder, Bell Boy Hybrid, Burpee's Fordhook, Canape Hybrid, California Wonder). (2) *Heart-shaped* (often called Pimento or Perfection; characteristically mild). (3) *Tomato-shaped* (Sunnybrook). (4) *Long* (about 2 inches wide at the top, and 6 to 8 inches long. These are all heavy producers, setting 30 or more fruits. Sweet Banana, also called Sweet Hungarian, is the best-known variety; it is yellow, turning red when mature).

A fifth type, not as easily found, is a small sweet pepper with fruits about an inch wide, used for pickling but also good when eaten fresh. Cherry Sweet is a variety of it handled by Olds', and one called Nosegay, developed at the University of New Hampshire, is stocked by Farmer. This house also lists a novelty white pepper and another that ripens to a chocolate brown.

RECIPES

The seeds and the white pulp inside a sweet pepper are always removed, sometimes after a preliminary cooking of the whole pepper. Many recipes also call for removing the skin of the pepper by roasting, grilling, or boiling. We seldom do this. For one thing, until a pepper is fully mature, the skin is hard to remove. For another, garden-fresh peppers usually have tender skin that doesn't need removing. You'll notice that we suggest in only one of the following recipes that peppers be skinned.

Really fresh sweet peppers need not be cooked at all to be enjoyed, for they are very good when sliced fresh and joined with lettuce or with lettuce and tomatoes in a salad. Peppers are high in vitamins A and C, higher than tomatoes, and using them fresh seems very natural to most of us, but we once knew a Russian woman whose American husband had a gardenful of sweet peppers, and she hadn't the foggiest idea *what* to do with them, cooked or fresh.

None of our recipes here calls for parboiling sweet peppers, but if you do so with garden-fresh ones, give them 6 to 8 minutes at a brisk boil.

ROAST-CORN STUFFED PEPPERS

We tasted this delicious dish for the first time after an outdoor steak and roast corn party. It was given by a neighbor on a farm next to ours in Missouri, and we had brought the corn, plucked from the garden as we were on our way over. Some of the ears, roasted over coals, were left over, and the hostess did this with them the next day and brought some of the results to us. Keep this recipe in mind for midsummer when tomatoes and peppers are bearing, and when the corn is coming in strongly. If some ears become a trifle more mature than you like for corn on the cob, roast them anyway and reserve them for this use. Here, they will come into their own.

> *2 or 3 ears Roasted Corn**
> *1 large thoroughly ripe tomato*
> *Salt*
> *Pepper*
> *4 large green peppers*
> *Butter*

Cut kernels off ears of corn. This can be done the day after the corn is roasted; store ears in plastic bag in refrigerator, and cut kernels off when needed. Chop tomato coarsely, mix with corn kernels, season with salt and pepper.

Cut tops off peppers, remove seeds and pulp, and stuff shells with the corn and tomato mixture. Dot stuffing generously with butter, stand shells in a baking dish in ¼ inch of water, and bake about 30 minutes in a 350-degree F. oven. *Serves 4.*

PEPPERS AU GRATIN

You can use whole anchovies, chopped, in this dish, but we find them too strong when used with most garden vegetables, so we almost always prefer anchovy paste if a touch of this flavor is welcome.

4 large sweet peppers, diced
1 tablespoon finely chopped Nasturtium Capers*
1 teaspoon anchovy paste
6 ripe olives (preferably Greek), chopped
Salt
Pepper
¼ cup fresh bread crumbs
2 tablespoons olive oil

Mix all ingredients except crumbs and oil, and put into an enameled metal casserole. Sprinkle crumbs over the top, dribble oil over crumbs, cover casserole, and bake for 20 minutes at 375 degrees F. Serves 4.

SWEET RED PEPPERS VINAIGRETTE

Try this way of preparing sweet peppers after they have matured and turned red—when they also take on a distinctive ripe flavor. In general, plan on 1 or 2 peppers per serving.

Mature sweet peppers
Ice water
Vinaigrette Sauce*

Put the peppers whole into a 375-degree F. oven for 6 to 8 minutes. Plunge them into a bowl of ice water immediately on removing them from the oven. This will loosen their skins, which can then be slipped off. Also cut off stem ends and remove seeds and pulp.
Put peppers into a bowl large enough to accommodate them easily, pushing them gently down. Pour over them enough Vinai-

grette Sauce* to cover them. Cover bowl with plastic wrap and refrigerate for at least 4 hours before serving.

You can use Herbed French Dressing* as an alternative here.

If we are blessed with more ripened peppers than we need at the time, here is how we can them: Peel them in the way just given, remove seeds and pulp, and pack peppers into wide-mouth pint jars. Seal and process in a pressure cooker for 15 minutes at 5 pounds.

BRAISED PEPPERS

3 tablespoons corn oil
*1 tablespoon Garlic Oil**
4 large mushrooms, sliced
4 sweet peppers, cut into 1/4-inch strips
Salt
Pepper
2 tablespoons soy sauce
2 tablespoons cream sherry

Heat oils to shimmering in a skillet. Add mushrooms and peppers, cover skillet, and cook over medium heat for 10 minutes, stirring several times. Remove lid, turn heat to medium-high, and cook for 2 or 3 more minutes, stirring. Add the rest of the ingredients, cook 2 more minutes, stirring, and serve at once. *Serves 4.*

SWEET PEPPER CASSEROLE

4 sweet peppers, cut into 1/4-inch rings
*1 tablespoon Garlic Oil**
1 tablespoon olive oil
8 scallions, coarsely chopped
*1/4 cup Kraft Stock**
1/4 teaspoon sugar
Salt
Pepper

Mix all the ingredients together in a casserole. Cover and cook for 20 minutes in a 375-degree F. oven. Inspect and stir halfway through, and add a little more stock if needed. *Serves 4.*

Chapter 25

POTATOES—WHITE AND SWEET

WHITE POTATOES (*Solanum tuberosum*)

Everybody knows the potato started out in Peru but when we tell visitors that the dahlia-like plants they see growing here and there about our house grounds are tuberous Peruvian herbs, they seldom guess that we are going a long way around to say "potatoes." The reason we plant some potatoes outside the garden is that they improve the soil and are attractive plants. Harvesting them is rewarding and fun, and if you ever want to see a child fascinated, invite one to help you dig a hill of potatoes.

Potatoes like their soil a bit acid. Half a handful of any acid plant food mixed well with the soil at the time of planting a hill of potatoes will take care of this. When we plant potatoes to improve the soil they have to get along with what they find, plus the plant food and a good deep spading, but we encourage them with a half-bucket of compost worked in.

You will almost always be advised to buy certified seed potatoes for planting, for a clean crop. This is a good idea, though we don't always follow it. The fact is, you can plant any potato, including the one you intended to have for dinner. We have a friend who often buys more potatoes than she can use before some start sprouting. When they do sprout, she brings them to us and we plant them.

We'll admit that when we have the space for a lot of potatoes we do buy certified ones to plant. Not every seed house carries potatoes but you can often buy them locally at a garden center. The mail order seed houses with the greatest number of potato varieties, so far as we have found, are Olds', Farmer, and Henry Field's, which list 16 varieties among them. Aside from getting healthy stock, there is another advantage in buying seed potatoes—

the choice you'll have of different maturity times. Waseca, for instance, is an extra-early russet baker, Chippewa is a white mid-season variety developed by the U. S. Department of Agriculture, and Red La Soda is late and is also tolerant of indifferent growing conditions.

You can plant a potato whole, or cut it into 4 or 5 squarish pieces. Each piece should have at least 1 eye, which is the bud of the potato tuber, a slightly sunken place on the surface. Let the pieces dry for 2 or 3 days, dig a hole, work in compost or peat moss, place each potato piece with the eye (or sprout, if it has started) pointing upward, and cover with 4 or 5 inches of soil.

In some mild climates you can plant potatoes the year around. In cold-winter ones plant early in the spring (one member of this household insists on St. Patrick's Day for planting), say 2 weeks before the last hard frost is due. This will produce a summer crop. For a second crop, plant again in mid-spring.

Potatoes do their best growing when the weather is cool but the days are fairly long. The best practice is to make an early planting with an early variety, and later plantings with late varieties. Sprouts will show above ground in 3 or 4 weeks. You can sometimes hurry growth by exposing seed potatoes to sunlight for a week or two before planting. The day temperature should be about 60 degrees for this.

When the leaves on the potato plants start to yellow, which will be in about 3 months for early varieties, you can expect to dig up to half a dozen nice potatoes per plant, and you'll then discover that the way to enjoy potatoes is to dig them as you need them. You have no idea how delicious a potato can be if you've never eaten freshly harvested ones. Some fanciers eat them raw like apples. Protect potatoes from the light after you dig them or they may turn green in spots. A green colored potato is mildly poisonous.

You need not dig a whole hill if you don't need that many potatoes at once, and you can let some late varieties remain undug for a month after they mature.

For a partial harvest, probe with your fingers and you'll find some potatoes near the surface. Gently detach them from the root, pat the soil back in place, and the plant will keep on growing; this is also a way to get tiny potatoes long before the plant matures its crop.

RECIPES

Freshly dug potatoes are superior for any cooking method. Remember that if you intend to bake them, however, you'll need to plant a baking variety of potato. You *can* bake any potato, but the non-baking variety will not have an agreeably dry and fluffy texture after baking. It will take longer to bake, too, about 90 minutes at 350 degrees F. If you want to cook such a potato in the oven, steam it, like this: Wash and dry it, rub it with butter, and wrap it securely in foil, crimping the edges of the foil to keep the air in. A medium-small new potato will be done in about an hour at 350 degrees F.

When steaming newly dug potatoes on a rack over boiling water, cook them gently, unpeeled, with the lid off. You can speed the cooking time by cutting the potatoes in half, steaming them with the cut sides up, and putting the lid on the pan for the first 10 minutes. The total time needed depends on the size of the potatoes and ranges between 15 minutes and 40 minutes. Test for doneness by seeing if a sharp fork will easily pierce the centers of the cut surfaces. Unlike most other garden-fresh vegetables, potatoes right out of the garden take a little longer to cook than do store-bought ones.

CHATEAU POTATOES

This recipe, adapted for freshly dug potatoes, is a superb way to compliment your guests, as the potatoes look like tiny new ones all the same size. You make balls from large potatoes with a ball cutter (like a tiny ice cream scoop). And the shells that are left over can be used in Chiffon Potatoes*.

2 tablespoons butter
4 large freshly dug potatoes
Salt

Melt butter in an enameled metal casserole in a 350-degree F. oven. Peel or scrape potatoes, rinse, and cut balls from them. You should get about 15 balls per potato. Reserve unused parts for another dish.[1] Put balls into saucepan with just enough *cold* water to cover. Put lid on pan and bring water to a boil. Drain immediately. Return pan to the heat for a minute, shaking it constantly, to dry potato balls.

Put balls into the hot butter in casserole. Stir them gently to coat each with butter. Bake uncovered about 40 minutes, shaking casserole 2 or 3 times. This is about 10 minutes longer than non-newly dug potatoes need. Salt lightly and serve. *Serves 4.*

You can surround a crown roast or a Divan* with spoonfuls of these little potatoes on nests of cress, each a single serving.

CHIFFON POTATOES

Employ the unused parts of potatoes left from cutting potato balls for this recipe. Such an unused part from a freshly dug potato, will cook in about 15 minutes at a moderate boil, covered. If you use a whole potato instead, slice it thickly and cook in the same way.

> *Unused parts of 4 potatoes left from Chateau Potatoes**
> *or 2 sliced potatoes, parboiled*
> *Salt*
> *2 small shallots, finely chopped*
> *4 tablespoons butter*

Chop potatoes finely with a fork, but don't mash them. Salt lightly, stir in shallots and 1 tablespoon of the butter cut into small dice.

Melt rest of butter in an 8-inch skillet, swirling it to cover entire bottom. Put potato mixture in, pressing lightly with a turner. Cook over medium-low heat about 15 minutes, till the down side lightly browns. Turn potato cake out by inverting skillet over a buttered plate, and slide it back into skillet to brown other side for about 10 minutes. *Serves 4.*

---

[1] You can keep the unused parts of the potatoes for a day or two by immersing them in ice water and storing in refrigerator. We usually cook them at once as described in Chiffon Potatoes*, then put them in a plastic bag in the refrigerator when they are cool; they will keep for 2 or 3 days.

If we are serving this dish at a hearty breakfast, and it is wonderful for this, we substitute fresh herbs for the shallots. A tablespoon of Italian parsley, or a teaspoon of savory or tarragon is good. Chop the herbs finely.

POTATOES PAT

This dish came about by chance one evening when we had worked all day checking several decades of newspaper files on microfilm, and were famished. The original point of the dish was its speed, even with freshly dug potatoes. It was named for Pat because she became infatuated with it. Like the well-known Dauphine Potatoes, it fools most people into thinking an excellent cheese is used in it. It is also a little like Potatoes Anna but takes much less time and work. Another point about it is that a single potato makes two generous servings.

> *4 tablespoons butter*
> *2 medium-sized potatoes*
> *Salt*
> *½ cup evaporated milk*

While butter melts over medium heat in a large skillet, peel potatoes with a razor-edged peeler, wash and dry them. Then slice them directly into the hot butter, using the peeler to make very thin slices. Cover skillet bottom evenly with the slices. Turn heat to low, cover skillet and cook for 15 minutes. Do not shake skillet or stir potatoes.

Then salt lightly, gently dribble milk over the potatoes, and cook for 5 more minutes, uncovered, while milk is absorbed. Tilt skillet if necessary to distribute the milk evenly. To serve, fold in half like an omelet. *Serves 4.*

HERBED BAKED STUFFED POTATOES

We usually double this recipe when we make it, as the surplus freezes well; to freeze, wrap each potato in plastic wrap and then in foil or a plastic bag. These make ideal potato servings to go into the "Visiting Gift Box" described in Chapter 2. Feel free to vary the herb combination given here, of course, though we suggest you include parsley in any combination.

4 large baking potatoes
4 tablespoons butter
1 cup evaporated milk
1 teaspoon finely chopped parsley
1 teaspoon finely chopped tarragon
1 teaspoon finely chopped chives
1 teaspoon finely chopped basil
Salt
Pepper

Pierce each potato ½ inch deep with a fork in several places, put into shallow pan and bake about 75 minutes at 375 degrees F., or until the fork will easily go through them.

Immediately cut an oval piece from each potato to make an opening from which you can scoop out the inside, leaving a thin shell. Break up this potato pulp in a warm bowl with a fork. Add the rest of the ingredients and whip with an electric or rotary mixer until fluffy. Carefully fill shells with this. Return to oven to heat through. *Serves 4.* (If you make extra ones for freezing, this reheating is done after defrosting.)

STUFFED BAKED POTATOES

This is a simpler dish than the preceding one, but very good. Evaporated milk can be used instead of the cream, but cream is better in this case.

4 baking potatoes
8 tablespoons well-chilled butter
½ cup cream
Salt
Pepper

Bake potatoes as for Herbed Baked Stuffed Potatoes*. Then cut each in half lengthwise and scoop out the pulp, leaving a thin shell.

Put potato pulp in a bowl and break it up finely with a fork but do not mash. Add butter, cut into small pieces, stirring it in well. Stir in cream and seasonings. Fill shells with this mixture and return to oven to heat through. Finish cooking under the broiler to brown the tops lightly. *Serves 4.*

BRAISED SHOESTRING POTATOES

With freshly dug potatoes this is an exquisite dish. You can use jellied drippings from a roast chicken in place of the stock.

3 medium-sized potatoes
3 tablespoons butter
⅓ cup Kraft Stock*
Salt
Pepper

Scrape or peel potatoes, cut them into slices ⅛ inch thick, and cut slices into strips ⅛ inch wide.

Melt butter in a large skillet, spread potato strips evenly in it, cover and cook over low heat for 15 minutes, shaking skillet several times.

Add stock and cook uncovered for a few more minutes while the potato strips absorb the stock. Tilt skillet a few times so that stock is evenly spread. Season and serve at once. *Serves 4.*

SAUSAGE-STUFFED POTATOES

We often have well-seasoned pork sausage for breakfast and this recipe came about as a way to introduce the sausage's robust flavor into a luncheon dish. The potatoes need not be bakers. Note that salt and pepper are not used; the sausage and bacon do the seasoning.

4 medium-sized potatoes
½ cup crumbled pork sausage
½ cup chopped onions
1 cup fresh bread crumbs

(1)

(2)

(3)

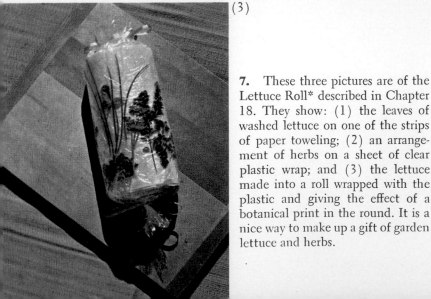

7. These three pictures are of the Lettuce Roll* described in Chapter 18. They show: (1) the leaves of washed lettuce on one of the strips of paper toweling; (2) an arrangement of herbs on a sheet of clear plastic wrap; and (3) the lettuce made into a roll wrapped with the plastic and giving the effect of a botanical print in the round. It is a nice way to make up a gift of garden lettuce and herbs.

8. Summer squash is one of the best plants in the home garden for high yield and good looks. This one is a zucchini and is one of the new hybrid varieties, bearing its attractive fruits over a long period starting less than two months after sprouting. *W. Atlee Burpee Co. photo*

2 tablespoons Vegetable Stock*
Butter
2 strips bacon

Scrape or peel potatoes. With a spoon or a ball cutter make "boats" of them by removing about ½ cup of the inside of each. This scooped-out pulp can be handled as unused and leftover parts are for Chiffon Potatoes*, for use in some other dish.

Put potato boats in a saucepan of cold water, bring just to a boil, and drain.

With a fork, mix the sausage, onions, and crumbs. Moisten this mixture with the stock, and spoon it into the potato boats. Butter a baking dish and set boats in it. Lay half a strip of bacon on each boat, and bake for about 1 hour in a 350-degree F. oven, or until boats are fork-tender. *Serves 4.*

OVEN-FRIED POTATOES

This is a good way to make almost-French-fried potatoes without a French-fryer. The procedure we use is for freshly dug potatoes, which are firmer than older ones. Some recipes similar to this one call for chilling potato strips in ice water, but we find it makes too little difference to bother with.

4 medium-sized potatoes
5 tablespoons butter
Salt

Scrape or peel potatoes. Cut them into ½-inch slices and cut the slices into ½-inch strips.

Melt butter in an enameled metal casserole by preheating it in a 300-degree F. oven. Put potato strips into casserole and coat each with butter by lifting and stirring with a turner.

Cover casserole and bake for 15 minutes. Stir potato strips by lifting with turner, and bake uncovered for 15 minutes more. Salt lightly and serve. *Serves 4.*

PAPRIKA POTATOES

Here, as with any recipe calling for paprika, it must be fresh.

3 tablespoons butter
3 shallots, finely chopped
3 medium-large potatoes
Salt
Paprika

Melt butter in a casserole in a 300-degree F. oven. Add shallots
and let them cook for a few minutes while you prepare potatoes.
Scrape or peel potatoes and cut into ½-inch cubes. Add them
to casserole, stirring well. Sprinkle with salt and with enough paprika
to color lightly top layer of potatoes. Do not stir again. Bake for
about 60 minutes, covered, or until a sharp fork will easily pierce a
potato cube. Serves 4.

HERBED POTATO CASSEROLE

This is an accommodating dish, willing to wait if guests are
late, and not suffering in flavor.

5 tablespoons butter
3 medium-sized potatoes
3 medium-sized onions
Salt
Pepper
Milk
4 sprigs thyme

Butter a shallow casserole with 1 tablespoon of the butter. Scrape
or peel potatoes and cut them and onions into ⅛-inch slices.
Spread half the potato slices, then half the onion slices in casserole, dot with half the remaining butter, and season with salt and
pepper. Repeat layers, and pour enough milk in casserole to cover

the two bottom layers. If you use evaporated milk, add an equal amount of water to it to thin it.

Lay thyme in the center and lay the wrapper from a stick of butter on top. Put lid on casserole and bake for 45 minutes at 300 degrees F. Remove lid and butter paper, and bake for 15 minutes more. Remove thyme before serving. *Serves 4.*

TOMATO-POTATO CASSEROLE

The tomato juice should not be seasoned for this dish. If fresh tomatoes are in the garden, you can use a finely chopped one in place of the juice.

> 2 *tablespoons butter*
> 3 *large potatoes*
> 1 *slice premium quality ham ¼ inch thick*
> 1 *clove garlic*
> 4 *sprigs thyme*
> 4 *peppercorns*
> *Salt*
> ½ *teaspoon sugar*
> 1 *cup tomato juice*

Melt the butter in an enameled metal casserole. Scrape or peel potatoes and cut into ½-inch cubes. Cut ham slice into 1-inch squares. Stir potatoes and ham into casserole.

Make a bouquet garni of the garlic, thyme, and peppercorns by tying them into a 6-inch square of muslin. Nestle it among the potatoes and ham in casserole. Season casserole contents with salt and the sugar, and pour in tomato juice.

Cover casserole and cook for 15 minutes in 325-degree F. oven. Add more tomato juice if needed and cook, uncovered, for 15 minutes more. *Serves 4.*

LITTLE LYONNAISE POTATOES

Done with newly dug potatoes, this easy variation of Lyonnaise potatoes was developed by us to accommodate those who like their onions on the light side. Scallions can be used in place of shallots.

3 *medium-large potatoes*
4 *tablespoons butter*
2 *shallots*
Salt

Scrape or peel potatoes and cut them into ¼-inch cubes. Melt butter in large skillet, spread potatoes in it, cover skillet and cook over medium-low heat for 10 minutes. Shake skillet several times.

Peel shallots and cut into slices as thick as a nickel. Sprinkle them on top of the potatoes, but *do not stir*. Cover skillet again and cook for 5 minutes more.

Uncover skillet, stir lightly, and cook for 5 minutes longer, reducing heat to low. Salt lightly and serve at once. *Serves 4.*

NEW POTATOES SUPREME

With newly dug potatoes this simple dish is food for kings.

4 *medium-sized potatoes*
Salt
4 *tablespoons butter*
1 *tablespoon finely chopped parsley*

Wash but do not scrape potatoes. Cut them in half and steam on a rack over boiling water as described in this chapter under RECIPES. Salt the cut surfaces lightly during steaming.

Melt butter in a large skillet. Roll potatoes in it, then turn the cut surfaces down and cook over medium heat until a crisp, lightly brown crust is formed, 12 to 15 minutes. Arrange potatoes on platter and sprinkle with the chopped parsley. *Serves 4.*

SWEET POTATOES (*Ipomoea batatas*)

Sweet potatoes are to white potatoes as Jerusalem artichokes are to globe artichokes—they share a name and not much else. On the table, a sweet potato is much more like a winter squash than it is like a white potato. We grew good sweet potatoes when we lived in places with hot summers, such as Virginia. Don't try growing them if your summers are cool—but if you can count on 4 or 5 warm months, don't be daunted by the feeling that sweet potatoes are strictly a Southern crop. Some home gardeners in Michigan and other parts of the upper Midwest grow them every year. They take up as much space as a vine crop such as melons, though, so they aren't for the small garden.

What you plant is a sprout that has grown from a sweet potato. You can grow your own sprouts by planting some sweet potatoes in sand and keeping them warm (at least 75 degrees F.) and moist. Each sweet potato will grow several sprouts. (Note: Sweet potatoes sold for eating are sometimes treated to keep them from sprouting.) It takes about a month for sprouts to grow to transplanting size, so start the whole process a month before it will be mild and warm outside.

Then carefully pull off the rooted sprouts and plant them 1½ feet apart on a 4-inch ridge of earth. They like a light, sandy soil, not a rich one. Fertilize them only a little, if at all, or they'll run to leaves. They don't need much water, either, and they provide their own "mulch" in the form of leafy shade.

You can buy sweet potato plants locally in some places, the South especially, but if you live somewhere else and don't want to grow your own, four houses that sell plants are Burgess, Henry Field's, Olds', and Farmer. Varieties carried include the well-known Porto Rico; a good yielder called Centennial; All Gold, which is early and a good keeper; and Gold Rush, an exceptional keeper. You can buy 25 plants for about 2 dollars, and should harvest about 30 pounds of sweet potatoes from them.

The way in which you harvest sweet potatoes and care for them immediately afterward will control the quality of your crop. Don't wait for frost before you dig them. Clip off the vines (you can compost them) and dig the sweet potatoes carefully with a spading fork, separating each one gently from its root. Dry them in the sun for 2 or 3 hours, then pack them 1 or 2 layers deep in grocery cartons and put them to cure (dry out excess moisture) in a warm airy room. We have put the boxes on top of furnace pipes in the basement at times, and in various warm places inside the house when we had no basement.

In 2 weeks the sweet potatoes will be ready to be stored. The ideal storage temperature is 55 degrees F., but just come as close to it as you can. Any sweet potato bruised or cut during harvesting should be used promptly, even if curing isn't yet completed, as it will quickly spoil.

RECIPES

Besides being rich and delicious, sweet potatoes are packed with some important health helps, especially Vitamin A. We give here three ways we cook them, and the way we freeze them.

Like winter squash, "garden-fresh" is not a factor in how good a sweet potato can be, but proper curing is. For this reason, if we can't raise our own sweet potatoes, we try to locate a good small roadside stand within driving distance, and get them there, uncured. We then cure them ourselves in a warm place in the house for about 2 weeks. As with pears, they are seldom ready for eating when one buys them.

We think that after you try the recipes that follow, you'll never be tempted to put marshmallows on good honest sweet potatoes.

BAKED SWEET POTATOES

4 medium-sized sweet potatoes
4 tablespoons butter
Salt

Scrub sweet potatoes under running water. Dry with paper towels, lay them in a shallow pan or on a cooky sheet, and bake for about 60 minutes at 375 degrees F. When done, they will begin to ooze a little syrupy liquid. Remove them from oven. Use a cloth to protect your hands, and massage each sweet potato gently to loosen the pulp. Then make a long gash down the top center of each and push the ends together enough to make the top gap open. Tuck 1 tablespoon of butter into each sweet potato, and salt lightly. *Serves 4.*

CANDIED SWEET POTATOES

2 large sweet potatoes
4 tablespoons butter
Salt

Cook sweet potatoes as in Baked Sweet Potatoes*. Let them cool, then peel with your fingers—the skin comes off easily. Cut sweet potatoes into ½-inch slices either crosswise or lengthwise.

Melt half the butter in a large heavy skillet and cook slices in it over medium heat until brown and glazed on bottom. Add the rest of the butter, turn slices and brown the other sides. Salt very lightly. *Serves 4.*

(Two tablespoons of brown sugar can be added while browning, but we don't think this necessary when sweet potatoes have been well cured. The sweetness is then built in.)

SWEET POTATO CASSEROLE

2 large sweet potatoes
⅓ cup cream sherry
Salt

Cook sweet potatoes as in Baked Sweet Potatoes*. Peel them, mash them well, and stir in sherry and a little salt. Put this mixture into a casserole and bake at 375 degrees F. for about 15 minutes. *Serves 4.*

You can use ⅓ cup melted butter in place of the sherry, or 3 tablespoons of each.

To Freeze Sweet Potatoes

Bake the desired number of sweet potatoes, following directions as given. Peel, and either slice crosswise in whatever thickness you prefer, or cut in half lengthwise. Wrap in foil to freeze, or freeze in containers. When thawed, the sweet potatoes are in a convenient form for candying or for serving as a casserole dish.

Chapter 26

RADISHES

RADISHES (*Raphanus sativus*)

Radishes have a name for being the easiest plant to grow. Only cress rivals the radish in speed. Both will give you a harvest in a mere 3 weeks. It will be a young harvest, as both mature later than this, but it will be a harvest. This is why we suggest radishes as a garden project for small children when we are asked. The speedy growth holds their interest, and the astounding reality of a pulled radish in the small hand that planted the seed can launch a lifetime interest.

As with any root crop, the radish grows best in well-spaded garden soil. Dig in compost and plant the seed ⅓ inch deep. We usually punch spots in a seed bed with a finger or trowel handle far enough apart to accommodate whatever size the variety of radish will become, and drop one seed per spot. This is more work than dribbling seed in a row, but you get better grown radishes, and also save the work of thinning.

Radishes are also often used as markers in a row of a slower-sprouting vegetable. The radishes come popping up, marking the row and helping the companion planting by breaking the soil. This is especially useful in clay soil, which can form a crust so hard for a plant to break that a brittle sprout such as beans have may snap off in the effort.

Radishes do best in cool, or at least non-sweltering, weather, and demand moisture. If their leaves start to wilt, water the garden. The time to feed them is when you plant them. Compost is both nourishment and humus, and we add a pinch of commercial fertilizer per seed or use a soluble fertilizer 2 weeks after planting.

Make plantings small and repeat them every 10 days. The idea is to keep your table supplied with only as many radishes as you can use. They are at their crisp best right after being pulled, and most varieties pass their prime a few days after maturing.

There are two main groups of radishes. The most important is the one we've been talking about—the summer radish. The other is called winter radish. It takes about three times as long to grow, and can be stored. An unimportant but interesting third group are oriental radishes, which grow perfectly immense roots, up to 50 pounds. Two houses, Burgess and Shumway, handle a variety called Sakurajima that grows to 15 or more pounds if the plant is not allowed to blossom.

Summer radishes have red or white skins, or a combination. Some good red ones are Cherry Belle, Red Giant, and Champion. Good white ones include Hailstone, White Icicle, and White Strassburg—which can take some hot weather. Our long-time favorite white variety, though, is Burpee White, for its mildness and for staying crisp long after other radishes have gone pithy. Two good red-and-white radishes are Sparkler and French Breakfast.

We have grown three varieties of winter radishes: Long Black Spanish, China Rose, and Celestial. Round Black Spanish is also listed by many seedsmen. All winter radishes are large compared to a typical summer radish.

Plant seeds of winter radishes in midsummer, in time for them to make about 10 weeks' growth before frost. We have usually left them in the ground, well mulched, until wanted, but you can store them in moist sand all winter in a cool place.

RECIPES

We use summer radishes fresh and see no point in cooking them. If you want to try it, they can be boiled whole or sliced paper thin and cooked gently in a little oil for 5 minutes.

Winter radishes are better subjects for cooking, though they too are very agreeable fresh. To use them fresh, peel them like a potato and slice off rounds with the peeler. We've added these slices to salads, but an elderly Dutch couple next door to us in Virginia used to make a winter-time breakfast of them, putting the slices on buttered homemade bread.

Thinly sliced in the same way, or cut into ¼-inch cubes, try cooking a winter radish in a small amount of water until the radish is tender-crisp and the water is cooked away, then finishing the cooking by simmering in milk. No seasoning besides salt and pepper are needed. Generally speaking, winter and oriental radishes can be cooked as turnips are cooked.

Summer radishes are one of the ingredients in our Salad Soup*, and we will conclude by mentioning two other culinary uses of this little vegetable: The younger leaves make a nice addition to a dish of mixed leafy greens for cooking (they are used in salads, too, but we don't like their texture for this). And, if a radish grows old and goes to seed, we are told that the seeds when sprinkled into a salad add an appealing peppery flavor. We haven't tried this but we offer the suggestion to the adventuresome.

(Note: If you have hummingbirds, let a few radishes form flowers. The hummingbirds are mad about them.)

Chapter 27

RHUBARB

RHUBARB (*Rheum rhaponticum*)

We've grown rhubarb and grown rhubarb, but we don't cook much rhubarb. We used to have a nice sunny southwest corner set off for handsome MacDonald rhubarb in our farm garden, and it grew beautifully, but the fact is, Pat just doesn't care much for rhubarb. So we didn't use much of it, but we made a lot of rhubarb lovers happy with gifts of the stalks, and the planting was a pleasure to look at. This is another of the garden plants that can take its place in the society of flowers with success, so feel free to plant it where it can be seen.

When you pick a spot for a rhubarb bed, remember that like asparagus it will be there for years. This makes the cost of starting it easier to bear, for the roots are dearer than asparagus roots. A family of four that likes rhubarb may want a dozen plants, and good roots of one of the best varieties will cost about a dollar apiece in that quantity.

You can also grow rhubarb from seed, but it takes a year or two longer and you can't buy seed of one of the better varieties, only the Victoria being commonly offered. Also, like fruit trees, plants from seed are off-type.

Except that you space the plants farther—3 or 4 feet apart—prepare the soil for rhubarb the same as for asparagus. Plant the rhubarb roots early in the spring, 4 inches deep, and don't harvest any stalks the first year.

Each fall spread 2 or 3 buckets of compost over each hill, and each spring spread a mulch. Remove any seed stalks that may form, as setting seed exhausts a plant.

In time the roots become crowded and you'll have to divide them and replant if you want continued good production. Do this every

6 years or so. Cut each root into several pieces, each with a bud, and plant as in the original planting.

When you harvest rhubarb, take the large outer stalks. Simply pull them loose with a little twist. *Do not eat the leaves.* They contain oxalic acid, a poison.

Spring is the big harvest season for rhubarb, but you can continue it to midsummer with a vigorous planting well cared for. During the rest of the season the plant needs its growth to build strength for the next year.

MacDonald continues to be an excellent variety. It is rather tart, and has red stalks, as has Valentine. Victoria's stalks are greenish with red tinting, and it is a little more tart than MacDonald. Canada Red is a good, well-known variety, and a new strain called Chipman's Canada Red is less tart than others and of a rich red color.

RECIPES

Discard the leaf of the rhubarb stalk, and peel the stalk, though some varieties have a tender skin that doesn't need peeling. Cut the stalk into chunks 1 or 2 inches long, for cooking.

Rhubarb is easy to freeze. Treat it as just described, put into plastic bags or containers, and freeze. No blanching is needed. When you defrost a package, cook it as you would cook fresh rhubarb.

We offer here the recipe we ordinarily use, a baked one because it makes a more richly flavored dish than does stewing or steaming.

BAKED RHUBARB

Garden-fresh rhubarb takes about the same cooking as rhubarb from the market, but has more flavor. Consequently we do not add spice as is sometimes suggested.

> *Rhubarb stalks, peeled*
> *Sugar*
> *Orange rind*
> *Salt*

Cut stalks into 1-inch chunks. Make a layer of them in a baking dish and sprinkle generously with sugar. Sprinkle grated orange rind over the sugar, and just a little salt. Repeat these layers until the baking dish is comfortably filled. Bake uncovered for about 1 hour at 350 degrees F., until the rhubarb is quite soft. It may be served hot or chilled.

Chapter 28

RUTABAGAS

RUTABAGAS (*Brassica napobrassica*)

Like kale, there is something hearty and winter-night cozy about rutabagas. Their distinctive flavor and good yellow color make them an outstandingly good accompaniment for roast pork and beef, and they are also valuable in the diet.

Rutabagas are a cool-weather crop, usually planted to mature in the fall. A spring crop may be possible if the summer heat doesn't catch them, since they take at least three months to mature. The plant originated in northern Europe, which seems to account for rutabaga's being called Swedish turnips, or just Swedes. They are a species of the genus that turnips also belong to.

Dig compost in when you seed rutabagas. They like a deep, fertile soil and some fertilizer rich in potash, to help their root development. A 5–10–10 formula will do. In nearly all respects you grow rutabagas the same way you grow beets.

Harvest rutabagas following the first light frost, or you can start harvesting at any time after the roots have grown enough to be worth while. Store the final harvest in a cool place, and they will keep all winter.

American Purple-Top is the most widely offered variety, in various strains. Laurentian is popular in Canada, where rutabagas are an important vegetable. There are also some white rutabagas, Macomber being a good one.

RECIPES

You will find that a garden-fresh rutabaga is sweeter, milder, and more subtly flavored than any you ever got at a store. For that reason we suggest that you not wait until frost comes before starting to use this vegetable from your garden. Also, a late planting will give you smaller roots but they will be of exceptional quality. The ruta-bagas you dig and store before the first hard frost comes will be of good quality if your storage conditions are good, but they will not be as different from store-bought ones as those you harvest early.

Each of the recipes we give here calls for a preliminary steaming. We do this by peeling the rutabaga, cutting it into slices ⅓ inch thick, and steaming them until barely fork-tender. This can be done over boiling water, or wrapped in foil and put into a 400-degree F. oven. Either way, they will take about 30 minutes. A whole ruta-baga, peeled, about the size of a baseball, will take about 1 hour over boiling water and 1½ hours in the 400-degree F. oven.

RUTABAGA BRAISE

Rutabagas and broccoli are in the garden at the same season, and their flavors complement each other beautifully, as this dish will demonstrate.

> *2 tablespoons olive oil*
> *1 teaspoon Garlic Oil**
> *2 cups broccoli*
> *1 medium-sized rutabaga, sliced and steamed*
> *1 teaspoon lemon juice*
> *Salt*
> *Pepper*
> *2 tablespoons cold butter, diced*

Heat oils in a skillet and add broccoli. Cover and cook over medium heat 8 to 10 minutes, shaking pan now and then.

Cut rutabaga slices into ½-inch cubes, add them to the broccoli, and sprinkle with lemon juice, salt, and pepper. Cover and cook for 5 more minutes until rutabaga is heated through.

Just before dishing up, drop in diced butter and stir gently as it melts. Serve at once. *Serves 4.*

RUTABAGA CROQUETTES

The mixture that is put into the refrigerator to chill can be made a day or two ahead, and the croquettes cooked when wanted.

¼ cup evaporated milk
1 medium-large rutabaga, sliced and steamed
1 tablespoon flour
1 tablespoon butter
1 egg yolk, beaten
¼ teaspoon nutmeg
Salt
Pepper
1½ cups fine, dry bread crumbs
1 egg, lightly beaten, with 2 tablespoons water
4 tablespoons butter

Warm milk but do not let it boil. Add rutabaga and mash with potato masher. Stir in flour, butter, egg yolk, nutmeg, salt, and pepper, in that order, and put into refrigerator to chill for at least an hour.

To make the croquettes:

Form the mixture into sausage shapes about 2½ inches long. Roll them in the crumbs, dip them in the egg-and-water, roll again in the crumbs. The lightness of the mixture makes it less easy to handle than a croquette stiffened with sauce, but the resulting delicacy is well worth the trouble, especially for a garden-fresh rutabaga.

Melt the 4 tablespoons of butter in a large skillet and cook croquettes over medium-high heat, turning them gently to brown all sides. *Serves 4.*

GINGER RUTABAGA

We sometimes use raw ginger root in this recipe, in which case we add a little sugar. But the candied ginger is more easily found in most localities, and is entirely satisfactory. We use the same amount of either.

> 2 *tablespoons corn oil*
> 2 *teaspoons Garlic Oil**
> 1 *medium-large rutabaga, sliced and steamed*
> 1 *tablespoon finely chopped candied ginger*
> *Salt*
> *Pepper*

Heat oils in a skillet. Cut rutabaga slices into ½-inch cubes. Add them and the other ingredients to the skillet, stirring over medium-high heat until rutabaga is heated through. *Serves 4.*

Chapter 29

SALSIFY

SALSIFY (*Tragopogon porrifolius*)

If you like oysters you'll like salsify. It is popularly known as the oyster plant, since the part you eat, the tapering white roots, have a light and agreeable oyster flavor. These roots look like narrow parsnips. They grow about 8 inches long and are about an inch thick at the top. Seedsmen often complain that gardeners don't appreciate salsify, and point out its virtues: It is a graceful plant, worthy of a place among the flowers; it is undemanding, wanting merely deep spading to start with, and fertilizer to keep it thriving; it is as immune to troubles as a weed; and it stores itself in the earth until you want it. Salsify is an old plant, and an old name for it is purple goatsbeard. Its flowers are an attractive lavender.

Plant and care for salsify exactly as you do parsnips. You can plant salsify a little earlier in the spring, but both need a long growing season—all spring and summer for salsify.

There is but one variety of salsify offered the home gardener: Sandwich Island Mammoth. A plant known as black salsify is not related.

You can dig salsify roots, leaving an inch or two of stalk on them, and store them in a sand box in the cellar for the winter, but they will do as well right in the garden where they grew. A winter-gardening friend of ours, Frederic C. Streland, does his gardening in the Philadelphia latitude and finds that salsify goes through the winter with no more protection than a straw mulch. And the mulch is there merely to keep the earth from freezing too hard for convenience in digging the roots.

RECIPES

You can cook the slender leaves of salsify in the way you cook any leafy green. They have a faint oyster flavor and combine well with the delicate flavor of lettuce if cooked together. Don't take many leaves from the salsify, though, or you'll rob the roots of nourishment.

The usual cooking procedure with the roots is to scrub them well, scrape them, and then parboil them until tender in enough water to cover them and with a tablespoon or so of lemon juice added. The lemon juice is to keep the roots from turning dark. With freshly dug salsify we have not found this darkening enough of a problem to need attention. We usually do the parboiling in Vegetable Stock*, covering the pan and cooking over medium heat until a sharp fork will pierce the thick part of the root with light pressure. This takes from 10 to 20 minutes, depending on the size of the root. An advantage of raising your own salsify is that you can harvest delicate young roots, something you never see in the stores.

CHESTNUT SALSIFY

Besides being available at the same time of year, chestnuts and salsify go together beautifully. This dish is a rich one, subtly flavored, and we suggest you try it as an accompaniment to broiled chicken. A salad with Herbed French Dressing*, a dry white wine, and a fresh pear and Port Salut cheese would round out a little feast.

> 3 tablespoons butter
> 3 tablespoons olive oil
> 1 cup sliced Processed Chestnuts*
> 6 large mushrooms, sliced
> 8 salsify roots, parboiled
> 1½ cups Béchamel Sauce*
> 1 egg yolk, beaten

Heat butter and oil, add chestnuts and cook covered over medium heat for 10 minutes. Add mushrooms and cook 5 minutes longer, stirring once or twice.

Slice salsify into ½-inch chunks. Put these into a casserole and over them the chestnuts and mushrooms.

Warm the Béchamel Sauce gently, stir 1 or 2 tablespoons of it into the beaten yolk, then stir this into the rest of the sauce and pour it over contents of casserole. Heat for 20 minutes, uncovered, in a 300-degree F. oven. *Serves 4.*

MOCK OYSTERS

This is a simple dish to prepare. Try serving it with a small helping of horse-radish mixed with cream, as described under RECIPES in Chapter 16, "Horse-radish."

2 cups parboiled, mashed salsify roots
4 eggs, beaten
Salt
Pepper
4 tablespoons butter

Thoroughly blend salsify, eggs, salt, and pepper.

In a large skillet melt butter and drop spoonfuls of the salsify mixture into it, keeping them separate. Cook over medium heat, browning each "oyster" on both sides. Remove from skillet and keep them warm until all have been cooked. You may need to add more butter. *Serves 4.*

SAUTEED SALSIFY

3 tablespoons butter
2 shallots, finely chopped
4 tablespoons Kraft Stock*
12 salsify roots, parboiled
Salt
Pepper
Grated nutmeg

Melt butter in a large skillet and cook shallots for a minute or two over low heat, shaking skillet now and then. Add stock, and when it has blended with butter and shallots, put salsify into skillet, coating them with the mixture by tilting skillet. Increase heat to medium and cook for a few more minutes, shaking skillet frequently. Season lightly with salt, pepper, and nutmeg. *Serves 4.*

SALSIFY AND POTATO POTPIE

This is one of those recipes that makes you think of a cozy fireside on a snowy night, and, in fact, Mr. Streland, whom we mentioned earlier and whose recipe this is, happens to be a wintertime enthusiast, at least in the garden.

> *2 or 3 cups peeled and sliced salsify*
> *2 or 3 cups peeled and sliced potatoes*
> *Salt*
> *Pepper*
> *Biscuit dough or pie pastry*

Put salsify in a saucepan with just enough water to cover, bring to a boil, reduce heat, and simmer for 20 minutes, covered.

Add potatoes, salt, and pepper. Bring to a boil again and simmer, covered, for about 5 more minutes, adding additional water if needed.

Put into a casserole, cover with biscuit dough or pie pastry, and bake about 20 minutes at 350 to 375 degrees F. *Serves 4.*

Chapter 30

SQUASH—SUMMER AND WINTER

SUMMER SQUASH (*Cucurbita melopepo*)

Squash deserves a more attractive name than "squash." We have known people who wouldn't eat it simply because they didn't like its name, which does seem ridiculous. Squash is a fine, tasty vegetable, good for you and willing to be cooked in a great variety of ways. It also comes in a variety of forms.

The ones you'll find offered by just about every seed house are zucchini, cocozelle, yellow crookneck, yellow straightneck, and scallop or patty pan. We've raised them all, and our favorites are zucchini and yellow crookneck. In the hot Midwest summers cocozelle did better for us than zucchini, but these judgments on squash are subject to frequent revision because the vegetable breeders keep bringing out talented new varieties and strains. If we find ourselves in a hot climate again, we'll plant the Burpee Hybrid Zucchini, which also grows prodigiously with limited summer heat and is a more compact grower than some. Both it and Zucchini Elite, a hybrid developed by Harris, give you their first fruits in about 7 weeks.

Squash, being like cucumbers a cucurbit, takes exactly the same care. See Chapter 13, "Cucumber," for details.

RECIPES

It is a good thing that summer squashes lend themselves to all sorts of cooking methods, because they bear so many fruits, you'd We lived in a place one summer where three families shared a va- get awfully tired of eating them cooked the same way every time. cant-lot garden of a dozen zucchini squash plants, and they couldn't

keep up with the production. As a result, some zucchinis became
the size of little watermelons before any of us could get to them.
Though such a huge summer squash is edible, the time to pick the
squash is when it is still small, not much more than 6 inches long.
If you can't easily pierce its skin with your thumbnail, summer
squash is too old. We used to hand such older squash over the
garden fence to our steers on our farm, and they became very fond
of them.

Because we are talking of cooking garden-fresh squash, you will
notice that no recipe calls for peeling the squash. Also, the cooking
times are shorter than for store-bought squash. Garden-fresh squash
is much moister.

Though squash will accept a great deal of flavorings, it makes a
nice dish merely sliced and cooked in a little butter for 10 minutes.
And we often pick a baby zucchini, about 4 inches long, for slicing
up raw in a salad, like a cucumber. A Chinese woman to whom we
once gave some zucchinis from our garden served them raw, in
slices dusted with monosodium glutamate, as hors d'oeuvres.

MATCHSTICK ZUCCHINIS

This dish takes constant attention during the cooking, but the
cooking is brief, and if the zucchinis are cut beforehand they can be
held till wanted, in a covered bowl in the refrigerator, making this a
fast last-minute dish.

2 *tablespoons butter*
2 *shallots, finely chopped*
3 *zucchini squashes about 8 inches long*
½ *cup Vegetable Stock**
¼ *cup Kraft Stock**
Salt
Pepper

Melt butter in a large skillet and cook shallots over low heat for a
few minutes while you prepare the zucchinis.

Cut each zucchini crosswise into 3 pieces, slice them lengthwise
into slabs ⅛ inch thick, then cut each slab into matchstick-size
strips. Spread them on paper towels for a few minutes to dry slightly.

Turn heat under skillet to medium-high, add squash sticks and cook for 3 or 4 minutes, shaking skillet frequently.

Add Vegetable Stock, turn heat to high and cook for 3 more minutes, stirring squash sticks by lifting them with a turner as they cook.

Add Kraft Stock and cook in the same way for 2 more minutes, or until liquid is absorbed and cooked away. Season with salt and pepper, and serve at once. *Serves 4.*

ZUCCHINI CURRY

This is a quick dish, since garden-fresh squash cooks fast, and cutting it into finger-thick sticks speeds it still more.

> 2 tablespoons olive oil
> 2 shallots, finely chopped
> 3 zucchini squashes 6 inches long
> 2 tablespoons butter
> 2 tablespoons flour
> ⅓ cup Vegetable Stock*
> 2 tablespoons dry vermouth
> Salt
> ¼ teaspoon curry powder

Heat olive oil and cook shallots over low heat while you prepare the squashes.

Cut squashes into 1-inch chunks and cut each chunk lengthwise into quarters. Add them to the shallots, cover pan, and increase heat slightly to finish the cooking while you make this sauce:

Melt butter in a skillet. Add flour, stirring until it turns golden. Add stock and wine, stirring over medium heat until sauce thickens. Stir in salt and curry powder, then squash and shallots. *Serves 4.*

SOY SQUASH

This starts out like a Chinese dish and ends up like a French one,
and it is an agreeable marriage.

> 3 *tablespoons corn oil*
> 1 *tablespoon Garlic Oil**
> 4 *zucchini squashes 8 inches long*
> 2 *green peppers*
> 4 *scallions*
> 1½ *tablespoons butter*
> 1½ *tablespoons flour*
> ½ *cup Vegetable Stock**
> *Salt*
> *Pepper*
> 2 *tablespoons soy sauce*
> ¼ *teaspoon sugar*

Heat oils in a large skillet. Cut each squash into 4 pieces crosswise and cut pieces into quarters. Add to skillet and cook, covered,
over medium heat for 10 minutes.

Meanwhile, cut peppers into ¼-inch strips, and chop scallions into
½-inch pieces. Stir these into skillet and cook, covered, for a few
more minutes while you make the sauce:

Melt butter in a saucepan, add flour, and stir till mixture bubbles.
Add the rest of the ingredients and stir over medium heat until
thick. Remove vegetables from heat, stir sauce into them, and serve
at once. *Serves 4 to 6.*

ZUCCHINI CASSEROLE I

> 1 *tablespoon butter*
> 3 *zucchini squashes 8 inches long*
> 2 *large mushrooms*
> 1 *small red onion*
> ¼ *cup tomato juice*
> ¼ *cup Vegetable Stock**

 2 tablespoons finely chopped parsley
 1 tablespoon finely chopped oregano
 12 Nasturtium Capers*, finely chopped
 1 clove garlic
 Salt
 Pepper
 2 tablespoons claret wine
 Grated Romano cheese

Melt butter in a large casserole in a 300-degree F. oven.

Meanwhile, cut squashes into 2-inch pieces crosswise, and quarter the pieces; slice mushrooms and onion. Add these to the casserole, along with tomato juice, stock, parsley, oregano, Nasturtium Capers, and garlic (with a toothpick through the garlic if you wish to remove it later). Cover casserole and bake 1 hour.

Remove casserole from oven, add salt, pepper, and wine, stirring gently. Sprinkle with enough grated cheese to cover the top, and return to oven, uncovered, for 10 minutes, increasing temperature to 400 degrees F. *Serves 4.*

ZUCCHINI CASSEROLE II

 4 zucchini squashes about 6 inches long
 6 tablespoons butter
 1 egg, beaten
 ¼ cup evaporated milk
 ½ teaspoon grated nutmeg
 ¼ teaspoon sugar
 ¼ cup grated Parmesan cheese

Slice squashes into ¼-inch rounds and cook, covered, in 2 tablespoons of the butter over medium-high heat for 4 or 5 minutes, shaking pan now and then. Remove squash to a casserole.

Melt the rest of the butter and remove pan from heat. Stir together the beaten egg, milk, nutmeg, sugar, and half the grated cheese. Stir in the melted butter. Pour this mixture over the squash in the casserole, sprinkle the rest of the grated cheese on top, and bake uncovered at 325 degrees F. for about 40 minutes. *Serves 4.*

HERBED ZUCCHINIS

The leafy greens used in this recipe are whatever your garden has growing at the same time you have squash. We use young kale, beet tops, or endive.

4 zucchini squashes, cut in half lengthwise
4 cups Vegetable Stock*
2 tablespoons butter
2 teaspoons Garlic Oil*
1 cup chopped and blanched leafy greens
2 scallions, finely chopped
3 mushrooms, finely chopped
2 tablespoons finely chopped parsley
2 teaspoon finely chopped basil
1 teaspoon finely chopped oregano
Salt
Pepper
¾ cup Croutons*
4 teaspoons olive oil

Parboil zucchini halves in the stock for 5 minutes. Drain. Scoop pulp from zucchinis, leaving shells ⅛ inch thick.

Heat butter and Garlic Oil, add pulp and all the rest of the ingredients except Croutons and olive oil. Stir well.

Put zucchini shells in a roasting pan, fill them with the pulp mixture, top them with the Croutons and heat for 15 minutes in a 300-degree F. oven. Then sprinkle olive oil over the tops and return to oven for 15 more minutes. *Serves 4.*

ZUCCHINIS MAUD

A friend gave us this recipe. It is a rich dish and sounds as if it originated in Italy or southern France.

5 zucchini squashes, cut in half lengthwise
4 cups Vegetable Stock*
1 tablespoon butter

   3 scallions, finely chopped
   Salt
   Pepper
   ¼ cup sour cream
   ¼ cup grated Parmesan cheese
   1 cup Croutons* browned in butter

Parboil zucchini halves in the stock for 5 minutes. Drain. Scoop
pulp from 8 of the halves, leaving shells ⅛ inch thick.

   Melt butter in a saucepan. Cook scallions in it over low heat
for a minute or two while you chop the zucchini pulp and the two
extra halves. Add this to saucepan and stir in all other ingredients
except Croutons.

   Arrange zucchini shells in a roasting pan. Quickly stir Croutons
into mixture in saucepan, heap the shells with it, and bake for 20
minutes in a 350-degree F. oven. *Serves 4.*

SAVORY ZUCCHINIS

   This is a useful recipe for using zucchinis that have grown a bit
bigger than you usually want them. It happens every season.

   4 zucchini squashes 9 to 10 inches long
   Butter
   8 slices bacon
   ½ teaspoon dry mustard
   ¼ teaspoon salt
   2 teaspoons sugar
   1 tablespoon finely chopped basil
   3 tablespoons cider vinegar
   1½ cups Croutons*
   2 tablespoons olive oil

Steam zucchinis whole for 12 to 15 minutes, until barely fork-
tender. Remove them to a buttered baking dish.

   Cook bacon in a skillet, cut it into small pieces, and stir into
the skillet all the rest of the ingredients except Croutons and
olive oil.

Heat olive oil and simmer Croutons in it until they have absorbed the oil and are lightly brown.

Stir Croutons into the mixture in skillet. Make a deep slit in each squash and fill with this mixture. Heat in a 350-degree. F. oven for 20 minutes. *Serves 4.*

BROILED SQUASH

This recipe comes from Mrs. David Burpee of Doylestown, Pennsylvania, to whom we are also indebted for the suggestions on harvesting and cooking tampala in Chapter 17. The squash here, Mrs. Burpee says, should be no more than 6 inches long.

> *6 young zucchini squash*
> *2 tablespoons melted butter*
> *· 1 cup dry bread crumbs*
> *Salt*
> *Pepper*
> *½ cup grated Parmesan cheese*

Drop the squashes whole into a stew pan of boiling water and cook for about 5 minutes, covered. They should be barely fork-tender when done.

Remove them and cut each in half lengthwise. Put them into a shallow pan and immediately brush them with the melted butter. Mix the crumbs with salt and pepper to taste, and spread over the squash halves. Finish by sprinkling the grated cheese over them. Slide the pan under the broiler and remove when cheese is lightly brown. *Serves 4.*

LEISURELY YELLOW SQUASH

You can cook yellow crookneck or straightneck squash in about half the time given here, but try them this way. The slower cooking brings out subtle flavors.

> *1 tablespoon butter*
> *1 tablespoon corn oil*
> *1 tablespoon Garlic Oil**

4 medium-sized yellow squashes, cut in ¼-inch slices
4 large mushrooms, cut in ¼-inch slices
½ cup Vegetable Stock*
1 tablespoon finely chopped parsley
1 teaspoon finely chopped basil
1 teaspoon finely chopped marjoram
Salt
Pepper

Heat butter and oils in a large skillet, add squash slices, and cook covered over low heat for 20 minutes, stirring occasionally, till slices are translucent but still firm. Add mushrooms and cook covered for 5 more minutes while making the sauce:

Put all other ingredients except salt and pepper into a saucepan and cook over high heat, stirring continually, until liquid is cooked down to about half and is slightly thickened. Add salt and pepper and pour over the squash as it is dished up. *Serves 4.*

STUFFED YELLOW SQUASH

4 medium-sized yellow squashes
4 cups Vegetable Stock*
4 tablespoons butter
½ clove garlic
2 large mushrooms, cut into small dice
1 green pepper, cut into small dice
Salt
Pepper
1 cup Croutons*

Cut squashes in half lengthwise and boil in the stock for 5 minutes. Drain. Scoop pulp from squash halves, leaving shells ⅛ inch thick.

Melt half the butter in a saucepan, add garlic, mushrooms, green pepper, and cook over low heat for 5 minutes. Discard garlic and stir in the squash pulp and salt and pepper. Arrange squash shells in a roasting pan and stuff them with this mixture, topped with the Croutons. Melt rest of the butter, drizzle it over the stuffed shells, and bake for 30 minutes in a 300-degree F. oven. *Serves 4.*

SKILLET SQUASH

A milk infusion seems particularly adapted to summer squash. We have used this recipe for zucchini also, and it would probably work as well with patty pan.

4 medium-sized yellow squashes, cut in ½-inch slices
Milk
½ cup flour
½ teaspoon salt
¼ teaspoon pepper
4 tablespoons butter

Put squash slices in a bowl, cover them with milk, and steep for 30 minutes. Drain well.

Mix flour, salt, and pepper, put into a strong white paper bag with half the squash slices. Hold bag closed and shake it up and down a few times to coat squash with flour mixture. Repeat with the rest of the squash.

Melt butter in a large skillet, add floured squash slices, and cook over low heat for about 20 minutes, turning slices halfway through. They should be golden brown when done. *Serves 4.*

BATTER-FRIED SQUASH BLOSSOMS

This is an Indian recipe and we are indebted for it to *The Art of American Indian Cooking* (Doubleday & Company, Inc., 1965), an unusual and good collection of native recipes as presented by Yeffe Kimball and Jean Anderson. The squash blossoms referred to can be from any variety of squash, winter or summer, or from a pumpkin vine. Ideally, pick them just before they open, preferably male blossoms, which are larger and won't grow fruits (but leave some for pollination purposes). We did not try this recipe but a friend did so for us and was so enchanted that we almost retitled it "Ella's Squash Blossom Breakfast." It would also make a luncheon side dish, or an appetizer with drinks. About 4 to 6 blossoms make 1 serving.

⅓ cup milk
1 teaspoon flour
¼ teaspoon salt
Pepper
1 dozen squash blossoms
¼ cup corn oil
Paprika

Make a light batter by beating together the milk, flour, salt, and pepper. Dip the blossoms in this one by one, and drain them on a plate.

Heat oil in a large skillet till it shimmers, add blossoms, and cook over medium heat until they are golden brown, watching them closely. Drain on paper towels, sprinkle with paprika, and serve at once. *Serves 2 or 3.*

WINTER SQUASH (*Cucurbita maxima, and others*)

As a food, winter squash is as different from summer squash as if they weren't related. Instead of being used green, winter squash is thoroughly ripened on the vine and can then remain good for months. Winter squashes taste entirely different too, having so rich an orange or yellow flesh that they are often used for pie instead of pumpkins, to which they are related also.

In our eyes, the supreme winter squash is the Hubbard. It is also one of the largest, and its vine takes more room than a small garden can afford, so we grow it only when we have such room, in a warm-summer climate.

Very close to Hubbard in quality are the smaller-fruited Butternut and Buttercup. A Hubbard grows to 10 or 15 pounds, and the others run to 5 pounds or so.

Some newer small winter squash varieties have edible seeds. One is Sweetnut, developed at the New Hampshire Experiment Station, and another is Eat-All. Farmer handles them. Hubbard seeds, too, are good to eat when dried for a few hours in a 150-degree F. oven, but you have to hull them before eating.

Acorn squash is probably the most popular winter one, though we think its quality inferior to some other small ones. However, an

Acorn squash once did us the favor of planting itself on a parking area we had covered with coarsely crushed limestone, and gave us a basketful of fruits that fall with no care whatever from us.

As to culture, you handle winter squash the same as any other cucurbit. See the cucumber chapter for details.

If your garden isn't big enough for winter squash, you might try one of the smaller bush varieties that have been developed. We have no personal experience with these but we have good reports. One variety is Gold Nugget, an All-America selection handled by several seed houses. Bush Buttercup is listed by Burgess. Sweetnut, mentioned before, is a compact grower. Burpee's handle two bush winter squashes: Baby Blue Hubbard, and a bush Acorn.

If you lack space for even one of these bush types, you may want to buy a whole winter squash at your food store, since it is one of the very few vegetables that do not lose quality quickly after harvesting. Be sure to buy a *whole* squash, and make sure it hasn't been cracked by rough handling. Hubbards are usually the best buys. You can store such a squash in any warm, dry place until you want to cook it, since they will keep for months.

RECIPES

For individual servings and immediate use, an Acorn squash is a convenient size. The procedure with it, as with any small winter squash, is: Split it lengthwise, remove seeds and fibers with a spoon; put 1 tablespoon of butter in the seed cavity, sprinkle a little salt over the cut surface, and bake at 350 degrees F. for an hour or more, depending on the size. A fork should pierce the flesh easily when done. A little sherry in the seed cavity adds to the taste, as does a trace of nutmeg. One squash half makes a serving, just as it comes from the oven.

Since we cook more Hubbards than any other winter squash, we freeze most of it after baking. We do the baking at 325 degrees F., putting the halves on cooky sheets, and a 15-pound Hubbard takes just about 4 hours. We do not season it at this time, or add anything to it. After it cools, we take a spoon and gently scrape the baked pulp from the thin shell of skin, blending the pulp with the liquid that forms in the bottom of each half during baking. We then spoon the pulp onto sheets of foil, in serving-size portions, and make packages which we put into individual plastic bags and freeze. These make nice gifts as well as being convenient for our own use.

When serving one of these packages, we merely heat it in a 300-degree F. oven after thawing at room temperature, sprinkling it with salt and dotting with butter. A dash of sherry or cognac during the last 5 minutes of reheating is a good addition, as are Blanched Almonds*, sautéed in butter until golden and then stuck into the Hubbard pulp.

Chapter 31

TOMATOES

TOMATOES (*Lycopersicum esculentum*)

If American home gardeners could raise only one vegetable it would be tomatoes. The people who sell the gardeners their seeds find the tomato the consistent leader in sales, with beans next in line. Pound for pound, tomatoes do compare well with most other garden vegetables in their contribution to a good diet, but if this were the chief criterion, beet greens or kale would have walked off with the popularity prize long ago. The answer appears to be that tomatoes are so good to eat, cooked or raw, and so versatile at combining with other vegetables, that almost everybody loves them.

As a result, you can get a dazzling assortment of tomato types. Tomatoes come in red, yellow, orange, pink, green (when ripe), and even white. You may have them huge, weighing 2 pounds or so, or as small as a boy's marble, or in many sizes in between. They come in sweet tastes, in tart ones, and in variations of each. There is even a hollow tomato you can stuff like a sweet pepper. And the plants range from dwarf bushes a few inches high, to climbers that can reach a second-story window.

A little surprisingly for so popular a vegetable, tomatoes are choosy about their environment, and the same tomato will taste different in different areas. A yellow tomato that was a great success in our garden in the Washington, D.C., vicinity proved hardly worth growing in east-central Missouri, which has almost the same summer climate. This is one good reason that hybrid tomatoes have become big news among gardeners. Their hybrid vigor can be the shade of difference between a middling-good harvest and a horn of plenty.

This does not mean that a hybrid tomato is always a better choice for you. We've planted hybrids that were shamed by the superior performance of old stand-bys such as Marglobe in a row beside them. Our practice has been to shop around a little each season, trying some new tomatoes along with proven performers.

To do such shopping around, you must raise your tomatoes from seed. No nursery offers many varieties of plants; even half a dozen is more than usual. Yet Burpee's, the leader in the development of first-generation hybrid tomatoes, listed seed for 33 tomatoes in 1969; Burgess listed 79 varieties; and Stokes an astounding 95, though the house serves Northern gardeners having a short summer season.

Among the standard big red tomatoes, Delicious and Rutgers are good ones that will give you fruit in about 11 weeks from transplanting, and Fireball will beat that time by 2 weeks. New hybrid tomatoes come out every year, but one that has held top honors for several years now is Burpee's Big Boy. A new one that promises well and is particularly resistant to disease is Burpee's VF. Among small fruited tomatoes, Red Cherry and Yellow Pear have been our choices.

If your summer is warm enough to suit tomatoes, they are not a hard crop to grow. They take up less space than the vine crops and they keep on producing until frost finally kills them. Even then the plants are usually full of unripe tomatoes, the best of which can be cooked green or ripened indoors.

Plant tomato seeds 6 or 8 weeks before all danger of frost will be past. You may have to plant them in a pot indoors, as they need a 70-degree temperature for good germination. You can then transplant the small seedlings to a flat or cold frame, protected from frost until the weather is warm enough for a final transplanting to the garden. A way that has worked well for us is to get seedlings started indoors, and after 2 or 3 weeks transplant them to the garden and put a Hotkap over each. This is like having a small paper greenhouse for each plant. We've tried planting tomato seeds under Hotkaps in the garden, too, but the plants tended to become leggy.

When transplanting a tomato plant, set it deeply—just about up to its leaves. It will develop extra roots along the part of the stem you put underground, and will be better anchored and will grow more sturdily.

Set plants 2 or 3 feet apart in as sunny a spot as you have, and water the planting holes well just before transplanting. When the hole is filled, tramp the soil down firmly with your feet. This is a good time to set a stake. It should be about as high as the variety is apt to grow. Nylon stockings make good fasteners, and the way to use them is to tie a strip of stocking firmly to the stake, then tie a loose loop around the stem of the tomato so that it is supported but not choked.

Average good garden soil will suit tomatoes, especially if you dig in compost. But a fertilizer heavy on nitrogen will make them grow leaves instead of fruit. We always mulch the plants well.

If your tomato plants blossom but do not set fruit, it may be that the nights are too cool for them. A remedy is to spray the blossoms with a hormone. Blossom-Set is one that many seed houses sell.

To keep a lusty tomato plant from spending more time growing than fruiting, pinch off the tips of the side shoots that sprout at the angles where branches join the main stem. This will keep these so-called sucker branches from growing but will retain plenty of leaves. The plant needs leaves for its own nourishment, and to keep fruits from being scalded by hot sun. The only exception is in cool-summer regions, where sunlight can hurry the fruit's ripening.

RECIPES

We are so partial to fresh tomatoes that we use most of them that way during the bearing season, sliced up and heaped on a platter. A vine-ripened tomato is simply wonderful when served this way with nothing more added than a light sprinkle of salt—or of sugar, as Ken's father preferred. And miniature tomatoes are a splendid item for a lunch box, a discovery made by one of our farm neighbors with four children, the first year she grew Red Cherry tomatoes.

However, we also use a lot of tomatoes in cooking, and we canned a great many for this when we had 100 plants in our farm garden, as well as cooking many just out of the garden.

A garden-fresh tomato, as well ripened as it ought to be, cooks quickly. There is some difference between types, due to the great variations of tomatoes. In each recipe here the temperature and the timing are for fresh tomatoes, and call for less cooking than store-bought or commercially canned tomatoes take.

TOMATO CASSEROLE

> 4 medium-large ripe red tomatoes
> Butter
> ½ cup grated Romano cheese
> 1 cup Green Sauce*

Trim the green stem end from each tomato. Make an X-gash halfway down through each with a knife. Put tomatoes into a buttered baking dish and sprinkle half the grated cheese over them, holding each gashed tomato open as you do so, to admit the cheese. Pour sauce over tomatoes and sprinkle with the rest of the cheese. Bake 12 to 15 minutes at 400 degrees F. *Serves 4.*

SCALLOPED TOMATOES

We use our Sourdough Bread* in this recipe and think it adds appreciably to the flavor. We slice it about ½ inch thick.

> 4 large ripe tomatoes, quartered
> Butter
> Salt
> Pepper
> 1 teaspoon sugar
> 1 tablespoon finely chopped basil
> 4 slices lean bacon, diced
> 3 slices bread

Arrange tomatoes in buttered casserole and sprinkle with salt, pepper, sugar, and basil.

Fry bacon in a skillet. Tear the bread into fairly small bits and stir them into the skillet, cooking over low heat until they have absorbed the bacon drippings and browned lightly. Spread this mixture over the tomatoes and bake for 30 minutes at 300 degrees F. *Serves 4.*

STUFFED TOMATOES

> 4 *large ripe tomatoes*
> 4 *scallions, chopped*
> 2 *tablespoons corn oil*
> 1 *tablespoon Garlic Oil**
> 1 *cup Croutons**
> 2 *tablespoons Vegetable Stock**
> ¼ *cup finely chopped parsley*
> 2 *teaspoons finely chopped thyme*
> *Salt*
> *Pepper*

Trim a slice off the tops of the tomatoes and scoop an egg-sized cavity out of each, reserving the removed pulp for some other use.

Make this dressing: Cook scallions in the oils over low heat for 5 minutes, stirring several times. Stir in the rest of the ingredients. Put tomatoes in a baking dish, fill them with the dressing, and bake for 12 to 15 minutes in a 400-degree F. oven. *Serves 4.*

GREEN TOMATO CASSEROLE

This is a season-end use of good-sized but unripe tomatoes (which though green outside will be partly ripe and pinkish inside).

> 4 *green tomatoes*
> 8 *large mushrooms*
> 1 *tablespoon corn oil*
> 1 *teaspoon Garlic Oil**
> 2 *shallots, finely chopped*
> 2 *tablespoons finely chopped parsley*
> *Bay leaf*
> ½ *cup tomato juice*

½ teaspoon sugar
Salt
Pepper

Cut tomatoes in half and put them into a shallow baking dish. Remove and chop mushroom stems. Heat the oils in a skillet and cook mushroom stems, caps, and shallots over low heat, covered, for 3 or 4 minutes, turning mushroom caps over halfway through.

Remove caps from skillet, add the rest of the ingredients, and cook over medium-high heat for 5 minutes, stirring. Remove bay leaf, and pour all but about 2 tablespoons of this sauce over the green tomatoes in baking dish. Then top each half with a mushroom cap, pour the rest of the sauce over, and bake covered for 40 minutes at 350 degrees F. *Serves 4.*

BROILED GREEN TOMATOES

4 medium-sized green tomatoes
⅓ cup Herbed French Dressing*
½ teaspoon sugar

Slice tomatoes ½ inch thick and arrange slices in a shallow pan you can put under the broiler.

Mix dressing and sugar and spoon about half of it onto tomato slices. Let them marinate for about 15 minutes, then bake for 30 minutes at 300 degrees F. Turn each slice, spoon over the rest of the dressing, and finish cooking under broiler for about 10 minutes. *Serves 4.*

DILLY GREEN TOMATOES

We use few pickles but try to put up a few jars of these pickled miniature tomatoes for Christmas presents. They are also nice as appetizers. Furthermore, this use of the small fruit turns disaster into triumph when the season's first killing frost approaches while the vines are still heavy with yet-green cherry or plum tomatoes. The amounts given here will fill about 10 half-pint jars. Choose the smallest tomatoes (the others can be ripened indoors for use fresh), and leave the green caps on them.

About 4 cups miniature green tomatoes
10 heads fresh dill
10 small hot red peppers
10 cloves garlic
2 cups white vinegar
2 teaspoons salt
4 cups water

Wash tomatoes, dill, and peppers. Peel the garlic. Fill 10 half-pint sterilized jars with tomatoes, adding 1 dill head, 1 pepper, and 1 garlic clove to each jar, arranged so they will make an attractive pattern with the tomatoes when seen through the glass.

Combine vinegar, salt, and water, bring to a boil, and pour immediately into each jar, almost filling them. Seal jars at once. Store in a cool, dry place.

Chapter 32

TURNIPS

TURNIPS (*Brassica rapa*)

Turnips have a kind of homely reputation for being all-around nourishing. If you include their leaves, they are, and we raise turnips because we like the whole plant. Here, we are talking about the roots. See Chapter 17, "The Leafy Greens," for recipes using leaves.

If you want to taste something delicate and yet with character, raise your own turnips and harvest them young and crisp a few minutes before you start cooking dinner. They are like a different vegetable from the discouraged ones you often see at the store, which are frequently softened and sometimes pithy, at times stored until in desperation they start to unfold the new green leaves of a second spring.

You can grow an early crop of turnips and also a fall one, in most sections. Plant early in spring and again in midsummer about 3 months before frost. In warmer sections a late fall planting may produce a winter crop. Culture is the same as for beets. If root maggots are a problem in your locality, work a powdering of chlordane into the soil when sowing.

Years ago you had to wait 9 or 10 weeks to grow any turnip to full size. Some still take that time, but there are speedier new ones. A hybrid called Just Right, developed in Japan, will mature a root in 6 weeks under just-right conditions. It is best when planted for a late crop. A newer early-maturing hybrid from Japan is Tokyo Cross, an All-America winner that is said to produce pure white 2-inch roots in 5 weeks, or can go on growing until the roots are enormous—6 inches wide—without going pithy. Among older varieties one of the most dependable is the 8-week Purple-top White Globe. It stores well too and is a convenient shape to handle.

Any turnip will grow leaves you can cook, but some work harder at it. The Shogoin is such a variety, and we've usually planted it, especially if we had to make the most of small space. The Just Right hybrid is also a good leaf producer.

Just as there are some white-fleshed rutabagas, there are some yellow-fleshed turnips. Golden Ball, also called Orange Jelly, is the one you are most likely to find offered.

RECIPES

Garden-fresh turnips that have been grown quickly are more delicate in flavor than someone used to other turnips may imagine. A test of this is a recipe you'll find in Chapter 39, Turnip Chicken Casserole*, in which a harmonious blending results.

And turnips are one of the vegetables that come to mind as belonging in a stew or ragout. We include one such recipe in Chapter 39, Beef Ragout*.

Fresh turnips cook quickly. Timing is somewhat complicated by their varying sizes, but 20 minutes is close to right for either steaming or boiling a garden turnip about the bulk of a tennis ball. And little turnip balls cut with a ball cutter will cook fork-tender in about 5 minutes.

STUFFED TURNIPS

When you make mashed potatoes, make an extra cupful for this recipe. The flavors of turnips and potatoes combine well.

4 medium-large turnips
1 cup mashed potatoes
⅓ cup grated Parmesan cheese
Salt
*4 teaspoons Parsley Butter**

Peel turnips and scoop an egg-sized hollow out of each, reserving the removed pulp for some other use. Parboil turnip shells in water, covered, for 15 minutes, until barely tender. Drain, and put into baking dish.

Mix potatoes, cheese, and salt together and fill turnip shells with it. With a spoon make a little well in the top of each stuffed shell and fill it with 1 teaspoon Parsley Butter. Bake for 20 minutes at 325 degrees F. *Serves 4.*

TURNIPS IN CREAM

We have used evaporated milk for this dish also, and find it gives approximately the same results as cream. As with Chateau Potatoes*, we use the unused parts of the turnips for some other dish. Chopped, they combine well with a leafy green when cooked together.

> 6 *medium-large turnips*
> 2 *cups Vegetable Stock**
> 4 *tablespoons butter*
> *Salt*
> *Pepper*
> ½ *cup cream*
> 1 *tablespoon finely chopped parsley*

Peel turnips and cut balls out of them. You can expect to get 60 to 70 balls. Put these into a saucepan with the stock, bring to a boil, and cook, covered, for 5 minutes. Drain, add the butter, and cook, covered, over medium heat for 5 more minutes, shaking pan several times. Season with salt and pepper, pour cream into pan, and cook, uncovered, 2 or 3 minutes longer, shaking pan a few times. Sprinkle with parsley and dish up. *Serves 4.*

TURNIP CASSEROLE

> 4 *medium-sized turnips*
> 3 *cups Vegetable Stock**
> 2 *tablespoons corn oil*
> 6 *scallions, chopped*
> 4 *large mushrooms*
> *Salt*
> *Pepper*
> ½ *teaspoon sugar*
> 1 *cup Croutons**

Peel turnips and cut into ½-inch cubes. Boil in stock for 5 minutes. Drain, and reserve ½ cup stock.

Heat oil in a skillet, add scallions and the mushrooms, broken into half a dozen pieces each. Cook, covered, over medium heat for 5 minutes, stirring now and then. Stir in the rest of the ingredients, then the turnips, and turn into a casserole. Moisten with the reserved stock and bake for 30 minutes at 300 degrees F. *Serves 4.*

Chapter 33

FOR FAMILY FUN—PEANUTS, POPCORN, PARCHED CORN

We recommend to you in this chapter three homemade delicacies you could call nibbling food. All are old-fashioned fireside and kitchen activities. Popping corn has never gone out of date as entertainment, but parching it, and roasting peanuts are so much a part of past times that now they seem brand-new again. Also, these are family pleasures just as gardening itself is, things all ages can join in doing. We can't help thinking this kind of activity is important and that this is a powerful endorsement for whatever enhances it.

And as a practical everyday note: Corn freshly popped or parched, and peanuts freshly roasted, are nutritious as well as delectable, and *you* control the amounts of salt and oils or butter added. Also, compare the cost of what you get to packaged commercial eat-along tidbits if you want a pleasant surprise.

PEANUTS (*Arachis hypogaea*)

If you have 4 months of hot summer weather you can grow peanuts, which may help reconcile you to the heat. Peanuts in the garden have two benefits to bestow. They are a most interesting plant to observe in growth, and newly dug peanuts, freshly roasted, are more delicious than you'd ever imagine peanuts could be.

We grew peanuts well in our sandy soil on the Gulf Coast of Mississippi. Commercially speaking, they are a chancy crop if grown much farther north than Arkansas (they are native to Brazil), but this restriction does not apply to diligent home gardeners. Even in southern Canada peanuts are grown in home gardens by dint of early planting in sandy soil, which warms up quickly, and by choosing a sheltered site that slopes to the south.

You can plant a peanut whole, or shell it out. We shelled our seed nuts, to speed them up, and did not plant until the weather was balmy. Shell them carefully so as not to harm the inner skin. The plants grow to a foot or so high and can become spready. Plant them about 18 inches apart.

In the garden the peanut is a leafy attraction, with showy yellow flowers, but a curious thing about it is another set of flowers that form the peanuts. They do so by bending over and burrowing into the earth, where the peanuts then develop.

Various strains of two varieties of peanuts are offered by most seedsmen. The earlier one is called Spanish, or Early Spanish. It bears 2 or 3 small sweet kernels to the pod and is the peanut you usually find in candy or as a salted peanut. The other variety, Jumbo Virginia, and also called Mammoth Virginia or Improved Virginia, bears 1 or 2 large kernels to the pod and is a heavy producer. In addition to these, a variety called Red Tennessee is offered by Park's, a Southern house.

To harvest your home garden peanuts, do this: Wait until just *before* frost in the fall, to give the plants all the time they can get for producing a crop. Then dig the plants up whole and shake the earth from the roots and from the dangling peanuts. Hang the plants in an airy place to start the curing. A carport is a good place. Give them 2 or 3 weeks there. Then pull off the peanuts and pile them loosely in a cardboard carton or on newspapers to finish drying. This will take another 2 or 3 weeks. You can then roast them, and we suggest you roast only part of the crop at a time because they are at their delicious best when freshly roasted.

Pat, having had a country childhood, remembers that roasting peanuts was part of the farm routine. From late fall to early spring, after supper was cooked and the range oven was still hot, a large shallow baking pan was filled with cured peanuts and left in the oven for an hour or more while the stove cooled off. The pan was shaken occasionally, and then the peanuts were poured into a big crockery bowl and brought into the living room to be shelled for before-bedtime snacks along with a bowl of popcorn.

We now use the electric or gas oven, but the procedure is much the same: Give the peanuts 20 to 25 minutes at a temperature of from 300 to 325 degrees F. If the peanuts are large, use the longer time and higher temperature. Remove the peanuts from the oven before they seem to be quite done, because they continue to cook along as they cool. This is something you'll catch on to after a trial run or two. A well-roasted peanut has a brittle shell, and its inner skin will flake off easily.

POPCORN (Zea mays everta)

When our garden wherever we were living at the time had room for sweet corn, we usually planted some popcorn too. Both take the same culture. You can buy good corn for popping, but it is easy to grow and in this way you can try several varieties.

The best popcorn we know of is South American Mushroom, and there are now some hybrids of it. The yellow kernels expand to 25 or 30 times their volume when popped and are better flavored, we think, than white varieties. South American Mushroom's drawback is that it takes a long time, 105 days, to mature. If your season is too short for this, Tom Thumb is a dwarf that takes only 85 days, and Minhybrid, a dwarf developed by the Minnesota Experiment Station, takes 83 days. If you'd like to try a novelty dwarf, Strawberry popcorn (100 days) has mahogany red kernels, and the little ears make effective decorations as well as being good to eat.

Harvest popcorn ears after they are completely dry and ripe. Husk them and store them in a dry place at any temperature except extreme cold. You can pop the corn at any time after this, though it pops better after being stored for a year. When you are ready to use it, do this: Rub 2 ears briskly together "against the grain," holding them over a pan. The kernels will drop readily, along with some fluffy chaff. To get rid of the chaff, shake the grains in a colander outdoors. Then store the corn in jars in the refrigerator. Cold corn pops better and bigger.

Our favorite popper is the old-fashioned wire basket type on a long handle, as we usually pop corn over fireplace coals. If not, we use a heavy skillet over medium-high heat on the kitchen stove. In either case, ¼ cup of kernels is about the amount to pop. Cover the skillet and keep shaking it by sliding it back and forth across the burner, or the corn will burn. When it starts to pop, reduce the heat.

When using the fireplace popper we melt butter separately to pour over the popped corn, but with a skillet you can melt a tablespoon or two of butter in it just before you put the kernels in to pop, and they will butter themselves. Caution: After you are sure every kernel has popped, remove the popper from the heat but keep its lid on for a few more seconds. A laggard kernel often picks this moment to explode, showering popcorn all over the place.

POPCORN BALLS

> *About 12 cups freshly popped corn*
> *Salt*
> *3 tablespoons butter*
> *3 cups brown sugar*
> *¾ cup water*

Put popped corn into a large bowl that will hold it with room to spare. Salt it lightly.

Melt butter in a heavy saucepan, add brown sugar and water, and stir until sugar is dissolved. Boil without stirring until syrup reaches the soft-ball stage, 238 degrees F. Then pour syrup slowly over popcorn, stirring popcorn gently to coat each popped kernel with syrup.

Flour your hands lightly and shape popcorn into balls. Work quickly and handle popcorn gently. Put balls on waxed paper, not touching each other, while syrup hardens.

Popcorn Ball Christmas Tree

This makes a delightful Christmas tree decoration for children, we've found—ornaments they can eat. Make miniature popcorn balls by the recipe above. When they are hard and dry, wrap each in a square of sheet plastic, twisting it shut at the top and tying with Christmas ribbon. Hang the balls on the tree by the ribbons.

PARCHED CORN

To parch corn, you expose it to heat without burning it, and the result is a convenient, cooked food. This was a staple with our pioneer forefathers. It was palatable, lightweight, kept well, and always ready to eat. A man could take a pocketful when hunting or clearing the woods, and it also satisfied a hungry child. What they used was field corn that was grown for the livestock. Today, Farmer Seed and Nursery Company offers a new hybrid corn that is particularly suitable for parching, White Crisp. We have tried it, and it is excellent. Here is their recipe for parching; any cooking oil can serve as the oil here, and the utensil used is a skillet:

PARCHED CORN

To parch, corn must be brittle dry, and proceed as if popping corn with popping oil and stirring. When kernels turn autumn brown, pour out to cool. Salt and serve.

Chapter 34

HERBS

Out of all the herbs with culinary possibilities we use comparatively few, after years of testing many, but those we use we grow ourselves and we use some every day. In the coastal climate where we are now living we grow these herbs: Basil, oregano and marjoram, parsley, rosemary, tarragon, and thyme. If you count these also as herbs, we grow them too: Celery, chives, and nasturtiums. We also grow spearmint but seldom use it, and we used to grow borage, dill, and sage, but used them too little to justify the space. This year we're going to see if summer savory and chervil thrive here.

The herbs named above, including tarragon, will grow from seed, the most inexpensive way to get a herb garden started, especially if you want a good many different kinds. Quite a lot of other herbs will also grow from seed, and once you have them started you can propagate some from cuttings or divisions. Oregano, rosemary, and thyme grow from cuttings with ease, and by pulling old clumps apart you can multiply tarragon, mint, marjoram, oregano, thyme, and chives quickly.

We grow herbs in the garden (and flower beds) for decoration and in some cases fragrance, as well as for use in cooking. In addition we have pots or planters of some near the kitchen for greater convenience, or for their protection if they are not winter-hardy and we are living in a cold-winter climate. Rosemary can die of the cold, for example, as can thyme and tarragon.

Each herb has its own cultural likes and dislikes, and some will refuse to grow at all in certain climates or even in certain spots in an otherwise favored climate. There is also a general rule that warns gardeners not to grow herbs in anything but poor soil if they want the most flavor. We pay scant attention to this, planting herbs where

we please, and we can't say we find them less satisfactory in good
soil. As a general rule for all herbs, this one, from the people at
Hemlock Hill Herb Farm, agrees with our experience: "Most herbs
require good drainage, and do best in good garden loam, in full sun."

The Hemlock Hill people sell plants. Nichols Nursery is a West
Coast source for plants and also for many kinds of herb seeds. Park's
also list an unusually good selection of seeds.

If you'd like to grow herbs indoors for winter use in a cold-
winter climate, choose a place near a window—a south one if possible—in a room that isn't very warm. About 60 degrees would suit
the herbs, though it wouldn't suit most persons. No plants do well
near gas appliances, by the way. Use a sandy loam and a low-
nitrogen fertilizer or no fertilizer at all. Among the herbs mentioned
below, these are most likely to succeed indoors: Basil, chives, marjoram, mint, parsley, rosemary, sage, summer savory, tarragon, and
thyme.

For garden culture, some herbs do well if seeded late in the year
for sprouting the following spring. In the South and mild coastal
areas, plant seed in December. In colder zones, spade the bed
after the first hard frost and leave it rough until the end of Indian
Summer. Then rake it, and in November just before cold weather is
due, seed the herbs, a little more deeply than for spring sowing, and
forget them. You need not mulch the bed. Among the herbs mentioned below, these can be fall-seeded: Borage, chervil, chives, dill,
marjoram, parsley, sage, summer savory, and thyme.

BASIL (*Ocimum basilicum*)

A tender annual. Its leaves have a sprightly fragrance that makes
it a pleasure to work near it in the garden. We have used it as a
garden hedge, and enjoyed the singing of the bees around it. Often
called sweet basil, it is one of the most useful herbs, its taste going
agreeably with many vegetables, especially tomatoes. We think it
too strong to be added to a salad, but it is a good flavoring for the
dressing. Basil grows about 2 feet tall, but there is a good dwarf
variety much favored in France, and we prefer it. A dark-leaved one

is also available in the 2-foot height, and Nichols list a lettuce-leaved green basil. Seed basil in the spring after frost is over, in a sunny or partly sunny place.

BORAGE (*Borago officinalis*)

An annual with hairy leaves that taste slightly of cucumber. You can cook them or cut them into salads. The plant grows about 18 inches high and has sprays of pretty little blue flowers which can be dipped in slightly beaten egg white, then in granulated sugar, and dried on waxed paper, as treats for children. Borage will seed itself and can get to be a weed. It wants a sunny spot, and spring or fall seeding.

CHERVIL (*Anthriscus cerefolium*)

An annual much cherished in France, where the delicately curled leaves are used to flavor all sorts of dishes, including ragouts. Plant chervil in spring or fall, in partial shade, and don't transplant it.

CHIVES (*Allium schoenoprasum*)

See Chapter 21, "The Onion Family." Chives are highly attractive in any flower border.

DILL (*Anethum graveolens*)

An annual that grows 2 or 3 feet tall in full sun, and has graceful seed heads, good in flower arrangements. The mature seed heads are used for flavoring pickles. The leaves have a limited usefulness for flavoring various dishes. They make a pretty garnish for a platter of fish or chicken, and the flavor goes nicely with some vegetables.

This is particularly a question of your own taste in dill's case. Seed in spring or fall, and don't transplant.

MARJORAM (*Majorana hortensis*)

A perennial (annual in cold-winter climates) of considerable usefulness in cooking. The leaves are quite aromatic, almost pungent. The plant grows 2 feet high and can make a nice low hedge in a sunny spot. Marjoram is supposed to be the perfect herb with mushrooms, and we use it in a great many other dishes, alone and with most of the other herbs listed here. It is splendid in bean soups. It is also called sweet marjoram. The seeds are small and take some coaxing to start, but once you have marjoram growing you can increase it from cuttings and by dividing clumps. Put some in a pot you can bring indoors if your winters are cold, and your marjoram will go on and on. Plant the seed in spring or fall.

OREGANO (*Origanum vulgare*)

This perennial is also called wild marjoram. Its stems are stiffer than those of marjoram, the leaves are slightly more pungent, and it is a stronger grower. Otherwise everything we have said about marjoram applies here. There really isn't any point in raising both for cooking purposes, but if you can't get one, the other will take care of you nicely.

PARSLEY (*Petroselinum crispum*)

A biennial, but usually planted every year because it goes to seed the second year. Curled-leaf parsley is more attractive as a garnish, but the flat-leaved (Italian) type has more flavor. The culinary uses of parsley are legion, and it not only combines with almost any other herb but helps bring out the other's flavor.

You aren't apt to eat such a lot of parsley that its vitamin content matters, but it is high in A and C, and also has more protein than most vegetables. We have noticed that child visitors to our garden eat parsley by the handful, as if they instinctively know it is good for them.

Parsley grows about a foot high. Seeds are slow to sprout, so sow them in a well-watered row, cover shallowly, and pat the earth down with your hand, then keep the soil moist with a mulch of peat moss. Seed in spring or fall. If you let a plant go to seed, it may do you the favor of planting next year's parsley for you, and you can transplant these seedlings.

A variety of parsley called Hamburg grows a 6-inch root like a fat parsnip, and tastes of both parsnip and parsley. It is used raw in salads, cooked in soups, and steamed tender for serving with butter or a simple sauce.

ROSEMARY (Rosmarinus officinalis)

A perennial (annual in cold-winter climates) often grown for its fine dark green foliage, something like spruce needles, and small blue flowers. A prostrate form makes a ground cover, and others grow upright to 18 inches, or trail. Rosemary is a good choice for a window box. As a culinary herb it is good with lamb and with chicken, but it is strong and must be used sparingly. When we broil lamb over coals we throw a few sprigs of fresh rosemary on the coals to give the meat an agreeable smoky fragrance.

Plant rosemary in the spring. It will grow from seed, and cuttings root easily. It likes full sun but will get along with less. It is said to prefer poor soil, and we have some growing in poor soil but some others are flourishing in rich soil.

SAGE (Salvia officinalis)

A perennial (annual in cold climates, though it wintered over for us in Missouri) with attractive gray-green leaves. The leaves are traditionally used in poultry dressings. Like rosemary, they are strong and should be used with restraint or everything will taste like sage.

Seed sage in spring or fall. Full sun is fine, but half as much will do. Incidentally, we've found that sage blossoms are one of the most attractive flowers to hummingbirds.

SPEARMINT (Mentha spicata)

A perennial that grows 2 feet high in a spot it likes, which usually means a moist one. Mint can become a nuisance, spreading by underground stems. You can propagate it by planting these stems. Sprigs of mint are good in lemonade and some other summer drinks, and are indispensable in mint juleps. Mint flavor harmonizes with globe artichokes, but we have never found many uses for it in cooking. There is mint sauce for lamb, of course, though we don't care much for it. And we carry a recipe for Cold Mint Sauce* in Chapter 19, for use with cantaloupe.

Seed mint in spring or fall, in sun or part sun.

SUMMER SAVORY (Satureia hortensis)

An annual that grows no more than a foot high and often less, especially if it doesn't get the full sun it wants. It won't take hard cutting, either, and can die of heat or drought, but it is a nice herb and adds something to many vegetable and meat dishes, and particularly to eggs. It also goes well with beans and with the cabbage family. It has a perennial and hardier cousin, winter savory, considered less delicate in flavor. Seed summer savory in spring or fall, and winter savory in spring or summer. Both like full sun.

TARRAGON (Artemisia dracunculus)

A perennial (annual in cold climates) highly popular in Europe. This is a good culinary herb that finds a place in a great many dishes. We've found it very temperamental about where it grows but if it likes a spot it grows like a weed. It seems to prefer snuggling

its roots against a wall. It grows well for us in planters. Propagate
it by digging it up and pulling these roots apart in early spring, as
this species of tarragon rarely sets seed. Stem cuttings also root easily.
Tarragon combines well with many vegetables and is splendid with
chicken and in omelets.

THYME (*Thymus serpyllum*)

A perennial with various varieties. The culinary ones grow about
a foot tall but can be kept shorter by pruning to a neat bush shape.
Thyme is one of the nicest edging plants in our garden, and we
sometimes make borders of it along garden paths, interspersed with
pansies, chives, or heuchera. We grow two varieties of thyme, a
gray-leaved one that we suppose is a mutation of the vulgaris
variety, and lemon thyme, the citriodorus variety. Thyme grows
from seed, from cuttings, and from plant divisions. Cuttings root
so readily that when we prune the little plants in wet weather many
of the clipped stems that fall to the ground take root and make tiny
plants.

Seed thyme in spring or fall, in sun or part sun. It will get along
in any soil, we find, but doesn't want soggy ground, especially in
winter. Once you get it started, divide the plants each year or two
or they will get woody, like miniature trees, and won't bear many
leaves.

Thyme is a strongly flavored herb so use it with caution. We
usually chop any herb before adding it to a dish, but you can use
a sprig of thyme as a bouquet garni all by itself, unchopped, and
remove it when the dish is cooked. Thyme is good with beef, and
blends well with potatoes, beans, and in fact with most vegetables.

Harvesting

For eye appeal—and this applies to all herbs mentioned here—
a few sprigs, say of basil, oregano, rosemary, and parsley, in a
pottery sugar bowl or cream pitcher, make one of the most pleasing
little kitchen bouquets we know of.

The best way to harvest herbs for any purpose is with a pair of scissors. We much prefer fresh herbs, as our recipes show, and to chop them we use a cook's knife and a board.

However, to have herbs on hand when the plants are dormant, or are annuals out of season, you must preserve them in some way. We use three ways: Drying, freezing, and steeping to make a herb vinegar.

To Dry a Herb: Cut sprigs at any time but preferably before blooming is far along. Sprigs can be dried on trays outdoors in the shade in warm weather, or tied in bunches and hung indoors, but we prefer to dry them quickly. We rinse them, shake them, and dry them on cooky sheets in a 225-degree F. oven. The time depends on the size and moistness of the leaves; some will dry in 30 minutes and others take hours, but when they are crisp but still greenish, they are done. Don't powder them; just strip the leaves from the stems, which will shatter the leaves somewhat, and store them in small jars tightly capped. Rosemary, dill, thyme, and marjoram are exceptionally good keepers.

To Freeze a Herb: Rinse it, dry it by patting between paper towels, put it into a plastic bag, and thence to the freezer. We usually do this with basil, which we think dries poorly. It keeps for about a month frozen. Tarragon also holds its flavor when frozen.

To Make Herb Vinegar: Rinse the herb, shake it dry, and put it into a jar of lukewarm vinegar. A rough rule is: To 1 cup of vinegar, ¼ cup of the herb. You can increase the amount of the herb, and bruising the leaves first will help release the flavor. White vinegar is best; it doesn't have to be wine vinegar, though tarragon is usually steeped in it. You can also use leftover white dinner wine such as a sauterne. We keep the jar of vinegar in which the herb is steeping at room temperature and shake it several times during the steeping. You can let the herb remain in the vinegar, but with a small-leaved one such as thyme we find it more convenient to strain the vinegar off after about 3 weeks, to keep the leaves from getting into dishes where we don't want them.

Herbs that take well to steeping are basil, marjoram, mint, tarragon, and thyme.

RECIPES

In judging how much of a dried herb to use, compared with the same herb fresh, you must take into account how old the dried one is and how well it has been dried and stored. Our general rule is to use only ⅙ or ⅛ as much of the dried herb as the fresh one. This is less than most rules call for, but we are basing our practice on our own garden herbs, which may be stronger than commercially sold ones. When in doubt, smell or taste the dried herb to test its strength.

We think the use of herbs should be a matter of personal taste, and we hesitate to pass along such rules as a French custom of using four herbs with meat and poultry—parsley, chives, and two strong herbs such as oregano and thyme. Most herbs go well with other herbs as long as you don't let a strong herb dominate the others by using too much of it. Our own practice is to go by taste, sampling a little of the dish we plan to add a herb to, and then tasting the herb to see if the flavors will marry well. Very often the fragrance of each is sufficient to gauge compatibility.

There is a temptation to add too many herbs or too much of them to too many dishes, especially for someone just discovering herbs. Like liquor they should be handled with the understanding that too much is worse than none at all.

Since herbs occur in many of the recipes in this book, the only ones we'll give here are for a very handy aid to cooking, Parsley Butter*, and one from a friend for biscuits with herbs.

PARSLEY BUTTER

> 1 tablespoon finely chopped parsley
> 2 tablespoons butter

Work the parsley into the butter with a knife or spatula, on a plate, until the two are thoroughly blended. Some recipes call for parboiling the parsley first, but we don't do this. We often do add 2 or 3 drops of lemon juice while blending.

HERBS 239

You can store parsley butter in the refrigerator, wrapped in waxed paper, for several days. It is used to add flavoring, frequently late in the cooking procedure.

SASSY'S HERBED BISCUITS

The "Sassy" here is Mrs. Gordon Baker Lloyd of Sierra Madre, California. Mr. Lloyd is a well-known West Coast gardening authority. We give you the recipe as it was given to us:

"Use your favorite biscuit recipe, but instead of milk use tomato juice, and add ½ teaspoon of finely chopped fresh oregano."

Chapter 35

FRUITS

Growing your own fruit can become one of the most intriguing pastimes you ever imagined. One man found it so, and grew so interested in and knowledgeable about choicely good fruits that a nursery now makes a specialty of those he recommends. He is Mr. Robert A. Nitschke of Birmingham, Michigan, and the nursery is Southmeadow Fruit Gardens of Wabash, Indiana.

A few years ago the only fruit planting most home gardeners had space for was a strawberry bed. Today there are such productive new dwarf fruit trees on the market that if you have ground enough for a fair-sized vegetable garden—say 20 by 30 feet—you could turn it into a thrifty little orchard of 3 apple trees, 2 pears, a peach or cherry, and a border of strawberries. Or some other combination of fruits. As you probably know, the word "dwarf" when applied to fruits means only that the tree is smaller than a standard tree. A standard apple tree is 25 feet high or more, but a dwarf apple may grow to only 8 feet. The *fruit* borne by a dwarf tree, however, is as large as that on a standard tree; if anything, it is a little larger.

What could you expect to harvest from such dwarf trees? Well, there are dwarf apple trees that produce up to 6 bushels apiece. Counting on something less than this maximum, a dwarf orchard such as the one just suggested on a 20 by 30 plot could give you 500 pounds of fruit a season without even trying hard.

Ah—but what about the care of such an orchard? There is good news there, too. A great deal of progress in better and simpler controls of diseases and insects was made during and right after World War II. For the home fruit gardener the most significant single item is the development of new all-in-one sprays and dusts. Years ago we had in our farmhouse basement a 4-foot shelf devoted solely to various chemicals we mixed into sprays for the fruit trees. Today, one combination spray will do most of the job. Every garden center has such a spray or dust. The cost? About 35 cents or less per dwarf tree for an entire season. And you can apply it with the same sprayer or duster you use for your roses.

But perhaps you've heard that pruning fruit trees is tricky? Listen again: Most dwarf fruit trees are better off with very little pruning. Some home fruit gardeners never prune their trees.

This whole subject of growing fruit is covered in detail in our *Fruits for the Home Garden* (Morrow, 1968), also available to members of the American Garden Guild Book Club. It also describes a considerable number of varieties. Here are some suggestions for dwarf fruit tree varieties suitable for a small home planting:

APPLES: If we could plant only one, it would be Golden Delicious. And we'd select a so-called double-dwarf tree. "Double-dwarf" is the Stark Bro's Nurseries' name for a tree dwarfed both by a graft in the trunk and by a naturally dwarfed top that has more fruiting wood than is usual for the variety. Golden Delicious is one of several apples offered as a double-dwarf. It is an autumn apple and a good keeper, and also one of the few apples that will set fruit without another variety near for cross-pollination. McIntosh is a good late summer apple, and Jonathan follows it by 2 or 3 weeks. A very good new cross of a Jonathan type and a Red Delicious is Stark Jonalicious. It somewhat resembles the famous English dessert apple Cox's Orange Pippin.

Unless you live far enough north for the winter temperature to drop to about 10 degrees above zero, you may not be able to raise apples. There are exceptions, and a check with your county agricultural agent is a good idea here. Also, there is a new apple called Tropical Beauty that will get along even in Florida and Hawaii.

PEARS: Moonglow is a good new variety developed by the U. S. Department of Agriculture. It can be picked in mid-August in the Midwest. Bartlett comes along 2 weeks later, and Seckel 2 weeks after that. Bartlett and Seckel are good pears but since they can't pollinate each other, don't plant only the two of them if you are planting only two pears. Another fine one that will take care of this (and is one of the few pears that are self-pollinating) is Duchess, ripening in September. Comice is a splendid old French pear.

Note: With a pear, "ripening" means in most cases "maturing," which isn't the same thing. To ripen a pear, pick it when it will easily come off in your hand as you tilt it upward, then wrap it in soft paper and put it in a cool room for from a few days to a few weeks, depending on the variety.

PEACHES: Most peaches will set fruit without another variety nearby. Golden Jubilee is a good early peach, Elberta is a favorite mid-season one, and Belle of Georgia is an old-time and popular late ripener. One of the newest and most interesting dwarf peaches is Bonanza. It and related peach and nectarine trees developed by Armstrong Nurseries stay smaller than others and have an abundance of attractive leaves. They start bearing crops when only 2 or 3 feet tall.

CHERRIES: A practical choice for a small garden is a fairly new tart cherry, North Star. Like all tart cherries it needs no others nearby for cross-pollination. It is hardy, grows to 8 feet, and the fruit makes delicious pies. If you want sweet cherries, you need at least two varieties for cross-pollination. Van and Stark Gold would be good choices among the dwarfs.

PLUMS: Pollination is a particular concern with plums, so we suggest for the restricted planting a good and widely carried self-pollinating one called Stanley. It is a prune, which merely means it is a plum sweet enough to be dried if wished. For preserves, a Damson is hard to beat and is also self-pollinating.

STRAWBERRIES: One of the best home garden strawberries is Ozark Beauty. Instead of bearing for only a few weeks, it bears from June to frost in the Midwest, and the plants last 3 years or so instead of only one. Surecrop and Dunlap are good June-bearing strawberries. A June bearer is a strawberry that has a big crop approximately in June, the plants then being discarded and only the new ones that have grown from runners (stems that grow along the ground) saved for the next year. An everbearing strawberry has a crop in June or earlier, and another in the fall, and the plants are usually allowed to bear for 2 seasons. Ozark Beauty is a longer-useful exception here, and it also produces some berries throughout the summer. Most everbearers do not have runners, but Ozark Beauty does.

OTHER BERRIES: Raspberries and blackberries are good fruits for the home garden, very little trouble to take care of, and fast to bear. An excellent argument for growing them is the high price and poor quality of berries usually offered on the market. This is especially true of red raspberries, which are almost too delicate to be shipped.

An everbearing raspberry planted in the spring will give you a crop that fall, and will keep producing for about 10 years. If you don't have room to space a bed of plants the 5 or 6 feet they need between them, you might try using them as a background or border planting.

Red raspberries and blackberries make new plants by throwing up shoots from the roots. You can transplant these shoots (suckers). Black and purple raspberries make new plants by touching the tips of canes to the ground, where they take root. A spadeful of earth on such a tip at the end of the summer will help it root. You can cut it free from the mother plant the next spring and transplant it.

Like strawberries, raspberries come in everbearing and non-everbearing types. Everbearers have a small crop in midsummer and a bigger one in early fall. The others produce their entire crop in midsummer, over several weeks.

Pruning raspberries and blackberries consists mainly of cutting off at ground level the canes that have borne fruit. Do it right after you've gathered the crop, for simplest handling. Other than that, merely remove weak canes and prune the others back in the spring to about 4 feet, and clip a few inches off any lateral branches growing from these canes.

Canby is a good red raspberry and is almost thornless. Latham is also good, and September is a leading everbearer.

The best purple raspberry we know of is Sodus. We raised it and found it a tremendous producer.

A good black raspberry for sections with dry hot weather is Black Hawk. Another and very productive one is Starking Black Giant.

El Dorado is a good older blackberry, and Raven is a new one that looks good.

RECIPES

If it were not that a home fruit garden can give so much more fruit than anyone can keep up with, we'd recommend that everyone eat it all fresh. There are not many more delicious, colorful, healthy, and economical desserts. Few persons, we think, have sung the praises of fresh home-grown fruit with more feeling than an English epicure, Edward Bunyard. He has written of apples in a delightful little book, *The Anatomy of Dessert:* "A Blenheim is one of the very few fruits which may be slightly warmed to advantage, let us say to room-temperature. There is an added richness of flavour in such fruit, and for a cold winter's evening how admirable a dessert!"

And of cherries: "I have a deep compassion for our town dwellers who know so little of fruit at its best. How many of them have ever tasted a ripe cherry, one of those we gather on a July day, so full of juice and tender of skin . . . ? No, cherries at their best are for the garden owner."

On pears he is equally poetic. Celebrating the birth of the variety Comice, he wrote: "Here at last was the ideal realised, that perfect combination of flavour, aroma, and texture of which man had long dreamed."

We are carrying in this chapter a very good apple dish, the simple and delicious recipe we use for Peach Melba, and one for a pie that is adaptable to many fruits. In addition we thought you might like to know a little about drying fruit. This is a good way to keep fruit a long time in ordinary pantry storage and any kind of container, and dried fruit makes a convenient and nutritious in-between snack for everyone in the family. It used to be the practice to dry sliced fruit in the open air, strung on lines or even basted with thread to an old sheet. The oven is a faster and better drying agent.

To Dry Fruit

In general terms the best temperatures for drying are 125 to 160 degrees F. Start at 125, go up to 160, and finish at 150 degrees for apples, peaches, and pears. For plums, start at 130, go up to 165, and finish at 165 without reducing the temperature. For peaches and nectarines, start at 125, go to 175, and finish at 150. Home drying is far from an exact procedure, but if you divide the total time evenly between the temperatures given here, the results should be satisfactory.

Fruits may sour if starting temperatures are too low, or may ooze before drying if temperatures are much higher than those given here.

The time it takes to dry fruit differs with the fruit. We have dried apples in 10 hours, for instance, but the best guide is the appearance and feel of the dried fruit. It is finished when it feels pliable and dry to the touch.

Prepare apples for drying by peeling, coring, and cutting into ¼-inch slices. Prepare plums, peaches, and nectarines by splitting in half and removing stones. Prepare pears by first ripening them off the tree as previously described; then remove stems, split in half, or quarter, and remove cores.

Not everyone who dries fruit does it, but exposing the fruit to fumes from burning sulphur before drying is a safety measure. The sulphur is a disinfectant, and is also a bleach. Here is how you sulphur fruit:

Estimate the weight of the prepared fruit and for each pound of fruit put 1 teaspoon of sulphur on a piece of paper about half the size of this book page. Roll up the paper loosely and twist the ends shut. Now take the twist of sulphur and the fruit *outdoors*. This is important. Make a sulphuring box by inverting a barrel or a tight wooden box over a rack (or a series of racks) holding the prepared fruit, with the sulphur twist in a shallow metal pan on the ground and far enough below the racks so the fruit and burning sulphur won't touch each other. Finally, tilt the covering box or barrel, touch a match to the paper holding the sulphur, lower the cover, and time the sulphuring as shown below. The cover should be tight enough to keep all the fumes inside. Don't inhale them.

Sulphuring times: Apples: 30 minutes. Peaches and nectarines: 3 hours. Pears: 3 hours. Plums: 20–30 minutes.

APPLE CRISP

With tree-ripened, just-picked, crisp apples, this is a great dessert. With poor quality, soft apples, it is not worth making.

> 8 *or* 9 *large fresh apples, peeled and sliced*
> ½ *cup flour*
> 1 *cup brown sugar*
> 1 *teaspoon cinnamon*
> ½ *cup butter*

Arrange apples in a deep glass pie dish (about 2 inches deep and 9 across). Mix flour, sugar, and cinnamon together. Cut in butter until light and crumbly, and spread the mixture over apples, covering them evenly.

Bake about 30 minutes at 375 degrees F. When done, the juice should begin to bubble up through the topping. Equally delicious warm or cold, this is an ideal breakfast dessert. On a leisurely morning, serve it with thick cream for a topping. And with a pot of fresh coffee.

PEACH MELBA

With your own tree-ripened peaches and vine-ripened red raspberries you have the basic ingredients for the most elegant dessert we know, Peach Melba. The amounts given here are for 1 serving, so multiply by the number being served.

> ½ *tree-ripened peach*
> *About* ⅓ *cup red raspberry sauce*
> ½ *cup finest vanilla ice cream*

Peel peaches this way: Starting at the indentation at the stem end, cut with a sharp stainless steel knife down to the bottom tip and back up to the stem end on the other side. Gently pry the halves apart with the knife. Lift out seed. Again starting at the stem end, pull the skin down to the bottom end. If the peach is properly ripened, the skin will pull off easily and smoothly. After having peeled bushels of really ripe peaches in this way for canning we find few small annoyances more annoying than peeling a store-bought peach.

Raspberry Sauce

Make the raspberry sauce by heating barely to a simmer freshly picked raspberries and then putting them through a sieve. Add no water or sugar. Have this sauce and the peach halves at room temperature.

Put a peach half in a dessert dish, fill cavity to overflowing with the ice cream, and pour the sauce over it. *There* you have a dessert worthy of the great Melba for whom it was named.

When we have red raspberries to spare, we heat sauce made as above to the boiling point, pour it into hot sterilized half-pint jars, and seal. Then we can still make Peach Melba with later peaches. We use nothing but fresh peaches, and preferably use homemade ice cream.

UPSIDE-DOWN PIE

Here is a quick and easy way to make a fresh fruit pie guaranteed to have a crisp crust and a juicy filling. Made with your own tree-sweet ripe fruit, this will be a pie to remember and remember.

Spread a pie plate, preferably glass, with butter. Then sprinkle over it about ½ cup sugar, depending on the acidity of the fruit. Fill generously with fresh fruit, dot with butter, and again sprinkle sugar as needed. Lay a piecrust over the fruit and crimp it around the edge but don't press it to the pie plate.

Bake for 25 minutes at 400 degrees F. Remove from oven, invert a serving plate over the top of the pie, and turn the pie out upside down on the plate.

A decorative topping can be made with the trimmings from the crust in this way: Stack trimmings, with a little butter between each piece, roll out thinly, then cut shapes with a pie cutter or cooky cutter. Bake them on a cooky sheet until light brown, at the time the pie is baking. Arrange them on top of the filling immediately after pie is turned out on the serving plate.

Thinly sliced sharp Cheddar cheese is particularly good with apple pie. Heavy cream poured over an upside-down peach pie is delicious. On berry pies, a spoonful of sour cream is a nice touch.

Chapter 36

NUTS

Except for the hazelnut, which is shrubby, and the almond, most nut trees don't come in dwarf sizes like most fruit trees. Consequently they need more space than some home gardeners can give them. The other side of this coin is that you can buy perfectly good nuts. The biggest advantage of growing your own is the greater quantity you'll have of this delicious and highly nutritious food. You aren't likely to buy 100 pounds of paper-shell pecans each year but one tree can yield that harvest. And 4 or 5 bushels is a likely harvest from an English walnut or a hickory tree. These figures can run a great deal higher, and a mature black walnut tree can produce 30 or 40 bushels.

So if you have a large lawn and you'd like to have a big shade tree on it about 50 feet from the house, you might try a nut tree. We advise this distance because nut trees stain walks and buildings, and some nuts may be destructive if they fall on breakable things.

Nut trees take very little care. Most of them on home grounds never get fed or sprayed or pruned by the owners, though they can use some of each at times, but they go quietly on producing all the nuts they can.

The best news in recent years for nut tree growers was the introduction of an English walnut that can grow in cold-winter zones. Sold under various sub-variety or strain names, this is the Carpathian English walnut. All English walnuts are botanically *Juglans regia.* The Carpathian strain you are likely to find available is the Lake. The trees grow to 40 or 50 feet high.

Another advance in nut tree development during the past several years has been the appearance of paper-shell pecan trees that will

bear a crop in Northern states. Their secret is speed—they don't
need as long a growing season as pecans take in the South, where
life is more leisurely. Colby and Major are 2 varieties of these new
pecans. Nuts are about 1 inch thick and 1½ inches long. Those of
the Starking Hardy Giant variety average about 60 to the pound.
One pecan tree planted alone will usually produce nuts, though
having others near will increase the harvest from each.

Chinese chestnuts grow to about the size of standard apple trees
—big but not enormous—and are resistant to the blight that killed
off the old chestnuts.

There are hardy almond trees on the market now, generally adaptable to the regions where peaches thrive but a little more sensitive to cold winters and late spring frosts. Almonds are touchy
about pollination, needing 2 or more trees to the planting. Check this
point with the supplier if you buy trees, as varieties differ in cross-
pollination needs.

As to hazelnuts, the American species are most apt to succeed,
but the European, usually called a filbert, has better quality nuts.
Both need cross-pollination.

<h2 style="text-align:center">RECIPES</h2>

Ever notice how often a picture of a family room in a home
magazine or an advertisement will have in it a large wooden bowl
of assorted nuts with nutcracker invitingly near? In both our homes
when we were children there was always when in season a bowl of
nuts anyone was welcome to enjoy, and we still think it is a fine
idea. Nuts are convenient little foods, high in protein, high in
calories, but low on the cholesterol factor. They are good with an
apple or a few raisins, and just right for an after-school snack or a
little bite before going to bed on a chilly night.

You will find nuts used in some of our meat and vegetable
dishes but most of our nut crop has always gone into cookies. At our
house the cooky jar is a set of square metal refrigerator pans. We
try to keep a variety of cookies on hand. We store drop cookies in the
refrigerator in the dough stage—just enough in one package to bake
on a cooky sheet. Icebox cooky rolls are stored in the freezer. Bar
cookies, baked when mixed, are cut in the pan when cool and immediately wrapped with sheet plastic. We wrap each of the other

9. Tomatoes are one of the most rewarding vegetables a home gardener can grow, and the most popular one. A single heavy-bearing plant can produce dozens of fruits during a season that can last from midsummer to frost.

W. Atlee Burpee Co. photo

10. Herbs have decorative as well as culinary uses—and your own dried garden herbs can make welcome gifts at small cost.

Geo. W. Park Seed Co. photo

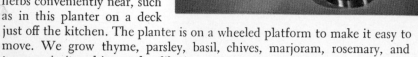

11. We like to keep a few herbs conveniently near, such as in this planter on a deck just off the kitchen. The planter is on a wheeled platform to make it easy to move. We grow thyme, parsley, basil, chives, marjoram, rosemary, and tarragon in it and in another like it.

12. A sweet pepper plant is an ornamental in its own right, especially when bearing its attractive fruits. The red ones here are the more mature. Some other varieties turn from green to yellow.

W. Atlee Burpee Co. photo

cookies in this way too when they have been baked and cooled, because it is a convenient way to serve them and they will keep almost indefinitely when wrapped and stored in the refrigerator in the metal pans.

Over the years we have tested many recipes for cookies, varying some to suit our own taste or available materials, as we have found that cookies make an ideal simple dessert. Served with coffee, at the table or in the living room or on the deck, they provide the right amount for each diner to choose for himself, they simplify serving, and they certainly reduce the dish washing afterward.

When we lived on the Mississippi Gulf Coast our own papershell pecans in one place we owned were young and barely coming into bearing, but we had a friend with a mature grove. He was happy to trade us pecans for help in picking up his crop. That winter we even fed the birds pecans, and the grove owner sold his surplus and still had heaps of pecans for the pralines he loved to make, one recipe for which he has given us for this chapter.

In Missouri we had black walnuts, hickory nuts, and hazelnuts. In California we have English walnuts and almonds. We find that most nuts can be interchanged in recipes, though each nut has a certain rightness for certain recipes. Black walnuts, for instance, have too heavy a flavor for many dishes but come into their own in rich chocolate cookies.

When we have no nut trees of our own we arrange with a grower for the amount we will need, and when they are ready he lets us know. In this way we know we are getting fresh nuts from a good clean crop, and the price is better. As soon as the nuts are well dried we shell most of them for storage.

With pecan and walnut kernels we ream out with the point of a sharp knife the part where the halves of the kernel join. This is where spoilage can start. Then we put the kernels in a large flat pan and put them in the oven at 140 degrees F. for 4 or 5 hours, shaking the pan every half hour.

Blanched Almonds

We blanch most almonds as soon as we shell them. Here is how to do it: Pour boiling water over shelled almonds, let stand 2 or 3 minutes, and then test one nut to see if the skin slips off. If so, drain the nuts, slip skins off quickly, pat skinned nuts dry on paper towels. Then put them in a large shallow pan and dry in the oven for 4 or 5 hours at 140 degrees F. Almonds tend to stick to the pan a little at first, so stir them about.

We store the almonds and other shelled nuts in the refrigerator in canning jars or coffee cans with plastic lids. At this moment we have English walnuts there that have been stored for 17 months, and they are fresh-tasting, sweet, and have an excellent color. It would never occur to us to buy our nuts in the small transparent bags you see in stores. Nuts are so good and so nutritious, they deserve the kind of handling we have just described, from harvesting to eating.

Chestnuts are handled differently from other nuts. They must be cooked, along with shelling. You do it this way:

Processed Chestnuts

Four steps are taken, in this order: 1. With a sharp knife make X-shaped gashes on the concave sides of the nuts, where there is air under the flexible shell. 2. Put nuts in a saucepan with enough cold water to cover them, bring water to a boil, and cook covered for 10 minutes. 3. Remove nuts one at a time from the water, peeling off shells and inner skins while the nuts are still warm. 4. Return the kernels to a saucepan of clean water, and cook over low heat for 20 minutes, or until kernels are tender. Drain and cool, and store in plastic bags in the refrigerator. The chestnut kernels keep for several weeks.

BOWKNOTS

The original version of this splendid recipe won first prize in the Pillsbury Company's first big bake-off several years ago under the name of No-knead Water-rising Twists. We do not use the water rising, and have made some minor adjustments in flavorings. We have found these sweet and delicate rolls a luncheon dish popular with both men and women.

½ cup shortening
¾ teaspoon salt

½ teaspoon vanilla
3 tablespoons sugar
½ cup scalded milk
½ teaspoon almond extract

Combine the above ingredients. Then stir in:

2 packages yeast mixed with ¼ cup lukewarm water

Add:

1½ cups sifted flour

Stir until well mixed, beat until smooth, then cover bowl and let rest for 15 minutes. Next, add one at a time, beating well after each addition:

3 eggs

Mix in thoroughly:

1½ cups sifted flour

The dough will be quite soft. Cover bowl and let rise for about 30 minutes in a warm place, 80 to 90 degrees.

Combine:

¾ cup chopped nuts (we prefer almonds)
½ cup sugar
1 teaspoon cinnamon

Divide dough into about 2 dozen small pieces with a tablespoon. Roll each piece in the sugar-nut mixture, stretching dough about 8 inches long and twisting into bowknot shape. Place the bowknots on 2 greased cooky sheets measuring 14 by 17 inches. Let bowknots stand for 5 minutes. Then bake 12 to 15 minutes at 375 degrees F. (We divide the sugar-nut mixture in half so the first cooky sheet of bowknots doesn't use it all.)

NUT-CHOCOLATE THINS

1 cup butter
1 cup brown sugar
1 egg yolk
1 teaspoon vanilla
2 cups sifted flour
1 (12-ounce) package semi-sweet chocolate bits
1 cup very finely chopped pecans

Cream butter and brown sugar until very light. Add egg yolk and vanilla, and beat until smooth. Blend in flour to a smooth paste, and spread it on a 14- by 17-inch cooky sheet. This is a rather tedious procedure, so give yourself enough time, and don't leave any bare spots on the sheet as you work the paste to each edge of the sheet. Bake for 20 minutes in a 250-degree F. oven.

Remove from oven and sprinkle the chocolate bits evenly over the baked layer. Return to oven for 2 or 3 minutes, then remove, and smooth the chocolate, to cover the entire bottom layer.

Sprinkle the chopped nuts evenly over the chocolate and return the sheet to the oven for a final 2 or 3 minutes while the nuts sink into the warm chocolate. Cool, and cut into bars about 1 inch wide and 1½ inches long.

If you cover the cooky sheet evenly each time, this makes a thin, crisp, and superb cooky. The recipe will make about 12 dozen.

OATMEAL MACAROONS

Here is a recipe for cookies a young mother who was a professional dietitian likes to keep in the cooky jar. It is a wholesome tidbit, and also good for anyone on a flour-free diet.

⅔ cup sugar
⅔ cup butter
3 cups quick-cooking (1 minute) rolled oats
1 egg, well beaten
1 teaspoon almond extract
½ cup chopped nuts (we prefer almonds)

Cream sugar and butter until very light. Stir in rolled oats, then the rest of the ingredients, until completely blended. This will make a rather dry mixture.

Pinch off small pieces, about the size of walnuts; place on buttered cooky sheet and flatten by criss-crossing with a fork. Bake for 10 minutes at 350 degrees F., until just light brown on the bottom. Do not overcook.

LAYERED NUT BARS

There are probably more variations of this recipe than there are cures for hiccups, but here is the one we find most popular.

½ cup butter
½ cup brown sugar (optional[1])
1 cup sifted flour

Cream butter and sugar until light, add flour and beat smooth. Spread in a 9- by 12-inch pan, working dough about ½ inch up the sides of the pan. Leave no bare spots in the bottom. Bake 10 minutes at 375 degrees F. Meanwhile, combine:

3 eggs, beaten
2 tablespoons flour
½ teaspoon salt
1½ cups chopped English walnuts
1½ cups brown sugar
½ teaspoon baking powder
1 teaspoon vanilla

Spread this mixture evenly over the baked cake when it is done. Return to oven for 20 minutes, or until brown. Cool in pan.

---

[1] Including the brown sugar gives a cooky-type base. Using the flour and butter alone will make a pastry base.

When cool, ice the cake with this mixture stirred well:

> 1½ cups confectioners' sugar
> 2 tablespoons grated orange rind
> 1 tablespoon lemon juice
> 1 tablespoon orange juice
> 1 teaspoon almond extract

Chill and cut into bars.

PRALINES

We offer this recipe through the kindness of our friend Mr. Ivan N. Anderson of Pass Christian, Mississippi. The amount of flavoring extract varies according to individual taste. About 1 teaspoon would suit most persons.

> 1½ cups light brown sugar
> ½ cup evaporated milk
> ½ teaspoon butter
> Salt
> Maple, rum, almond, or vanilla extract
> 1 cup pecan halves

Put all ingredients except extract and pecans into a heavy saucepan and stir until sugar is dissolved. Then cook over low heat until the soft-ball stage is reached, 236 to 238 degrees F. Remove from heat, allow to cool for a few minutes, stir in the flavoring, and then beat vigorously until the mixture begins to thicken. This is important. If it becomes too stiff, stir in 1 teaspoon lukewarm water.

Fold in the pecans, then drop the mixture by spoonfuls on waxed paper spread on a cold surface. Wrap pralines immediately in foil or sheet plastic.

CHESTNUT OMELET

We fixed this omelet for breakfast one New Year's Day and liked it so well we include it here. We served it with broiled ham

and with sprigs of cress for garnish. Pecans and English walnuts
also combine well with eggs.

2 tablespoons butter
4 Processed Chestnuts*, thinly sliced
3 large eggs
2 tablespoons cream
Salt

Melt butter in omelet pan or Teflon skillet over medium heat,
and drop chestnut slices in. While they are cooking, beat eggs
well, beat in cream, and pour this mixture into the pan, seeing
that the chestnuts are well distributed over pan bottom first. Cover
pan and cook until omelet is slightly puffy but still glossy. Season lightly with salt, remove from heat, and fold into a half circle. Serve at once. *Serves 2.*

Chapter 37

SAUCES

Several sauce recipes are carried in other chapters, and we list them at the end of this one. Here, we take up six other sauces, a special mayonnaise, and our version of French dressing. We use sauces a good deal but we keep them as simple as we can. We have two reasons for this. One is that garden vegetables do not need the help from a sauce that store vegetables often do. The other reason for simplicity in sauces is to save time. We don't think a sauce should require the attention an entire dinner may need, or should call for twenty different operations.

On the other hand we think canned sauces lack character and are expensive. We prefer to make most sauces when we need them, with the exception of the mayonnaise and French dressing. And we think one sauced dish per meal is usually enough, though we don't count salad dressing.

Making a sauce is sometimes a last-minute thing, and if your dinner guests are like ours you may find them leaning over your shoulder at the range as you do the sauce. In such case, try this: Ahead of time, line up the ingredients for the sauce *in the order in which you'll use them*. Then all you have to do is reach, leaving your mind free for conversation.

Although we carry no recipe for it, we often make a simple sauce by merely cooking down the liquids left after preparing certain dishes. For a change from flour-thickened sauces, this has its points. If the dish will accept it, a spoonful of cognac, dry vermouth, or sherry in such a sauce can be a sprightly addition.

BECHAMEL SAUCE

There are as many ways to make Béchamel Sauce as there are cooks. At bottom it is what most diners think of as a white sauce or cream sauce. In other words, it is a basic sauce you can add to and vary as you wish. Here is the way we make it, this recipe making 1 generous cupful.

3 tablespoons butter
1 shallot, finely chopped
½ small garden-fresh carrot, finely chopped
½ teaspoon finely chopped thyme
1 teaspoon finely chopped parsley
2 tablespoons flour
½ cup Kraft Stock*
½ cup evaporated milk
Salt
Pepper
Grated nutmeg

Melt butter, add shallot, carrot, thyme, and parsley. Cook over low heat for 5 minutes. Stir in flour, cooking until the mixture bubbles. Add stock and milk, turn up heat to medium, and stir until sauce thickens. Remove pan from heat and add seasonings. Only a little nutmeg is needed. Traditionally this sauce is strained before use, but you don't have to do so.

MORNAY SAUCE

This very useful sauce is one of the most frequent variations of Béchamel. To make it, simply add grated cheese to Béchamel Sauce*. Either Parmesan or Romano cheese is usually used. Grated Swiss, Monterey Jack, or Cheddar is sometimes favored. It is a matter of taste, availability, and harmony with the dish the sauce is to dress.

A good proportion is: 3 or 4 tablespoons of cheese to 1 cup of Béchamel. Additional cheese is often sprinkled over the sauced dish, which is then sometimes put under the broiler to melt and brown the topping lightly just before serving.

PEKIN SAUCE

> ½ teaspoon dry mustard
> ½ teaspoon sugar
> 2 teaspoons cornstarch
> 1 tablespoon soy sauce
> ¾ cup Kraft Stock*

Mix the first 3 ingredients together. Stir in soy sauce. Add this mixture to the stock in a saucepan and cook over medium heat, stirring, until the sauce thickens. Figure on getting a good ⅔ cup of sauce.

GREEN SAUCE

We often use this sauce over sliced chicken we are heating in a casserole, and it makes a fine topping for such vegetables as kohlrabi, carrots, celeriac, and turnips. This recipe will make about 1 cup of sauce. When tarragon and basil are out of season, we use 2 teaspoons of thyme, which is ⅓ the amount of the others.

> 2 tablespoons butter
> 2 tablespoons flour
> ¾ cup Kraft Stock*
> 2 tablespoons dry white wine
> Salt
> Pepper
> ⅛ teaspoon sugar
> 4 tablespoons finely chopped parsley
> 1 tablespoon finely chopped tarragon
> 1 tablespoon finely chopped basil
> 5 stalks chives, finely chopped
> ½ teaspoon soy sauce

Melt butter, stir in flour over low heat for a minute. Add stock and wine, turn up heat, and stir continuously until mixture thickens.

Lower heat, add other ingredients, and cook for a few more minutes, stirring. This is a medium-thick sauce that thickens a little more when used as topping for an open casserole or for a Divan*.

SAUCE BERCY

This famous sauce is especially good with fish but we have found it an interesting accompaniment to chicken and to some vegetables. There are many recipes for it. This is one we worked out to suit our own taste. It can be made in advance and reheated when wanted. The recipe makes about ½ cup.

    2 shallots, finely chopped
    ⅓ cup dry vermouth
    2 tablespoons jelled drippings from roast chicken
    2 tablespoons butter
    ½ teaspoon lemon juice
    1 teaspoon finely chopped parsley
    Salt

Put shallots and vermouth into saucepan and cook over medium-low heat, tilting pan now and then, until the vermouth is cooked down to about half. Stir in the jelled drippings until melted. Remove pan from heat and add the rest of the ingredients. Reheat just to the simmer stage immediately before serving.

SHALLOT SAUCE

This sauce is excellent over broiled fish, steamed broccoli, broiled eggplant, or a Divan*. The recipe yields about 2 cups.

    2 tablespoons finely chopped shallots
    2 tablespoons white wine vinegar
    3 tablespoons butter
    3 tablespoons flour
    1½ cups Kraft Stock*
    1 tablespoon finely chopped parsley
    1 tablespoon finely chopped tarragon

Put shallots and vinegar into a saucepan and cook over low heat until vinegar is almost all evaporated. Remove shallots to a dish for the time being, and melt butter in the pan. Stir in flour, stirring until it is barely brown. Add stock and cooked shallots, increase heat to medium, and stir until sauce thickens. Remove from heat, stir in herbs, and serve at once.

SHALLOT MAYONNAISE

Try using this mayonnaise next time you make stuffed eggs. It will be a revelation. It also makes a beautiful spread for club sandwiches and goes well with most cold meats. The recipe yields about 1½ cups.

1 egg
1 tablespoon white wine vinegar
1 tablespoon lemon juice
¼ teaspoon salt
1 teaspoon finely chopped basil
1 teaspoon finely chopped marjoram
⅛ teaspoon pepper
¼ teaspoon dry mustard
½ teaspoon honey
2 shallots, peeled
¼ cup Garlic Oil*
¼ cup corn oil
½ cup olive oil

Put everything but the corn oil and olive oil into a blender and run at medium speed for 10 seconds. Add the other oils ¼ cup at a time, running blender until well mixed, and pushing mixture down from sides of jar with a rubber spatula between runs. Store in refrigerator. It will keep for weeks.

HERBED FRENCH DRESSING

2 sprigs marjoram
¼ teaspoon salt
¼ teaspoon dry mustard

1 *tablespoon lemon juice*
1 *tablespoon white wine vinegar*
2 *tablespoons Garlic Oil**
2 *tablespoons olive oil*
4 *tablespoons corn oil*

Bruise the marjoram with your fingers and put it and all the other ingredients into a jar with a tight lid. Shake well. Discard marjoram before using the dressing. This recipe makes about ⅔ cup of dressing, and if kept longer than 2 or 3 days, it should be stored in the refrigerator.

Here are some other sauces and dressings, and the chapters in which they can be found:

Caesar Salad Dressing (Chapter 18)
Cold Mint Sauce (Chapter 19)
Horse-radish Sauces (Chapter 16)
Vinaigrette Sauce (Chapter 4)
Wilted Lettuce Dressings (Chapter 18)
Raspberry Sauce (Chapter 35)

Chapter 38

SOUPS AND STOCKS

KRAFT STOCK

Many recipes in this book call for Kraft Stock. This is our version of chicken stock and we keep it on hand at all times. When we trim the bones of a roasted or broiled chicken we unjoint them and store in the freezer until we have enough to make a pot of stock. The difference between our procedure from this point, and that of most recipes we know of, is the scant amount of liquid we use. This makes a stock that jells and is easier to store and more satisfactory to use because its flavor is more intense. Consequently, we often cut this stock with a vegetable stock to make the total liquid called for.

In making the stock we always add lemon juice or vinegar, which dissolves calcium from bones and makes a better stock as well as shortening cooking time. We also refrain from skimming the stock. You will find that stock made in this way makes a fine glaze.

KRAFT STOCK

> *Bones from 4 chicken breasts or 2 roast chickens*
> *2 cups liquid (water or Vegetable Stock*)*
> *1 tablespoon lemon juice, or 1 teaspoon vinegar*

Put ingredients in large saucepan, bring to a boil, cook covered over very low heat 3 or 4 hours, pushing bones down and stirring gently halfway through, and adding ½ cup more liquid if needed during last hour.

Strain remaining liquid into bowl. Store in refrigerator in 1-cup
jelly glasses. The fat that rises to the top will form a seal. The
recipe yields about 2 cups of stock.

HAM STOCK

When we finish with a ham we break the bone at the joint
and make a stock as in the preceding recipe. We reserve this ham
stock for cooking beans. A tablespoon of it is excellent for brais-
ing snap beans, and ham stock is a necessity for any dried bean
dish we make, as in Minestrone*. Remember that ham stock is
salty, so taste before you add salt to a recipe using it.

BEEF STOCK

Since leaving our farm we buy more boneless beef than otherwise, so we don't usually have beef stock on hand. With leftover bones, the procedure is the same as for chicken or ham bones.
When we make a quantity of beef-vegetable soup we buy a meaty
soup bone, cook it for a day, trim the meat and store it, put
the stock through a strainer and chill overnight. Next day we remove the fat, add Vegetable Stock* to make the total amount of
liquid wanted, and put in the vegetables to cook. We add the
meat, cut into pieces, during the last 30 minutes of cooking.
We think the best beef-vegetable soups are made in early fall
when hearty-flavored vegetables are at their peak. Tomatoes, corn,
okra, snap beans, onions, parsley, carrots, and potatoes can make
a memorable soup. And include a cubed turnip. Incidentally, when
we are freezing vegetables and don't have enough of any one to
fill a last container, we put several in one, and label it "Soup
Mix," for winter use in a robust beef-vegetable soup.

VEGETABLE STOCK

In the interests of nutrition and flavor we often use vegetable
stock in place of water. We usually do so when parboiling. In
each such case we drain and save the stock for another use, and

this seems so natural a pattern that we have not taken the space
to say so in each recipe. We keep such a jar of stock in the
refrigerator. It gets used up in making sauces or soups, or as
liquid added to a casserole, so we must keep replacing it. One
way to do so is to save the water in which vegetables are cooked,
except unpared ones such as potatoes. Another way is to cook
vegetables for the purpose of making stock, using surplus or coarser
parts you are not serving. To do so, add about 1 cup of water
to 2 cups of the chopped vegetable and simmer in a saucepan
with the lid on for an hour. We cook this until the vegetables
can be mashed. After mashing, we drain off the liquid, also pressing it from the mashed pulp. We do not season this stock, as
this would show up in any dish where it was used.

Parboiling in such stock does not affect the flavor of the vegetable being parboiled. It is the other way around—the vegetable
flavors the stock. A white vegetable, however, may pick up some
color from a stock.

MYSTERY SOUP

We call this Mystery Soup because the mystery is where the
leftovers went. The amounts given here will serve 2 persons a
nutritious, quick, and most economical luncheon.

> 2 tablespoons butter
> ½ cup Croutons*
> 1 cup leftover casserole dish (such as Rice Pilaf*,
>   Tomato-Onion Casserole*, etc.)
> ½ cup Kraft Stock*
> ½ cup Vegetable Stock*
> 1 large can evaporated milk

Melt butter in a saucepan and brown Croutons lightly in it. Remove Croutons and set aside to keep warm.

Put the cup of leftover dish in the saucepan, stir well over
medium heat, add both stocks, and blend by mashing with a
potato masher until mixture is smooth. Reduce heat to low and
cook for 10 minutes. Then add milk slowly, stirring. Bring just

to a simmer and serve at once, in warm bowls, topped with the Croutons.

The combinations of leftovers are of course endless, and the jelled stock and milk give a smooth texture, with the Croutons offering a crisp variation.

VICHYSSOISE

This well-known leek and potato soup is usually served cold, but we almost always serve it hot, especially on a cold, wet, miserable day.

4 tablespoons butter
4 medium-sized leeks
1 onion, or 4 scallions, chopped
4 medium-sized potatoes, peeled and chopped
2 cups Vegetable Stock*
2 cups Kraft Stock*
1 large can evaporated milk
1 tablespoon finely chopped parsley

Melt butter in heavy saucepan. Slice leeks thinly, using part of the tender green tops. Stir in these and onions, then potatoes and Vegetable Stock. Cover pan and cook over medium heat until vegetables are quite soft, about 15 minutes.

Instead of next using a blender, as is often done, or a sieve, we pulp the vegetables with a potato masher (ours has a flat circular bottom made in a grid pattern, and efficiently reaches anywhere in the saucepan bottom). When vegetables are well mashed, add Kraft Stock, blending it by continuing to mash for a minute or so. Then bring soup to a boil, reduce heat, stir in milk slowly, and continue stirring until soup begins to simmer. Remove from heat, put the lid on saucepan, and let soup stand 2 or 3 minutes before serving. Warm the bowls, and sprinkle a little parsley over each serving. *Serves 4.*

Made in this way, both cooking time and clean-up time are shortened, and using evaporated milk gives a velvety texture.

BORSCH

In this Russian vegetable soup made with meat stock, you can vary the kinds of vegetables to suit your taste, or according to what the garden is supplying at the time. Be sure to include beets and cabbage, however. The beets are not pre-cooked for this recipe.

> *2 cups coarsely chopped beets*
> *½ cup coarsely chopped carrots*
> *1 cup chopped onions*
> *1 cup chopped snap beans*
> *1 cup coarsely chopped cabbage*
> *1½ cups Vegetable Stock**
> *1½ cups Kraft Stock**
> *Sour cream*

Put all the vegetables into a saucepan with the Vegetable Stock and bring to a boil, covered. Reduce heat to medium-low and cook for about 20 minutes, until vegetables are soft enough for you to mash them as in the Vichyssoise* recipe.

Add Kraft Stock, continuing to mash while blending it. Reduce heat to low, cover pan again, and cook for 10 minutes. To serve, warm the bowls, and float a little island of sour cream on top of each bowl of soup. A slice of lemon can be used instead, but the cream is better, and makes an attractive contrast with the beautiful rose-red soup. *Serves 4.*

MINESTRONE

With a vegetable garden to call on, you can make a feast of this fine, full-bodied Italian soup. Serve it with Sourdough Bread*.

Soak overnight in enough water to cover them:

> *2 cups dried beans, any kind*

Next morning, cook beans over low heat until just tender, adding a little more water if needed.

In a large skillet, put:

>2 tablespoons olive oil
>2 large onions, chopped
>1 clove garlic, finely chopped

Cook slowly until onions are translucent. Then add:

>2 large tomatoes, peeled and chopped
>3 tablespoons finely chopped parsley
>1 teaspoon finely chopped basil
>1 teaspoon finely chopped oregano or marjoram

Cook for 10 minutes, then add contents of skillet to the beans. Next, add these ingredients to the beans:

>5 scallions, chopped
>1 cup chopped cabbage, preferably Savoy
>1 cup chopped snap beans
>2 zucchini squash, cut in ½-inch cubes
>1 carrot, cut in ¼-inch cubes
>1 large potato, cut in ½-inch cubes
>½ cup shelled peas
>1 cup Ham Stock*
>2 quarts Vegetable Stock*

Cook soup about 2 hours, covered, until vegetables are tender and flavors blended. Then cook separately until tender, in salted boiling water as directed on package:

>1 cup pasta in an attractive shape: shells, bows, etc.

Drain pasta. Stir it gently into the soup. Serve in hot bowls topped with grated Parmesan or Romano cheese.

SALAD SOUP

This is an almost-miracle dish for luncheon on a blistering hot day, guaranteed to cool and soothe while it nourishes.

Early in the morning while the dew is still on the garden, gather cucumbers, radishes, scallions, zucchini squashes, chives, a Jerusalem artichoke or two, and some very ripe tomatoes. Wash them and put them to chill in your refrigerator's vegetable compartment. Also chill the soup bowls you will use.

A few minutes before serving time, cut the vegetables into easily handled and attractive pieces right into the separate bowls. In this way the combinations can be altered to suit individual tastes if wished.

The Jerusalem artichokes add a crisp, nut-like flavor, and the vine-ripened tomatoes provide juice enough to permit eating the soup with a spoon. Season with salt and pepper to taste.

Chapter 39

CASSEROLES, ETC.

This chapter covers several dishes that have become favorites with us but did not seem to fall naturally into other chapters.

In mentioning the baking dish called a casserole in other chapters, we have occasionally specified "an enameled metal casserole." This was done in cases where the timing was based on the superior conduction of heat by metal as compared to glass or ceramics. We tend to favor enameled metal casseroles but we have used all kinds with satisfaction. A familiarity with your own utensils and appliances frees you to read any recipe's time/temperature factor in terms of your own needs.

One appeal of such dishes as are covered in this chapter is that most can be prepared ahead, and so save time when time is short. In our eyes an even stronger appeal is the subtle harmony that emerges when flavors intertwine.

We don't often use rice, but we carry a recipe for a pilaf here and rice appears in two other recipes that follow. We have noticed that when it comes to boiling rice, everybody feels about his particular method the same way everybody does about his own sense of humor: It's excellent. One cook assured us the only way is to bring the water to a boil, then let the pan stand over the stove's pilot light all day. Another puts the rice in the oven after boiling it soft. A Chinese friend still buys her rice by the 100-pound sacks because it gives her a feeling of security after experiencing famine scarcity in China when she was young, and she has a cooking method based on a careful measurement of the water, as nearly as we can recall. We didn't pay much attention because we seldom boil rice anyway. We fry it, according to another friend, who had been an Idaho camp cook in his youth and fried everything but coffee. Whatever it is, the recipe for Rice Pilaf* that follows is a way to make a delicious rice dish providing you also have a selection of fresh garden vegetables to put in it.

RICE PILAF

The measurements of the vegetables here are approximate. In practice, we take what is choice and plentiful at the time in the garden, and shift proportions to suit. This dish is superb with broiled lamb, whether the lamb is in the form of chops or budget-priced lamb breast. Another good combination is with a steak broiled on the patio, and the casserole can be ready ahead of time, for easier entertaining.

> 2 cups Kraft Stock*
> 2 cups Vegetable Stock*
> 8 tablespoons butter
> 2 cups long-grained rice
> ½ cup chopped celery heart
> 1 cup ¼-inch cubes carrots
> ¾ cup chopped scallions
> ½ cup finely chopped parsley
> 1 cup coarsely chopped English walnuts
> Salt

Put a large, heavy casserole in a 375-degree F. oven to heat through. Bring the stocks to a boil in a saucepan while butter is melting in a large heavy skillet over medium-high heat. When butter is bubbling hot, add rice and stir constantly until rice browns lightly, about 7 or 8 minutes.

Working quickly, put rice into the *hot* casserole, add the *boiling* stocks, cover casserole, and return to oven for 30 minutes.

Then add the rest of the ingredients, stirring them in with a fork to fluff rice. Cover and return to oven for 30 more minutes. This dish can be reheated if wished. Stir it well with a fork before doing so. *Serves 6 to 8.*

CHICKEN GUMBO

This dish can be made a soup by adding more stock and cooking the rice in the same pot. We prefer the dish as an entrée, the rice being cooked separately. A stewing hen comes into its own here, adding flavor to a flavorful main course. Note: the okra must be young and garden-fresh. We make this dish only when we are where we can grow okra.

Flour
1 chicken, cut up
4 tablespoons bacon drippings
2 cups Vegetable Stock*
3 large tomatoes, peeled and coarsely chopped
1 cup sliced okra
½ cup chopped scallions
1 teaspoon file powder[1]
Salt
Cooked rice

Put flour in a bag and shake the chicken in it, 2 or 3 pieces at a time. Melt bacon drippings in a heavy stew pan and lightly brown chicken in it. Add the stock, cover pan, and cook over low heat for 3 hours or until chicken is tender.

Remove and bone chicken, and set aside to keep warm. Add to the pan the tomatoes, okra, and scallions. Cover and cook over medium heat for 20 minutes. Season with file powder and salt. Add the chicken meat, heat through, and serve on a hot platter surrounded by rice. *Serves 4.*

ARROZ CON POLLO

This is another recipe from our friend Mr. Jerome Kantor, whose wife brought it from her homeland, Costa Rica. Mr. Kantor has cooked it for us and we have prepared it several times since. We always brown the chicken first in the oil, on top of the stove,

[1] File powder is made from sassafras; it adds an authentic Southern touch, though it is not indispensable.

then finish cooking in the oven while the rest of the dish is done as described here.

> *¼ cup olive oil*
> *4 cloves garlic, very finely chopped*
> *1 medium-sized onion, chopped*
> *1 green pepper, chopped*
> *2 cups rice*
> *1 frying chicken, 3 to 4 pounds, cut up*
> *Salt*
> *Pepper*
> *2 cups coarsely chopped green olives*
> *½ cup capers*
> *12 whole cloves*
> *Water*
> *1 cup shelled peas*

Bring oil to a simmer in a large skillet, add garlic, onion, and green pepper. Cook for a few minutes, then add rice, chicken, salt, and pepper. Simmer, shaking pan now and then, until rice is golden.

Add olives, capers, cloves, and water to cover. Put lid on and cook over medium heat until chicken is tender.

Add peas and cook for 10 more minutes. Serve at once, or put into oven for 10 minutes if you want a drier rice and if your skillet is oven-proof. *Serves 4.*

DIVAN

So far as we know, the name "Divan" for this kind of a built-up main course comes from a New York restaurant, Divan Parisien. We used to eat there when we lived in New York, and considered it one of the best places there to dine. The restaurant's version of the sauce was, we believe, a blend of two others, with additions, but for home cooking with garden vegetables, Béchamel Sauce* is delightfully adequate. The vegetable in a Divan is a matter of choice. We suggest asparagus here, but garden-fresh Belgian endive or broccoli are other good choices. Breast of chicken is probably the ideal meat but here again it is a matter of taste. We often add ham to the chicken. See Chapter 4, "Asparagus," for how to cook the asparagus here.

24 cooked asparagus spears
Salt
2 cups Béchamel Sauce*
Sliced chicken sufficient to serve 4
½ cup grated Romano cheese

Arrange asparagus in 1 or 2 layers in a shallow baking-serving dish, season very lightly with salt, and pour over it ½ cup of the sauce. Place the chicken on top, cover with the rest of the sauce, and sprinkle over it the grated cheese. Heat in a 300-degree F. oven until sauce bubbles. Brown cheese lightly under the broiler and serve at once. Be careful the cheese does not burn. *Serves 4.*

BEEF RAGOUT

There is a great deal of variation in ragouts. Basically they are well-flavored stews using wine and stocks in place of water. This version of ours makes a good company meal and can be prepared ahead except for the addition of turnips and carrots and the lacing with cognac, which should be done during the reheating, in that case.

2 pounds beef, cut into 1-inch cubes
½ cup dry red wine
½ pound pork sausage
1 tablespoon flour
½ teaspoon salt
¼ teaspoon pepper
¼ teaspoon sugar
1 cup Kraft Stock*
1 onion, chopped
2 tomatoes, coarsely chopped
1 clove garlic
1 bay leaf
2 whole cloves
2 sprigs parsley
1 sprig thyme
6 carrots, cut into ½-inch slices
4 medium-large turnips, cut into ½-inch chunks
1 tablespoon cognac

Put beef into bowl, pour wine over, and marinate 2 hours, stirring several times.

Cook sausage in stew pan, breaking it up with a fork. Add beef, brown over medium-high heat, stir in flour, salt, pepper, sugar. Add stock, onion, and tomatoes. Tie garlic, bay leaf, cloves, parsley, and thyme in a 6-inch square of muslin, and nestle this bouquet garni in pan. Cover and cook over low heat 2 to 4 hours. Halfway through, add the marinade wine, and 15 minutes before serving, add carrots and turnips. Immediately before dishing up, remove bouquet garni and stir in cognac. *Serves 4.*

VEGETABLE-MEAT LOAF

We have made this meat loaf with various combinations of meats, including venison once when we were marooned by a flood. We find the beef and pork sausage a good accompaniment to the vegetables, and if the sausage is strongly seasoned we omit the poultry seasoning. If baked in 2 small loaf pans, one of these little meat loaves makes a nice hot or cold main course to include in the Visiting Gift Box* described in Chapter 2.

1 tablespoon Garlic Oil*
8 scallions, chopped
¼ cup Vegetable Stock*
2 medium-sized carrots, finely chopped
1 stalk celery, finely chopped
1 teaspoon poultry seasoning
Salt
Pepper
2 tablespoons bourbon whisky
1 cup Croutons*
1 pound ground beef (chuck)
½ pound pork sausage
1 egg, slightly beaten

Heat Garlic Oil in skillet and cook scallions over low heat 2 or 3 minutes. Add stock, carrots, and celery, cover skillet, and cook over medium heat for 5 minutes. Remove from heat and stir in the rest of the ingredients with a fork, blending well. Form into a loaf to fit a loaf pan, and bake for 60 minutes at 350 degrees F. *Serves 4.*

TURNIP CHICKEN CASSEROLE

With fresh garden turnips the combination here with the delicate flavor of chicken is very fine—but the turnips must be garden-fresh. The chicken meat we use is that which is left over from a roast chicken or from broiled chicken breasts.

> 2 cups Vegetable Stock*
> 2 large carrots, cut into ⅛-inch slices
> 2 medium-sized turnips, cut into ½-inch cubes
> 3 stalks celery, cut on the bias in ¼-inch slices
> 3 cups sliced cooked chicken
> 4 tablespoons butter
> 4 large mushrooms, sliced
> 3 tablespoons flour
> ½ cup Kraft Stock*
> Salt
> Pepper
> ½ cup Blanched Almonds*, slivered

Bring Vegetable Stock to a boil in a saucepan, add carrots, turnips, and celery, cover pan, and cook over medium heat for 5 minutes. Drain, reserving ½ cup stock. Put vegetables in a casserole and arrange chicken over them.

Melt butter, cook mushrooms in it over medium heat 3 or 4 minutes, remove mushrooms, and arrange them on chicken slices. To remaining butter, add flour, stirring over medium heat. Add the ½ cup of reserved vegetable stock and all the rest of the ingredients except almonds. Stir until thick, pour over ingredients in casserole, sprinkle almonds over the top and bake, uncovered, for 20 minutes at 300 degrees F. *Serves 4.*

TOMATO-ONION CASSEROLE

We don't remember where the original of this recipe came from but we have been making the casserole ever since World War II, when it was a highly appreciated dish in a food-stamp-cramped cuisine. We had to make do with less butter then, but the recipe's simplicity admits of few changes. When tomatoes are out of season, home-canned ones will do. This dish will keep for several days in the refrigerator after cooking, and is good either hot or cold.

2 *large onions*
4 *large tomatoes*
Salt
Pepper
Butter
*Croutons**

Cut onions in ⅛-inch slices and tomatoes in ¼-inch slices. Place a layer of tomatoes in a casserole and a layer of onions on it. Sprinkle with salt and pepper, and dot generously with butter. Repeat layers until tomatoes and onions are used up. Spread Croutons over the top, dot with butter, and bake covered for 60 minutes at 325 degrees F. *Serves 4.*

JERUSALEM ARTICHOKE CHICKEN

This is a spendid way to use leftover chicken. We broil chicken breasts and use what is left in this way the next day.

2 *tablespoons corn oil*
½ *cup Blanched Almonds* or English walnuts, slivered*
4 *Jerusalem artichokes, parboiled and scraped*
2 *shallots, finely chopped*
4 *large mushrooms, chopped*
2 *inside stalks celery, chopped*
3 *cups slices or chunks cooked chicken*
Salt
Pepper
2 *teaspoons soy sauce*
¼ *teaspoon sugar*

Heat oil in a large skillet and cook nuts in it over medium heat until they brown lightly. Slice Jerusalem artichokes in ⅛-inch rounds and add to nuts, along with shallots, mushrooms, and celery. Cover and cook for 10 or 12 minutes, stirring a few times.

Add chicken and seasonings, stirring gently several times until chicken is heated through. *Serves 4.*

Chapter 40

WHERE TO GET IT

A home gardener can get most of his tools, fertilizers, and other garden staples at his local garden center or other supplier. Plants and seeds are also available from the same places. But in gardening more than in other pastimes the mail order houses traditionally do a great deal of the supplying. Aside from offering good value in price, quality, and controlled handling of the product, the mail order houses also offer the gardener the great advantage of wide choice. No seed rack could afford to devote 30 or 40 units of space to nothing but different kinds of tomatoes, for instance, but you can find that many in a seed catalogue, or even twice as many.

In repayment for ordering by mail, the catalogues offer gardening information and suggestions, sometimes a great deal of it. Some houses include bonus items in the order, and all of them offer certain discount buys.

January 1 is the date seedsmen consider the start of their catalogue-mailing season, but you can get a catalogue at any time during the year. Most of them are free, but to offset production, mailing, and handling expenses that can run to more than a dollar apiece for some catalogues, some houses make a charge. Charges are usually from 25 cents to a dollar, and are sometimes refundable if an order is placed.

Also reflecting the rising cost of service is a growing tendency by mail order houses to include a fixed handling charge on orders. Those making such a charge show it on their order blanks. Charges range from 35 cents upward.

The following list is in alphabetical order, and includes several suppliers other than seedsmen.

ARMSTRONG NURSERIES, Ontario, California, 91764. Primarily an ornamental-plant nursery and famous for its rose breeding, Armstrong is in this list because of its notable introductions of genetic dwarf peaches and nectarines.

BRECK'S OF BOSTON, 200 Breck Building, Boston, Massachusetts, 02210. One of the oldest American seed houses, Breck's dates back to 1818. Its colorful catalogue lists some European varieties not often found.

BURGESS SEED & PLANT COMPANY, Galesburg, Michigan, 49053. Stressing hardy strains for "Blizzard Belt" conditions, this house carries a large and interesting list of vegetables, and is one of the few places offering Jerusalem artichokes. The helpful catalogue also lists fruits and nuts.

W. ATLEE BURPEE COMPANY, Philadelphia, Pennsylvania, 19132; Clinton, Iowa, 52732; Riverside, California, 92502. A clean piece of catalogue work in book-page size, this one has stayed the same size for more than 90 years, and is helpful and concise. Burpee's are famous for their exclusive varieties, which in recent years have included their outstanding first-generation hybrids. They have consistently been a quality house, aggressive in carrying forward both scientific and field development, and are the world's largest mail order seed house. The number and kind of varieties carried indicate Burpee's non-regional character. Fruits and nuts are also listed.

CALIFORNIA NURSERY COMPANY, Niles, California. Fruit and nut trees are available here, including varieties not easily found, some being Luther Burbank's developments. A number of wine grapes are offered, and other special-climate plants such as globe artichokes, avocados, and olive trees.

FARMER SEED AND NURSERY COMPANY, Faribault, Minnesota, 55021. The interesting catalogue features Northern-adapted varieties (12 early-ripening green peppers, for instance), and lists a number of novel items also adaptable to many areas. Catalogue descriptions are unusually helpful. Fruits are also listed.

HENRY FIELD SEED AND NURSERY COMPANY, Shenandoah, Iowa, 51601. Considerable space is given to garden plans and planting advice in this many-paged and profusely illustrated catalogue. A good selection of vegetables is carried, along with nuts and fruits, including bush cherries for the Northern non-cherry country.

JOSEPH HARRIS COMPANY, Rochester, New York, 14624. This highly respected house puts out a well-written catalogue every year. Listings include their own hybrid vegetables and a representative selection of the well-known ones and some unusual ones. Descriptions are frank and informative.

HEMLOCK HILL HERB FARM, Litchfield, Connecticut, 06759. Herb plants are the main stock in trade here, about 50 being listed. The little catalogue also lists shallots, not an easy item to find.

J. W. JUNG SEED COMPANY, Randolph, Wisconsin, 53956. This 60-year-old house in the upper Midwest has a selection of standard and some unusual varieties, with the accent on adaptation to Northern growing conditions. Some fruits are also handled.

KERR GLASS MANUFACTURING CORPORATION, Sand Springs, Oklahoma, 74063. For an excellent booklet on canning and freezing foods, send 35 cents to this company for the *Kerr Home Canning Book*. Address Miss Hattie Kilgore, who directs their research and educational department.

HENRY LEUTHARDT NURSERIES, East Moriches, Long Island, New York, 11940. This nursery specializes in dwarf fruit trees. Its neat catalogue well deserves the name handbook, over half its space being devoted to culture and allied topics. Espaliered trees are a specialty here.

NEW YORK STATE FRUIT TESTING COOPERATIVE ASSOCIATION, Geneva, New York, 14456. We include this nursery, which is connected with the New York State Agricultural Experiment Station, because it has been outstanding for 50 years in testing new fruits through its members, and has developed some excellent varieties. We joined it years ago and tested several new apples and pears. The only requirement for membership is an interest in new fruits. The membership fee is 2 dollars a year, which can be applied to any order placed during the fiscal year. The catalogue is objective and helpful, and assumes some working knowledge on the reader's part. Tree fruits, grapes, and small fruits are listed.

NICHOLS GARDEN NURSERY, 1190 North Pacific Highway, Albany, Oregon, 97321. A regional seed house and nursery offering a selective list of both standard and unusual plants, and one of the few places offering shallots. They are especially strong on herbs, both plants and seeds.

L. L. OLDS SEED COMPANY, P.O. Box 1069, Madison, Wisconsin, 53701. The chatty and informative catalogue offers a good selection of vegetables for the home garden, and with an eye on regional growing conditions. The house is strong on potatoes, listing 11 varieties. (Note: They do not accept potato orders from California, Alaska, or Hawaii.)

JOHN OSTER MANUFACTURING COMPANY, 5055 North Lysell Avenue, Milwaukee, Wisconsin, 53217. This company makes, for use with its blenders, a small jar you may find convenient for the use mentioned in Chapter 2 under the heading "Preparing Fresh Vegetables and Fruit for Baby."

GEORGE W. PARK SEED COMPANY, P.O. Box 31, Greenwood, South Carolina, 29646. Although this Southern house emphasizes flowers, it offers a carefully chosen selection of the more popular vegetables, and manages to include some unique ones too. Such Southern favorites as Crowder peas are among the listings. The number of herbs carried as seed is unusually large, nearly 50.

R. H. SHUMWAY SEEDSMAN, 628 Cedar Street, Rockford, Illinois, 61101. If you miss the old-fashioned look seed catalogues had years ago, Shumway's catalogue will be a joy. Though carrying an up-to-date selection of vegetables, fruits, and nuts, this largest-page-size catalogue in the field chats along with here a handy hint (how to grow a "parsley sponge" on the window sill), and there a country-life comment ("Parsnips will improve the richness of your cows' milk.").

SOURDOUGH JACK'S KITCHEN, 1095 Kansas Street, San Francisco, California, 94107. You can order a package of sourdough starter in dried form here for about a dollar.

SOUTHMEADOW FRUIT GARDENS, 2363 Tilbury Place, Birmingham, Michigan, 48009. The small catalogue lists, as it states, only "choice and unusual fruit varieties for the connoisseur and home gardener." The varieties are those selected by a serious hobbyist fruit grower, Mr. Robert A. Nitschke, and the number of apple varieties is especially large and noteworthy.

STARK BRO'S NURSERIES, Louisiana, Missouri, 63353. This house, largest such nursery in the world, also has one of the largest catalogues in page size and one of the most lavishly illustrated. A long-established nursery, dating from 1816, Stark's offer many exclusive varieties of fruits and some nuts, and are very active in their scientific breeding program, as well as searching out good chance seedlings and mutations that occur in nature. The house took over Luther Burbank's developments after the famous plant breeder died. Stark's are especially famed for their apples. They pioneered in semi-dwarf spur-type trees during the past two decades. All their small dwarf apples are dwarfed by trunk grafts, to permit them to have particularly vigorous root systems.

STOKES SEEDS, Box 15, Buffalo, New York, 14205. With a page size not much larger than *Reader's Digest,* this plump little catalogue is one of the more informative. Variety descriptions are well handled, and careful attention is given to culture of each vegetable. Many of the customers are Canadian, so the emphasis in varieties is on growing conditions in the Great Lakes areas of Canada. The number of varieties is nevertheless quite large in several cases, such as tomatoes (95) and onions (39).

STRIBLING'S NURSERIES, P.O. Box 793, Merced, California, 95340. We include this West Coast nursery because, for those who live where such things will grow, figs, almonds, and citrus are offered, as well as globe artichoke plants.

GENERAL INDEX

34; perennial, 17; plants, 282; rosemary, 234; sage, 234–35; spearmint, 235; summer savory, 235; sweet basil (*see* basil); sweet marjoram (*see* marjoram); tarragon, 235–36; thyme, 236; wild marjoram (*see* oregano); winter savory (*see* summer savory)
"Hill," 12
Honeydew melons, 139
Hormone sprays, 216
Horse-radish, 125
Hotkap, 113, 215
Hummingbirds, 189
Hybrid vegetables, 92, 281, 282

Indians (American), 38, 54, 105, 128, 210
Indoors, growing seeds in pot, 9
Insects, 8, 12; control, 240
Italian broccoli, 73
Italians, 150
Italy, 206, 233

Japan, 221
Jerusalem artichokes, 38–39, 281
Jung Seed Co., J. W., 282

Kale, 85–86, 127
Kantor, Jerome, 56, 140, 155, 273
Kerr Glass Manufacturing Corp., 282
Kerr Home Canning Book, 282
Kilgore, Hattie, 282
Kimball, Yeffe, 210
Knob celery. *See* Celeriac
Know-how. *See* Seed catalogues
Kohlrabi, 13, 88–89

Leafy greens, 127–28
Leaves, mulch, 6
Leeks, 13, 145, 146, 151
Legumes (peas and beans), 9
Lettuce, 13, 127, 133–34; Deer Tongue, 4; types, 133; varieties, 133
Leuthardt Nurseries, Henry, 282
Life-span of seeds, in storage, 12–13
Lima beans, 57–58
Lloyd, Mrs. Gordon Baker, 239

Maggots, 12
Mail-order houses, 281–84
Malabar spinach, 127

Marjoram, 233
Mediterranean region, 33, 89
Melons, 13, 139–41. *See under* type
Michigan, 183; State University, 73
Middle Ages, 158
Midwest, 38, 51, 85, 92, 97, 133, 152, 158, 161, 183, 201, 241, 242
Minnesota, 45; Experiment Station, 140, 227
Mint. *See* Spearmint
Mississippi Gulf Coast, 113, 166, 225, 251
Missouri, 3, 21, 45, 66, 112, 166, 168, 214, 234, 251; farm garden, 18–19, 50, 147
Mulching, 6–7, 12, 18
Mustard, 13
Mustard greens, 127

Nectarines, 281
New Hampshire Experiment Station, 211
New York State Agricultural Experiment Station, 282
New York State Fruit Testing Cooperative Association, 282
New Zealand spinach, 127
Nichols Garden Nursery, 33, 38, 146, 231, 232, 282–83
Nitragin, 161
Nitschke, Robert A., 240, 283
North Africa, 44
Nurseries, 5; California, 33; list, 281–84
Nurseryman, 10, 11; seeding flat, 10–11
Nuts: trees, 249–50; varieties, 249–50

Okra, 13, 142; "dwarf," 142; varieties, 142
Olds Seed Co., L. L., 167, 172, 183, 283
Onion family, 145–46, 147, 148–50, 151, 153; chives, 145, 146, 148–49; garlic, 145, 146, 149–50; (globe) onions, 145, 146, 153–54; leeks, 145, 146, 151; scallions, 145, 146, 147; shallots, 145, 146
Onions, 13, 145, 146, 153–54, 284
Orchard, care of, 240–41
Oregano, 233
Organic gardeners, 5

INDEX OF RECIPES

curing, 184
freezing, 186
Sweet red peppers vinaigrette, 169–70
Sweet-sour cabbage, 84–85

Tarragon, 235–36
Temperatures, 21
Thyme, 236
Tomatoes, 216–20
 casserole, 217
 green:
  broiled, 219
  casserole, 218–19
  dilly, 219–20
  -onion casserole, 277–78
  -potato casserole, 181
  scalloped, 217–18
  stuffed, 218
Turnips, 222–24
 boiling, 222
 casserole, 223–24
 chicken casserole, 277
 in cream, 223
 steaming, 222
 stuffed, 222–23

Upside-down pie, 247–48

Vegetables:
 freezing ("Soup Mix"), 265
 meals, 26–28
 -meat loaf, 276
 preparation for baby, 26
 stock, 22, 265–66

Vermouth, dry, 24
Vichyssoise, 267
Vinaigrette sauce, 48–49
Vinegar, herb, 237
Vinegars, 22–23

Walnuts, drying, 251
Wax beans, dilled, 54
White sauce. See Béchamel sauce
Wild marjoram. See Oregano
Wilted lettuce I, II, 135–36
Wine and spirits, 24
Wine vinegar, 23
Winter savory. See Summer savory
Winter's night kale, 88
Winter squash, 212–13
 freezing, 212–13
 See Acorn squash and Hubbard squash

Yellow squash:
 leisurely, 208–9
 skillet, 210
 stuffed, 209
 See Summer squash

Zucchini:
 broiled, 208
 casserole I, II, 204–5
 curry, 203
 herbed, 206
 matchstick, 202–3
 Maud, 206–7
 savory, 207–8
 soy squash, 204